Study Guide

Frank H. Selto
University of Colorado at Boulder

Dudley W. Curry
Southern Methodist University

Introduction to Management Accounting

Fourteenth Edition

Charles T. Horngren

Gary L. Sundem

William O. Stratton

Dave Burgstahler

Jeff Schatzberg

Upper Saddle River, New Jersey 07458

D1401127

AVP/Executive Editor: Steve Sartori
Project Manager: Kerri Tomasso
Production Editor: Kevin Holm
Buyer: Michelle Klein

Pearson Prentice Hall^{TM} **is a trademark of Pearson Education, Inc.**

10 9 8 7 6 5 4 3 2 1

ISBN-13: 978-0-13- 234745-7
ISBN-10:   0-13- 234745-8

Table of Contents

This student guide is designed for use with the fourteenth edition of *Introduction to Management Accounting* by Horngren, Sundem, Stratton, Burgstahler, and Schatzberg. For each textbook chapter there is a corresponding guide chapter that presents the main focus and objectives and contains a detailed review of key concepts, plus a comprehensive set of practice test questions and problems. The solutions, which appear immediately after each practice test, can provide useful feedback to reinforce your learning.

HOW TO USE YOUR TEXTBOOK AND STUDENT GUIDE

Have you already developed a general study system or learning style that is most effective for you? Whether your answer is yes or no, please consider some time-tested ideas and procedures for the successful use of these materials in the study of management accounting.

1. First, this study requires more than the mere memorization of a few rules and definitions. Actually, it is essential that you develop for each chapter a clear understanding of the main concepts and their logical relationships. Remember that many of the chapters depend heavily on the earlier chapters in the textbook.

2. Don't try to digest an entire assignment in one long study session. This approach can be tiring, frustrating, and ineffective -- or at least an inefficient way to use your time. Instead, profitably divide your study time into several shorter periods:
    (a) If an entire textbook chapter has been assigned for a class meeting, you may want to first read the chapter from beginning to end without interruption. Next, study the chapter in detail.
    (b) During this second study, carefully proceed through each step of all the examples and illustrations. Note particularly the "Summary Problems for Your Review." These cover the most important ideas in the chapter. Conscientiously trace each step in these problems to their solutions until your understanding is complete.

3. After your textbook study of a chapter, read the corresponding chapter in this student guide:
    (a) The "Review of Key Concepts" is a descriptive outline that can aid your retention of the most important concepts and relationships presented by the textbook chapter.
    (b) Use the Stop and Review sections as an opportunity to view charts and exhibits that correspond to the outlined concepts.
    (c) The Study Tip boxes will help you to understand a concept before you move on to the next one.
    (d) The right margin has been left open for note-taking purposes. Taking quick notes will reinforce your understanding of the key concepts.

(e)   Solve the "Practice Test Questions and Problems." By checking your answers with the solutions, you can generate valuable feedback for mastering the chapter contents. At this point, don't hesitate to refer to your textbook as needed for more complete understanding.

4.   Next, solve the textbook problems that have been assigned as homework by your instructor. *Work alone*, at least initially, and not with a "study buddy." Try to develop reliance on yourself, not on somebody else.

5.   After the class discussion of the assigned problems, you can decide whether to restudy selected parts of the textbook.

REVIEWING FOR TESTS AND EXAMS

1.   If you have regularly completed all of your study and written assignments on time, the necessary review for an exam probably will be minimal. In any case, you will find it not feasible to cover everything in detail. Be selective. Concentrate your review on either the most important matters or the textbook sections that seem most difficult for you.

2.   You may find it helpful to "top off" your review by rereading selected parts of the student guide and reworking some of the practice test questions and problems.

Good luck!

Frank H. Selto
University of Colorado at
Boulder

Dudley W. Curry
Southern Methodist
University

CHAPTER 1

Managerial Accounting, the Business Organization, and Professional Ethics

> OVERVIEW
>
> This preview chapter emphasizes the partnership roles of managers and accountants in planning and controlling the operations of an organization. Our broad aim is to understand how accounting systems can aid management decisions. The chapter presents the three themes that govern the practice of management accounting: the concept of cost-benefit analysis, the behavioral focus, and adaptation to change. Your learning objectives for this chapter are to:
>
> I.   Describe the major users and uses of accounting information
>
> II.   Explain why ethics is important to management accountants
>
> III.   Describe the cost-benefit and behavioral issues involved in designing an accounting system
>
> IV.   Explain the role of budgets and performance reports in planning and control
>
> V.   Discuss the role accountants play in the company's value-chain functions
>
> VI.   Contrast the functions of controllers and treasurers
>
> VII.   Explain why accounting is important in a variety of career paths
>
> VIII. Identify current trends in management accounting
>
> IX.   Appreciate the importance of standards of ethical conduct to professional accountants

REVIEW OF KEY CONCEPTS

I.	Describe the major users and uses of accounting information

A.   All accounting information is prepared to help someone make decisions. In many cases, accounting information is absolutely critical to making good decisions. Users of accounting information and the decisions include:

       1.   Internal managers making short-term planning and control decisions

       2.   Internal managers making investment and long-term planning decisions

       3.   External parties, such as investors who decide whether to invest in the company and government authorities who decide on various policy and regulatory matters

B.   Note how the primary users and decisions of accounting information are different:

       1.   The first two categories deal with the internal use of information by managers: this is *management accounting* and is the focus of this text and study guide.

       2.   The third category is concerned mainly with the use of information by individuals who are external to the organization: this is *financial accounting*.

       3.   Different needs and different users indicate either different accounting *systems* for each category or a complex, multi-purpose accounting *system* that serves all.

> **Stop and Review**
>
> See textbook Exhibit 1-1

C.   Income tax and other regulatory authorities set allowable accounting practices for external, financial accounting (e.g., GAAP). There are no similar constraints on management accounting.

Important Abbreviations

AICPA   American Institute of Certified Public Accountants

CMA   Certified Management Accountant

GAAP   Generally Accepted Accounting Principles

GAO   General Accounting Office

IMA   Institute of Management Accountants

> **Study Tip**: *Before going on to the next section, be sure that you understand the different users of accounting information and how different accounting systems provide information for their decision-making needs.*

II.	Explain why ethics is important to management accountants

A. Ethical behavior is paramount in the accounting profession.

       1.   Companies rely on accurate reporting from accountants to make business decisions.

       2.   Businesses run better when a high level of ethical integrity is established.

B.   The basic ideas of management accounting apply to service and nonprofit organizations as well as to manufacturing organizations.

    1.   Service organizations produce a service instead of a tangible product.

        a.   They include banks, insurance companies, railroads, theaters, and medical clinics.

        b.   Nearly all nonprofit organizations are engaged in service activities--for example, universities, public libraries, churches, charitable organizations, and government agencies.

    2.   The main distinctive characteristics of service organizations are:

        a.   They are **labor-intensive** and not capital-intensive.

        b.   Their outputs are **difficult to define and measure.**

        c.   Their major inputs and outputs are **intangible** and therefore **cannot be stored.**

    3.   The last two items are the reasons why management accounting in service organizations (1) is especially challenging and (2) may have the most opportunity for improving decision making.

III.   Describe the cost-benefit and behavioral issues involved in designing an accounting system

A. Three major themes govern the design of management accounting systems:

    1.   **Simplicity** – an overall watchword for systems design.

    2.   The **cost-benefit** theme of choosing among accounting systems and methods:

        a.   All accounting information and systems are economic goods available at various *costs*.

        b.   More extensive management accounting information is desirable only if the *benefits* (through improved decision making) exceed the costs of the information.

        c.   Often it is easier to identify the costs of new information (e.g., computer hardware, software, and personnel) than the benefits.

    3.   **Behavioral implications** of operating a management accounting system:

        a.   The use of budgets stimulates planning activities. This is a beneficial behavioral effect.

        b.   Individual motivations are strongly influenced by performance reports and incentives that are used to appraise both decisions and managers. This can be a favorable behavioral effect **if** the performance reports and incentives are designed properly. Otherwise, adverse behavioral effects may result.

> **Study Tip**: *Can you explain the three major influences on management accounting systems?*

B.   Management decision making is composed of two basic functions:

    1.   **Planning:** deciding on objectives and ways to attain them.

    2.   **Controlling:** evaluating performance through **feedback,** modifying plans if necessary, and implementing plans.

Stop and Review
See textbook Exhibit 1-2

IV. Explain the role of budgets and performance reports in planning and control

A. **Budgets** are the main type of planning information. A **budget** is a quantitative expression of a plan of action. It is also an aid in coordinating and implementing the plan.

B. **Performance reports** are the main type of controlling information that compares results with plans and highlights deviations from plans.

C. **Management by exception** means focusing attention and effort on the more significant deviations from expected results. In accounting these deviations are called **variances**.

Stop and Review
See textbook Exhibit 1-3

> **Study Tip:** *Before going on, be sure that you understand the different types of information that accounting systems provide and how this information is consistent with the management process.*

D. Many management decisions relate to a single good or service, or to a group of related products.

    1. It is the responsibility of accountants to plan for and control the production of these goods and services. To do this effectively, accountants and managers often consider the **product's life cycle**.

    2. A **product's life cycle** refers to the stages that a product goes through, from development and introduction to the market, to maturation, and, eventually, withdrawal from the market.

E. The development stage of the product life cycle determines most of the costs of products and programs.

    1. During the production or delivery stages, typical accounting systems do not report past development costs or future phase-out costs.

    2. Thus, product costs over the entire life cycle may be understated by ignoring development and phase-out costs.

    3. Proper decision making for current products (and importantly for planning future products) requires that managers consider the costs over the entire product life cycle.

Stop and Review
See textbook Exhibit 1-4

V. Discuss the role accountants play in a company's value-chain functions

A. All businesses must assess and design activities to meet needs and values of their customers.

    1. The linked functions that a business uses to meet these needs and values together are called a **value chain**.

    2. Businesses must assess whether functions really add value to the products or services of an organization.

> **Stop and Review**
>
> See textbook Exhibit 1-5

B.   Accountants play a key role in all **value-chain functions.** Accountants affect each step of the product life cycle.

    1.   Providing estimated revenue during research and development

    2.   Giving feedback as to cost reductions that can be made long before any commitments must be made

    3.   Tracking the effects of continuous improvement programs during development

    4.   Planning for efficient distribution of the product (direct retail vs. wholesale; shipping and transportation)

    5.   Providing cost data for customer service activities (warranty and repair costs, cost of returned goods)

VI.   Contrast the functions of controllers and treasurers

A.   The chief accounting executive, or chief management accountant, is often called the **controller** (or **comptroller** in government organizations).

    1.   The controller's authority is basically of the **staff type**, that is, giving advice and service to other departments.

    2.   The **controller** has direct control, called **line authority**, only over subordinates, such as staff accountants (sometimes called financial analysts), internal auditors, cost clerks, and the general ledger bookkeeper.

        Staff authority, however, may be exerted to an equal, superior, or subordinate. This is the authority to advise not command.

> **Stop and Review**
>
> See textbook Exhibit 1-6

    3.   The main functions of the controller are preparing information for planning and reporting and interpreting and evaluating information in consultation with other managers.

D.   In contrast to the controller's functions, the **treasurer** of a company is concerned mainly with such financial activities as investor relations, banking, long- and short-term borrowing, and investments.

Controllership	Treasurership
1. Planning for control	1. Provision of capital
2. Reporting and interpreting	2. Investor relations
3. Evaluating and consulting	3. Short-term financing
4. Tax administration	4. Banking and custody
5. Government reporting	5. Credits and collections
6. Protection of assets	6. Investments
7. Economic appraisal	7. Risk management (insurance)

VII.	**Explain why accounting is important in a variety of career paths**

A.   There are many types and levels of career opportunities available in the field of accounting.

    1.   Certified public accountants (CPAs) in the U.S., or chartered accountants (CAs) in many other nations, work externally ensuring the reliability of companies' published financial statements.

    2.   Certified management accountants (CMAs) are internal employees of companies. The CMA program is overseen by the Institute of Management Accountants (IMA).

B.   Entry-level accounting positions are springboards into the world of business. By learning about all aspects of business, accountants make themselves prime candidates for management positions.

VIII.	**Identify current trends in management accounting**

A.   External environments and internal decision making change over time.

B.   Management accounting systems will provide useful information in the future only if they evolve along with the environment and the organization. Many accountants, managers, and academics have criticized accounting systems for not evolving and, therefore, for impeding good decision making.

C.   Current changes include:

    1.   Increased emphasis on service

    2.   Increased global competition

    3.   Advances in technology and electronic commerce

    4.   Changes in business processes (e.g. JIT and CIM)

D.   Management accountants themselves must be willing and able to learn and evolve.

IX.	**Appreciate the importance of standards of ethical conduct to professional accountants**

A.   High standards of ethical conduct are essential to the practice of management accounting.

    1.   Without acknowledged ethical behavior, accountants and their information are not credible.

    2.   The public recognizes accountants as adhering to high ethical standards.

    3.   To a large degree, the accounting profession's ethical reputation is responsible for its high social status.

    4.   The Institute of Management Accountants has developed standards of ethical behavior that address:

       a. Competence   - Maintain a high level of competence through ongoing development of knowledge and skills.

          - Perform professional duties in accordance with relevant laws, regulations, and technical standards.

          - Prepare complete and clear recommendations after appropriate analysis of relevant and reliable information.

       b. Confidentiality   - Do not disclose any confidential information unless authorized to do so.

          - Inform subordinates appropriately of the confidentiality of the information and monitor their activities in order to maintain confidentiality.

          - Do not use, or appear to use, confidential information in an unethical or illegal manner.

c. **Integrity**   - Avoid conflicts of interest.

- Engage in no activity that would affect the company's ability to function ethically.

- Refuse any favor that may influence or appear to influence the company's actions.

- Do not subvert the company's attainment of ethical objectives.

- Communicate professional limitations.

- Communicate professional opinions and information, favorable as well as unfavorable.

- Refrain from engaging in or supporting any activity that may discredit the profession.

d. **Objectivity**   - Communicate fairly and objectively.

- Disclose all relevant information that could influence user actions.

Stop and Review
See textbook Exhibit 1-7

Study Tip: *The previous sections described the organizational and professional roles of management accountants. Can you describe the practice and profession of management accounting?*

PRACTICE TEST QUESTIONS AND PROBLEMS

This section will help you find out how well you have absorbed the content of the textbook. Try to answer all of these questions and problems *with your textbook closed*. Then, check your answers with the *solutions that immediately follow this practice test*. In this way, you can determine which parts of the textbook chapter to restudy.

True or False Statements

Determine whether each of the following statements is True (T) or False (F) and enter your answer in the space provided.

_____1.   Management control refers primarily to the setting of maximum limits on expenditures.

_____2.   The treasurer of a company is concerned mainly with planning, reporting, evaluating, and interpreting.

_____3.   Compared with the typical management accounting reports, financial accounting reports are more likely to focus only on the actual results of the preceding period.

_____4.   One feature common to both financial and managerial accounting is that the methods and practices of both are strictly constrained by external authorities.

_____5.   There are essentially no conceptual differences between management accounting for service and for manufacturing organizations.

_____6.   Management by exception refers to assigning the most difficult management control tasks only to exceptional managers, who are identified by accounting performance reports.

_____7.   It is important to understand a product's life cycle so that costs from one stage of the cycle are not mixed with costs from another stage.

_____8.   The controller of an organization exercises both line and staff authority.

_____9.   Risk management is one of the usual duties of the controller.

_____10.   One of the objectives of the IMA's code of ethics is to establish management accounting as a recognized profession.

Multiple-Choice Questions

For the following multiple-choice questions, select the best answer(s), and enter identification letters in the spaces provided.

_____1.   Management accounting for an organization is aimed mainly at the decision needs of: (a) its stockholders, (b) its creditors, (c) government regulators, (d) internal managers.

_____2.   Analyzing variances from the budget of the cost of materials used in making a particular product should be classified as: (a) problem solving, (b) attention directing, (c) scorekeeping, (d) financial auditing.

_____3.   Controlling is done by: (a) accountants, (b) managers, (c) internal auditors, (d) accounting systems.

_____4.   The controller has direct line authority over: (a) line departments, (b) staff accountants, (c) staff departments, (d) executives.

_____5.   The management controlling function includes which of the following?   (a) formulating plans, (b) implementing plans, (c) evaluating results, (d) providing feedback.

_____6.   What two functions do performance reports serve? (a) the planning function, (b) the evaluation function, (c) the feedback function, (d) the audit function.

_____7.   Budgets primarily serve: (a) the financial reporting function, (b) the feedback function, (c) the planning function, (d) the controlling function.

_____8.   Unique difficulties of management accounting in service organizations *do not* include: (a) labor intensity, (b) diverse output, (c) ill-defined output, (d) perishability of output.

_____9.   The effective restrictions on measurements that can be reported by a management accounting system *do not* include: (a) GAAP, (b) the cost-benefit philosophy, (c) behavioral impacts, (d) adaptation to change.

_____10. The most useful scorekeeping information is the evaluation of performance made by comparing actual results for a month with: (a) the budget for that month, (b) actual results of the preceding month, (c) actual results of the same month a year ago, (d) actual results with results of a competitor.

Completion

Complete each of the following statements by filling in the blanks:

1.   The two basic functions of the management process are _____ and _____.

2.   The three main types of useful information that the management accountant should supply are:

_____-keeping information,

_____-directing information, and

_____-solving information.

3.   Concentrating on areas that deviate from the plan and ignoring smooth-running areas is called _____.

4.   The three distinctive features of service organizations are:

(a)_____

(b)_____

(c)_____

5.   The chief accounting executive, or chief management accountant, is often called the _____.

6.   Interpreting and evaluating information in consultation with operating managers is an example of the exercise of the controller's _____ authority.

7.   Comparison of this year's actual results with this year's budget is an example of a _____.

8.   Write out in full the words for each of the following initials:

(a) CMA:_____

(b) GAAP:_____

(c) IMA:_____

9.   The major areas of responsibility for ethical conduct by management accountants are:

(a)_____

(b)_____

(c)_____

(d)_____

Exercises

1. Identify each of the following features as being *more* identified with management accounting (MA) or with financial accounting (FA):

   _____1. Measuring actual performance against actual results of preceding period

   _____2. Less freedom in choosing measurement methods and principles

   _____3. Flexible timespan

   _____4. Detailed reports on subunits of an organization

   _____5. Stronger orientation to investors

   _____6. Constrained by GAAP

   _____7. Affects employees' daily behavior

   _____8. Focus on prior period's results

2. For each of the following activities within a company, identify the main function that is being performed: SK = scorekeeping; PS = problem solving; AD = attention directing.

   _____1. Preparing the variance of actual dollar sales from budgeted sales by type of product and by name of salesperson

   _____2. Tabulating spoiled rejected product units at the end of a manufacturing process

   _____3. Entering checks in the cash disbursement journal

   _____4. Estimating future cash inflows and cash outflows relating to the contemplated acquisition of specialized manufacturing machinery

   _____5. Computing and recording end-of-year adjustments for accrued wages and salaries

3. For each of the following pairs, use the code shown below to indicate the usual type of authority of the first-named party over the second-named party: L = line authority; S = staff authority; N = no authority

   _____1. controller/payroll clerks

   _____2. production superintendent/accounts payable bookkeeper

   _____3. engineering vice president/storekeeper

   _____4. controller/production superintendent

   _____5. president/chairman of the board

   _____6. manufacturing vice president/receiving clerk

   _____7. assistant controller/accounts receivable bookkeeper

   _____8. controller/purchasing officer

   _____9. internal auditor/assistant controller

Problems

Prepare solutions for each of the following problems in the spaces provided.

1.   The Parent Teacher Organization (PTO) of Eisenhower Elementary School held a fund-raising fair in the school gymnasium. The PTO president had prepared the following budget assuming 200 attendees who spend an average of $20 each and donations of all other resources:

Revenues	$4,000
Costs:	
Food and beverages	800
Prizes	500
Supplies	300
Custodial services	200
Total costs	$1,800
Income	$2,200

Afterwards, the PTO treasurer (the PTO has no controller) determined that 150 people had attended the fair, and total revenues were $2,250. Cost of food and beverages was $750. All prizes were awarded. Supplies cost $180, and custodial services were $500 due to damage to the gymnasium floor.

Prepare a performance report that shows how actual results differ from budgeted results. Which variances deserve further examination?

Item	Actual results	Budgeted results	Variance	Explanation
Revenues		$4,000		
Costs:				
Food and beverages		800		
Prizes		500		
Supplies		300		
Custodial services		200		
Total costs		$1,800		
Income		$2,200		

2.   The Evergreen Chamber of Commerce prepared the following budget for its annual Fourth of July concert and fireworks show:

Sources of revenue:

Merchant donations	$10,000
Public donations	5,000
Total revenue	$15,000

Costs:

Fireworks	$12,000
Rentals (band tent, audio equipment, portable toilets, barricades)	2,000
Police and fire protection services	3,000
Total costs	$17,000
Budgeted loss	$ (2,000)

Donations totaled $13,000. Due to an unusually wet first week of July, police and fire protection services cost $1,000 less than expected. Some fireworks did not ignite, and the distributor issued a $500 refund. One of the portable toilets was destroyed by members of the public and had to be replaced for $400.

Prepare a performance report that shows how actual results differ from budgeted results. Which variances deserve further examination?

CHAPTER 1 SOLUTIONS TO PRACTICE TEST QUESTIONS AND PROBLEMS

True or False Statements

1. False   This is spending control. Management control is exercised by coordinating, planning, evaluation, and feedback.

2. False   These are controller's duties. The treasurer is concerned with financing activities, investor relations, and so on.

3. True   Though both types of accounting reports contain past results, management accounting reports also focus on future outcomes (e.g., through budgets).

4. False   In general, management accounting practices are not constrained by external authorities.

5. True   In concept they are the same, though in practice, management control is likely to be more difficult in service organizations.

6. False   Management by exception refers to focusing efforts on exceptionally large variances.

7. False   Consideration of the product life cycle is important for consideration of total product costs, from development to phase-out.

8. True   The controller has staff authority with other line departments and has line authority over the accounting department.

9. False   Risk management (insurance) is usually a treasurer function.

10. True   This is an objective of the Institute of Management Accountants (IMA). The AICPA is concerned primarily with independent auditors and tax practitioners.

Multiple-Choice Questions

1. d   Though management accountants are involved with providing information for stockholders, creditors, and government regulators, the primary focus is providing information for internal managers.

2. b   Identifying causes for variances directs attention to problem areas. Preparing the performance report (variances) is scorekeeping. Financial auditing is concerned with assessing the effectiveness of internal controls and determining whether financial statements have been prepared in accordance with GAAP.

3. b   The actual task of controlling operations is a management task. Accounting systems provide information as designed by accountants. Internal auditors give guidance to managers about internal and management control strengths and weaknesses.

4. b   The controller directs, and is responsible for, the activities of staff accountants. The controller has staff authority to advise line and staff departments and executives.

5. b, c, d   Control encompasses all these activities; whereas formulating plans is a planning activity.

6. b, c   Performance reports are scorekeeping information that aid in control of operations; thus, they primarily aid evaluation and feedback. Through feedback, managers may learn from these reports, however, and use them as input for planning.

7. c	Budgets are one of the primary planning tools because they quantify the resources needed to attain organizational objectives. Budgets are used as part of performance reports, so they also serve the controlling and feedback functions. Financial reporting for the most part is not concerned with budgets.
8. b	Any type of organization may have diverse products (and services). Service organizations, however, are more labor intensive and their output is less well-defined and is more perishable than other (manufacturing) organizations.
9. a	GAAP technically does not apply to management accounting, though management accounting systems may rely on financial accounting systems that do comply with GAAP. Management accounting must meet cost-benefit and behavioral criteria and adapt to changing conditions.
10. a	The budget for the current month is the best benchmark for comparing actual current performance. The results of the preceding month and the same month a year earlier may be irrelevant to current performance; they may help identify trends, however. Comparisons to competitors' results are difficult, but may be useful if enough is known about them to make comparing their results meaningful.

Completion

1. planning and controlling

2. scorekeeping, attention-directing, and problem-solving

3. management by exception

4. (a) highest costs are related to payroll (labor is intensive), (b) output is hard to define and measure, (c) major inputs and outputs cannot be stored

5. controller

6. staff

7. performance report or scorekeeping activity

8. (a) Certified Management Accountant, (b) Generally Accepted Accounting Principles, (c) Institute of Management Accountants

9. professional competence, confidentiality of information, integrity, objectivity

Exercises

1. 1. FA, 2. FA, 3. MA, 4. MA, 5. FA, 6. FA, 7. MA, 8. FA

2. 1. AD, 2. SK, 3. SK, 4. PS, 5. SK

3. 1. L, 2. N, 3. N, 4. S, 5. N, 6. L, 7. L, 8. L or S, 9. N

Problems

1.

Item	Actual results	Budgeted results	Variance	Explanation
Revenues	$2,250	$4,000	$1,750 U	Fewer attendees who spent less per person than expected
Costs:				
Food and beverages	750	800	50 F	Less consumption in total, but greater per person
Prizes	500	500	0	
Supplies	180	300	120 F	Probably due to fewer attendees
Custodial services	500	200	300 U	Due to damage to gymnasium floor
Total costs	$1,930	$1,800	$ 130 U	
Income	$ 320	$2,200	$1,880 U	

The revenue and custodial service variances probably deserve the most attention. Why did so many fewer people attend the fair and spend less than expected per person? How was the floor damaged, and can damage be avoided in the future?

2.

Item	Actual	Budget	Variance	Explanation
Sources of revenue:				
Merchant donations		$10,000		
Public donations		5,000		
Total	$13,000	$15,000	$ 2,000 U	Merchants or public?
Costs:				
Fireworks	$11,500	$12,000	$ 500 F	Refund for defective fireworks
Rentals (band tent, audio equipment, portable toilets, barricades)	2,400	2,000	400 U	Replacement of portable toilet
Police and fire protection services	2,000	3,000	1,000 F	Lower staffing due to weather
Total	$15,900	$17,000	$ 1,100 F	
Loss	$ (2,900)	$(2,000)	$ 900 U	

Though the total variance is relatively small, the Chamber of Commerce might consider whether the defective fireworks and lower police staffing (and resulting vandalism?) could affect future attendance and financial support. The Chamber also should determine the source of the shortfall in donations (merchants or public). Support for the activity may be diminishing from both.

CHAPTER **2**

Introduction to Cost Behavior and Cost-Volume Relationships

OVERVIEW

This chapter presents a powerful planning model to assist decision making. It is called cost-volume-profit analysis or break-even analysis. When you are finished studying this chapter you should be able to:

I.   Explain how cost drivers affect cost behavior

II.   Show how changes in cost-driver levels affect variable costs and fixed costs

III.   Calculate break-even sales volume in total dollars and total units

IV.   Create a cost-volume-profit graph and understand the assumptions behind it

V.   Calculate sales volume in total dollars and total units to reach a target profit

VI.   Differentiate between contribution margin and gross margin

VII.   Explain the effects of sales mix on profits (Appendix 2A)

VIII. Compute cost-volume-profit relationships on an after-tax basis (Appendix 2B)

I.	**Explain how cost drivers affect cost behavior**

A. Suppose a computer manufacturing company changes its levels of various activities (orders taken, computers produced, labor hours worked, material used, etc.). How these activities affect an organization's costs is called **cost behavior**.

1. Costs may be affected by these changes in activity. **Cost drivers** are activities that affect costs.

> **Stop and Review**
>
> See textbook Exhibits 2-1 and 2-2

II.	**Show how changes in cost-driver levels affect variable costs and fixed costs**

A. Changes in cost-driver activity affect fixed costs and variable costs as follows:

Cost Type	*Total Cost*	*Unit Cost*
Variable	Increase or decrease	No change
Fixed	No change	Increase or decrease

The logic that supports these effects is tied directly to the definitions of these two basic types of costs:

1. **Variable costs** are costs (expenses) that *change in total* in direct proportion to changes in the related level of cost-driver activity.

   a. Therefore, variable costs stay the same per unit of activity, but increase in total as activity increases.

   b. *Example: Assume that activity increases. Each unit of activity causes total costs to increase by the variable cost per unit of activity. If the computer company has variable material cost of $500 per computer and makes 10,000 computers, the total variable materials cost is $500 x 10,000 = $5,000,000. Making one more computer would raise total variable material cost to $5,000,500 because the variable material cost per unit is constant at $500 per computer.*

   c. Other examples of variable costs include sales commissions and most kinds of purchased merchandise, supplies, and parts.

2. **Fixed costs** are the costs that *are not affected in total* by changes in cost-driver activity over a given time span.

   a. Therefore, fixed costs *do not stay the same per unit of cost-driver activity*: fixed costs on a per-unit basis vary *inversely* with changes in activity volume.

   b. *Example: Assume that activity increases. There will be more activity supported by the same total fixed costs. If the computer company has $1 million of fixed costs to make 10,000 computers in one year, the fixed cost per computer is $1,000,000 ÷ 10,000 = $100. Next year, if 20,000 computers are made with no change in total fixed costs, the fixed cost per computer is reduced to $1,000,000 ÷ 20,000 = $50. Thus, when activity increases, fixed costs on a per-unit basis decrease.*

   c. Examples of fixed-cost items per period include factory rent, executive salaries, and periodic depreciation.

d. A fixed cost is fixed only in relationship to a given planning period for the expected band of activity level, which is called the **relevant range.**

e. Activity below or above this range may require major adjustments in operations that would change the amounts of total fixed costs.

> **Stop and Review**
>
> See textbook Exhibit 2-6

f. Activity outside the relevant range could also affect the *variable cost per unit of activity*, caused by changing efficiencies at very low or very high levels of activity; for example, because of material purchase discounts.

3. Accountants usually assume that costs behave in a *linear* or *straight-line* manner.

a. Some costs may be *nonlinear*, that is behave not as a straight line, and they may be affected simultaneously by *several different* activities; therefore, we cannot always classify them into perfectly variable and perfectly fixed categories.

b. Usually, however, we associate a given variable cost with only one measure of activity, and we assume that relationship is *linear*. (It is possible to test this assumption with statistical techniques.)

c. As mentioned above, we also assume that fixed costs behave as a straight (horizontal) line within the relevant range.

> **Study Tip:** *Before going on, be sure that you understand the distinctions between fixed and variable costs and that you understand the relationship between the relevant range and fixed and variable-cost behavior.*

B. **Cost-volume-profit analysis** facilitates management planning decisions by quantifying the effects on net income of (1) alternative activity levels and (2) combinations of product selling prices, variable costs per unit of activity, plus total fixed costs per period. This approach is often called **break-even analysis,** although the more appropriate term is **cost-volume-profit analysis**, often abbreviated as **CVP analysis.**

1. The most common CVP approach considers sales activity as the primary cost driver. We will assume that sales activity is the appropriate cost driver. Chapter 3 considers other cost drivers.

2. The **break-even point** is that level of activity (e.g., level of sales activity) where total costs equal total revenues. At this point there is zero net income.

3. The **margin of safety** is the difference between the planned level of sales activity and the break-even sales activity.

4. **Contribution-margin** or **marginal income** is the excess of sales over variable costs, and it can be expressed as total dollars, dollars per product unit, percentage of sales, or ratio to sales.

III. Calculate break-even sales volume in total dollars and total units

---

A. **Contribution-margin technique** for computing *break-even point* in terms of sales activity:

Formula: Break-even point in units = Fixed expenses ÷ Contribution margin per unit

> *Example*: Selling price $5, variable cost per unit $2, total fixed costs $600 per month

Break-even point in terms of sales units: *divide total fixed expenses by contribution margin per unit:*

Contribution margin per unit is $5 - $2 = $3.

$600 ÷ $3/unit = 200 units

Prove this answer by filling in the blanks:

Sales: 200 units x $_____per unit $_____

Less: Variable costs 200 units x $_____per unit   _____

Fixed costs per month $_____per month   _____

Net income $_____0

B.   **Formula: Break-even point in total dollar sale = Fixed expenses ÷ Contribution-margin ratio or percentage of sales:**

Example: Contribution-margin ratio is $3 ÷ $5 = .6 = 60%.

$600 ÷ .60 = $1,000

Prove this answer by filling in these blanks:

Contribution margin $1,000 x _____ $_____

Less fixed costs per month $_____per month   _____

Net income $_____0

C.   The **equation method** of determining the break-even point is based on the fundamental relationships among the principal elements of the income statement:

1.   Sales   xxx

Less:

Variable expenses   xxx

Fixed expenses   xxx

Total expenses   <u>xxx</u>

Net income   <u>xxx</u>

2.   The equation form of this income statement is:

Sales - Variable costs - Fixed costs = Net income

Example: Selling price $5, variable cost per unit $2, total fixed costs $600, break-even sales units N, net income zero:

$5N - $2N - $600 = 0

$3N - $600 = 0

$3N = $600

N = $600 ÷ $3

N = 200 units

3. The break-even point in total dollar *sales* for this example is 200 units x $5 = $1,000.

4. The contribution-margin and the equation techniques are equivalent. Use whichever technique you wish. Note that the contribution-margin technique is merely the final step of the equation technique.

    a. Note that sometimes you have only enough data to use the contribution-margin ratio approach.

    b. This happens most often when analyzing competitors' profitability.

5. Either method can be used, for example, to compute the sales necessary to attain a certain **target net income,** for example $300:

    a. Contribution-margin technique (sales units):

        Target sales units = (Fixed expenses + Target net income) ÷ Contribution-margin per unit

        Target sales units = ($600 + $300) ÷ $3/unit

        Target sales units = $900 ÷ $3/unit = <u>300 units</u>

    b. Contribution-margin technique (sales dollars):

        Target sales dollars = (Fixed expenses + Target net income) ÷ Contribution-margin ratio

        Target sales dollars = ($600 + $300) ÷ .60

        Target sales dollars = $900 ÷ .60 = <u>$1,500</u>

    c. Equation technique (sales units and sales dollars):

        $5N - $2N - $600 = $300

        $3N = $300 + $600

        $3N = $900

        N = $900 ÷ $3 = <u>300 units</u>

        Target sales dollars = $5/unit x 300 units = <u>$1,500</u>

> **Study Tip:** *Be sure that, through practice in solving problems, you are comfortable using the two equivalent methods for making a cost-volume-profit analysis: the contribution-margin technique and the equation technique.*

IV. Create a cost-volume-profit graph and understand the assumptions behind it

A. The **graphical technique** is useful in portraying the concept of CVP analysis and the relationships among costs, volume, and profit.

> **Stop and Review**
>
> See textbook Exhibit 2-7

1. This technique can effectively communicate profit potentials over a wide range of sales activity.

2. When operating budgets are being considered, CVP graphs can improve management's understanding of budget relationships and effects.

V.   Calculate sales volume in total dollars and total units to reach a target profit

A.   Cost-volume-profit analysis helps managers identify critical levels of product sales, selling prices, variable costs per unit, and fixed costs per period.

   1.   However, it is often necessary in practice to make *trade-offs* (strike a balance) among the elements. For example, advanced technologies usually decrease variable costs per unit at higher fixed costs per period.

   2.   *Computer spreadsheet software* is widely used in planning activities to analyze trade-offs between different decisions about the elements of CVP relationships. Spreadsheet software eliminates mathematical errors and allows the decision maker to vary each CVP element systematically and observe the effects on, for example, break-even or target sales. Spreadsheet software is an indispensable management tool.

   3.   **Operating leverage** is the ratio of fixed costs to variable costs and is a measure of the riskiness of operations.

      a.   Companies with high operating leverage (large fixed costs relative to variable costs) are *riskier* than companies with low operating leverage (relatively low fixed costs). Small changes in sales activity cause large effects in the net income of high operating leverage companies, whereas small changes in sales activity do not affect low operating leverage companies as much.

> **Stop and Review**
>
> See textbook Exhibit 2-9

      b.   When a company has high operating leverage, it has low variable costs and high contribution-margins. Even small increases in sales cause large increases in net income (and vice versa).

      c.   In contrast, companies with low operating leverage find that small changes in sales activity do not change net income greatly.

   4.   The **margin of safety** is a measurement that uses planned sales and break-even sales to assess whether an operating loss is expected in the future.

      Formula: Margin of safety = Planned unit sales - Break-even unit sales

VI.   Differentiate between contribution margin and gross margin

A.   Do not confuse contribution margin with gross margin.

   1.   Recall *contribution margin* is the excess of sales over *total variable costs,* including both variable cost of goods sold and variable operating expenses, if any.

   2.   **Gross margin** (or **gross profit**) is the excess of sales over *total cost of goods sold,* including both variable cost of goods sold and fixed cost of goods sold, if any.

> **Stop and Review**
>
> See textbook Exhibit 2-10

VII. Explain the effect of sales mix on profits (Appendix 2A)

A. The *expected* **sales mix** is the relative proportions of products that a company expects to sell. The *actual* sales mix may vary from the planned mix.

    1. CVP models can be modified to reflect sales mix assumptions.

        a. The simplest approach is to express each product as a multiple of the one product with the *least* unit sales.

            Example: Assume the Alphabet Company expects that 2/3 of its unit sales will be Betas (B) and 1/3 of its unit sales will be Alphas (A); that is, a ratio of 3 Betas to 1 Alpha.

            The sales mix assumption can be expressed as $B = 3A$

            Substitute the value "3A" into the CVP equation for each occurrence of "B" and solve for the break-even or target level of A unit sales.

        b. The break-even or target level of B sales is three times that of A.

    2. This analysis does not find the level of sales that will maximize profits. Another technique called linear programming can accomplish this analysis.

> **Study Tip:** *Can you express the product mix assumption as an equation?*

VIII. Compute cost-volume-profit relationships on an after-tax basis (Appendix 2B)

A. When the organization pays taxes on its income, the amount of before-tax sales must be high enough to leave target profits after paying taxes.

    1. Ordinarily, break-even analysis is not affected by taxes, because income is zero at breakeven.

    2. In order to pay taxes on positive income, target income *before taxes* must be computed and entered into the CVP model.

        Example. Assume a tax rate of 30% and a target after-tax income of $210. What must the level of before-tax income be?

Net income before tax – taxes   = Net income after tax

Net income before tax - (tax rate) x (Net income before tax)= Net income after tax

Net income before tax x (1 - tax rate)   = Net income after tax

Net income before tax   = Net income after tax ÷ (1 - tax rate)

Net income before tax   = $210 ÷ (1 - .30)

                          = $300

$300 would be the target income used in the CVP model, not $210.

> **Study Tip:** *Be sure that you can express an after-tax profit target in its before-tax equivalent before going on.*

PRACTICE TEST QUESTIONS AND PROBLEMS
True or False Statements

Determine whether each of the following statements is True (T) or False (F), and enter your answer in the space provided.

_____1.   Cost-driver activities refer to the levels of activities that cause total costs to vary.

_____2.   Over the relevant range of activity, variable costs stay the same per unit of activity.

_____3.   The break-even point can be determined simply by measuring the fixed and variable expenses in a given income statement and finding their total.

_____4.   Over the relevant range of activity, fixed costs per unit of activity stay the same.

_____5.   In the very short run, all costs may be fixed.

_____6.   The excess of planned sales units over break-even sales units is the gross margin.

_____7.   Contribution margin, marginal income, and incremental income are synonymous terms.

_____8.   The number of product units that must be sold to earn a specified amount of net income can be computed by dividing the sum of fixed expenses and target net income by the unit contribution-margin ratio.

_____9.   As sales exceed the break-even point, a small contribution-margin ratio would result in less additional profit than would a large contribution-margin ratio.

_____10.   A firm with high operating leverage enjoys more stable income than a firm with low operating leverage.

Multiple-Choice Questions

For the following multiple-choice questions, select the best answer(s), and enter identification letters in the spaces provided.

_____1.   Costs that tend to vary inversely with changes in activity level are: (a) total variable costs, (b) variable costs per unit, (c) total fixed costs, (d) fixed costs per unit.

_____2.   Total fixed costs are $60,000 when 20,000 product units are produced. When 30,000 units are produced, fixed costs would likely be: (a) $90,000 in total, (b) $3.00 per unit, (c) $40,000 in total, (d) $2.00 per unit.

_____3.   Total variable costs are $100,000 when 20,000 product units are produced. When 25,000 units are produced, variable costs would likely be: (a) $5 per unit, (b) $100,000 in total, (c) $4 per unit, (d) $105,000 in total.

_____4.   Monthly production of a company consists of 2,000 units sold at $5.00 per unit. Total costs are $2,200 fixed and $6,000 variable. The break-even point per month is: (a) 440 units, (b) 733 units, (c) $10,000, (d) 1,100 units.

_____5.   Monthly sales of a company are $20,000 with total costs of $6,000 fixed and $8,000 variable. The break-even point per month is total sales of: (a) $14,000, (b) $15,000, (c) $10,000, (d) $20,000.

_____ 6.   A company produces a product for sale at $24 per unit. Costs are $48,000 per month for total fixed costs and $16 for variable costs per unit. The number of units to be produced and sold per month to break even would be: (a) 7,500, (b) 6,000, (c) 3,750, (d) 3,000.

_____ 7.   If sales remain constant but the contribution-margin ratio increased by 25%, total contribution would: (a) increase by the same percentage, (b) decrease by the same percentage, (c) be unaffected, (d) the answer depends on the level of fixed costs.

_____ 8.   Gross margin is: (a) sales minus all variable costs, (b) sales minus cost of goods sold, including both variable and fixed elements, (c) sales minus break-even sales, (d) sales minus cost of goods sold, excluding the fixed element.

_____ 9.   (Appendix 2A) A company produces and sells two products at contribution-margins of $2 for X and $5 for Y. Fixed costs are $10,500. If the planned mix is five units of X for each unit of Y, the break-even units of Y would be: (a) 3,500, (b) 700, (c) 1,500, (d) 3,000.

_____ 10.   (Appendix 2B) A company produces a product for sale at $24 per unit. Costs are $48,000 for total fixed costs and $16.00 for variable costs per unit. The number of units to be produced and sold to obtain a $4,800 profit after income taxes of 40% would be: (a) 6,600, (b) 10,000, (c) 6,000, (d) 7,000.

Completion

Complete each of the following statements by filling in the blanks:

1.   Whether a given cost is really fixed or variable depends heavily on:_____ ,

_____ , and

_____.

2.   High operating leverage means that _____ are relatively _____ compared to _____.

3.   As production volume decreases, _____ costs become larger on a per-unit basis.

4.   The typical break-even graph shows a _____ type of behavior for costs and revenues over the relevant range.

5.   A decrease in total fixed costs in a given case would cause the break-even point to _____.

6.   The unit sales in excess of breakeven necessary to meet a before-tax profit target can be found by dividing _____ by _____.

7.   Break-even sales dollars can be found by _____ _____ by _____.

8.   The _____ technique and the _____ technique are equivalent methods of modeling _____ relationships.

9.   The _____ defines the limits of valid cost and revenue behavior relationships.

10.   Different types of costs may have different _____ other than sales activity levels.

Problems

1.   This is a relatively simple review exercise that differentiates the behaviors of fixed and variable costs. All of the data pertain to the usual monthly production and sales of Como Company. Fill in the blanks, assuming that all costs and expenses are divided into strictly fixed and strictly variable elements.

Sales Activity	Total Fixed Costs	Total Variable Costs	Fixed Costs per Unit	Variable Costs per Unit
5,000	$180,000	$120,000	$ (a)	$ (b)
6,000	$ (c)	$ (d)	$ (e)	$ (f)
4,000	$ (g)	$ (h)	$ (i)	$ (j)

2.   Using the data given below, construct a cost-volume-profit graph in the format of the textbook Exhibit 2-5:

   Sales: $10 per unit

   Variable expenses: $6 per unit

   Fixed expenses: $2,000 per week

Dollars (in thousands)

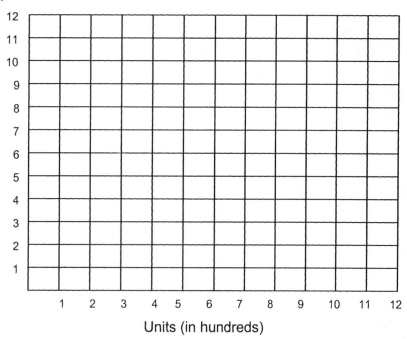

Units (in hundreds)

What is the weekly break-even point?

(a)   In units: _____ units

(b)   In total sales dollars: $_____

Exercises

1. Given for one of the products of Juarez Co.

Sales price per product unit	$50
Variable expenses per product unit	$35
Total fixed expenses per month	$27,000

a. Contribution margin per product unit $_____

b. Break-even sales in units per month _____units

c. Sales in units that will produce a net income of $9,000 per month _____units

d. Sales in units that will produce a net income of 20% of sales per month _____units

e. Net income if 2,500 product units are sold per month $_____

f. The break-even sales in units if variable expenses are decreased by $3 per unit and if total fixed expenses are increased by $9,000 per month _____units

g. If the company desires a net income of $15,000 on a sales volume of 5,000 units per month, what must the unit selling price be, assuming no changes in the $35 variable expenses per unit or the $27,000 total fixed expenses? $_____

2. Another good practice problem.

Monthly data given for Minturn Corporation:

Sales	$50,000
Total fixed expenses	$12,000
Total variable expenses	$35,000

Find:

a. Variable-cost ratio _____%

b. Contribution-margin ratio _____%

c. Break-even sales dollars $_____

d. Sales that would produce a net income of $9,000, assuming no change in the variable-cost ratio or the total fixed expenses $_____

e. Break-even sales if total fixed expenses are reduced by $3,000 *and if selling prices are* reduced by 20% per product unit, assuming no change in variable cost per product unit $_____

3. (Appendix 2A) Summa Products, Inc., produces and sells two products as follows:

	Magna	Laude
Selling prices per unit...	$50	$36
Variable costs per unit...	$40	$30

Total fixed costs are $20,160 per week.

Compute the break-even point in terms of units per week for each of these planned mixes:

	Units of Magna	Units of Laude
a. Three Magnas for each Laude	_____units	_____units
b. Three Laudes for each Magna	_____units	_____units

4. (Appendix 2B) Monthly data given for Peripheral Storage, Inc.:

Product selling price per unit	$20
Variable expenses per unit	$14
Fixed expenses	$12,000
Target profit *after* taxes	$3,600
Income tax rate	40%
Required unit sales?	_____

CHAPTER 2 SOLUTIONS TO PRACTICE TEST QUESTIONS AND PROBLEMS

True or False Statements

1. True   Fluctuations in cost-driver activity cause variable costs, which are components of total costs, to vary.

2. True   The relevant range is the range of activity over which variable costs per unit are assumed to be constant.

3. False   This is an incorrect approach to CVP analysis. Find the break-even point by dividing total fixed costs by the contribution margin per unit.

4. False   Fixed costs in total stay the same over the relevant range, but fixed cost per unit, which is another way of saying averaged fixed cost per unit, varies in proportion to activity level.

5. True   In the short run, one may not be able to vary costs at all; conversely, in the long run, all costs may be variable.

6. False   The margin of safety is the excess of planned unit sales over break-even sales. Gross margin is sales less total cost of goods sold.

7. True   These terms all refer to the amount of additional income earned by selling additional units of product or service.

8. False   This operation yields the target sales in dollars, not units. Dividing by unit contribution margin yields target sales in units (which can be multiplied by sales price to get sales dollars).

9. True   Additional profit beyond breakeven depends on the magnitude of the contribution margin per unit and the additional units sold.

10. False   High operating leverage means high fixed costs relative to variable costs (relatively high contribution margins). Small changes in sales activity (either way) can cause wide swings in profitability.

Multiple-Choice Questions

1. d   As activity level increases, fixed costs support more activity, and average fixed costs per unit decrease. Variable costs per unit and total fixed costs are constant, and total variable costs vary *directly* with activity.

2. d   Assuming we are within the relevant range, total fixed costs should remain at $60,000. Fixed costs per unit would be $60,000 ÷ 30,000 units = $2 per unit.

3. a   Again assuming we are within the relevant range, variable costs per unit should remain unchanged at $100,000 ÷ 20,000 = $5 per unit. Variable costs in total should increase to $5 x 25,000 = $125,000.

4. d   Variable cost per unit is $6,000 ÷ 2,000 = $3 per unit. Unit contribution-margin is $5 - $3 = $2 per unit. Dividing fixed costs by the contribution-margin per unit yields the break-even sales activity in units: $2,200 ÷ $2/unit = 1,100 units.

5. c   The contribution-margin ratio is $(20,000 - 8,000) ÷ $20,000 = .60. Dividing the fixed costs by the contribution-margin ratio yields break-even sales in dollars: $6,000 ÷ .60 = $10,000.

6. b   Break-even units are: $48,000 ÷ $(24 - 16) = 6,000 units.

7. a   This is easiest to show by example. Let sales = $10,000 and variable costs = $6,000. The total contribution margin (CM) = $4,000 and the CM ratio = $(10,000 - 6,000) ÷ $10,000 = 40%. Increasing the CM ratio by 25% yields a CM ratio of 50%. This would raise the total CM to .50 x $10,000 = $5,000, which is 25% higher than before. Fixed costs are irrelevant to CM; fixed costs affect the percentage increase in net income, however.

8. b   Gross margin is sales less total cost of goods sold. (a) and (d) are the contribution margin, and (c) is the margin of safety.

9. b   Using the equation technique: $2X + $5Y - $10,500 = 0 (break-even profits)

The product mix assumption is: X = 5Y (in units)

Substituting 5Y for X yields: $2(5Y) + $5Y - $10,500 = 0

$10Y + $5Y = 10,500

$15Y = $10,500

Y = 700 units

For extra practice, find break-even units of X and prove that these are the break-even sales units (e.g., show that profits are zero).

10. d   First, find the before-tax profit target: $4,800 ÷ (1 - .40) = $8,000

Using the equation technique:

$(24 - 16)N - $48,000 = $8,000

$8N = $8,000 + $48,000

$8N = $56,000

N = 7,000 units

For extra practice, prove that this level of sales units will generate a profit of $4,800 after tax.

Completion

1.   the relevant range, length of planning period, specific decision situation

2.   fixed costs, high, variable costs

3.   fixed

4.   a linear (or straight-line)

5.   decrease

6.   the target profit, the contribution margin per unit

7.   dividing, fixed costs, the contribution-margin ratio

8.   contribution-margin, equation, CVP

9.   relevant range

10.   cost drivers

Problems

1. Como Company

     a. $180,000 ÷ 5,000 = $36

     b. $120,000 ÷ 5,000 = $24

     c. $180,000, constant in total within the relevant range

     d.   6,000 x $24 (from part b) = $144,000

     e. $180,000 ÷ 6,000 = $30

     f. $24, constant per unit within the relevant range (from part b)

     g. $180,000, constant in total within the relevant range

     h.   4,000 x $24 (from part b) = $96,000

     i. $180,000 ÷ 4,000 = $45

     j. $24, constant per unit within the relevant range (from part b)

2.

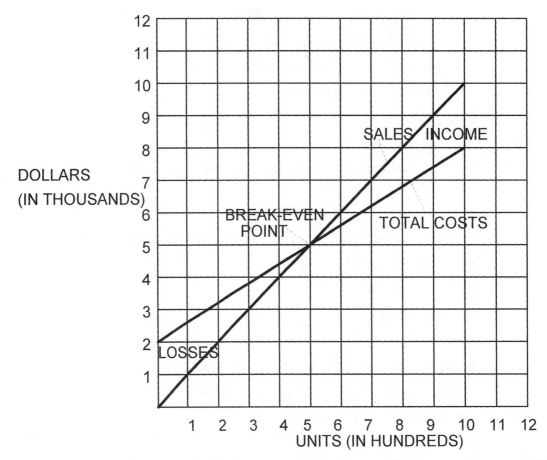

Break-even point can also be computed: fixed expenses divided by contribution-margin per unit: $2,000 ÷($10 - $6) = $2,000 ÷ $4 = 500 units, or, in dollars: 500 x $10 = $5,000.

Exercises

1. Juarez Co.

a. Unit contribution margin is unit selling price less unit variable expenses: $50 - $35 = $15.

b. Break-even sales in units is total fixed expenses divided by unit contribution margin:

$27,000 ÷ $15/unit = 1,800 units.

c. Unit sales to produce a target net income would be the sum of the total fixed expenses and the target net income divided by the unit contribution margin:

$(27,000 + 9,000) ÷ $15/unit = 2,400 units.

d. Using the equation approach:

target profits = .20 x total sales = .20 x $50N = $10N

$(50 - 35)N - $27,000 = $10N

$15N - $10N = $27,000

$5N = $27,000

N = 5,400 units

e. Each unit would contribute $15 toward total fixed expenses. Therefore net income would be: $(15 x 2,500) - $27,000 = $37,500 - $27,000 = $10,500.

f. The new unit contribution margin would be: $50 - $(35 - 3) = $18 per unit. The new total fixed expenses would be: $27,000 + $9,000 = $36,000. Therefore the new break-even sales in units would be: $36,000 ÷ $18/unit = 2,000 units.

g. Using the equation technique: Let P = the unknown sales price

[$(P - 35) x 5,000] - $27,000 = $15,000

5,000P -$35 x 5,000 -$27,000 = $15,000

5,000P = $15,000 + 27,000 + $175,000

5,000P = $217,000

P = $43.40

2. Minturn Corporation:

a. Variable-cost ratio is total variable expenses divided by sales: $35,000 ÷ $50,000 = 70%.

b. Contribution-margin ratio is the complement of the variable-cost ratio:

100% - 70% = 30%; or $(50,000 - 35,000) ÷ $50,000 = $15,000 ÷ $50,000 = 30%

c. Break-even sales are total fixed expenses divided by the contribution-margin ratio:

$12,000 ÷ 30% = $40,000.

d. Divide the sum of the fixed expenses and the desired net income (target net income) by the contribution-margin ratio:

$(12,000 + 9,000) ÷ 30% = $21,000 ÷ .30 = $70,000.

e.   The new total fixed expenses would be: $12,000 - $3,000 = $9,000. The new variable-cost ratio (to total dollar sales) would be:

$$\$35,000 \div \$(50,000 - 20\% \text{ of } 50,000) = \$35,000 \div \$40,000 = 7/8, \text{ or } 87.5\%.$$

Therefore the new contribution-margin ratio would be 1/8, or 12.5%. The new break-even sales would then be the new total fixed expenses divided by the new contribution-margin ratio:

$$\$9,000 \div 1/8 = \$9,000 \times 8 = \$72,000.$$

3. Summa Products, Inc.

Contribution margins are $50-$40 = $10 for Magna and $36 - $30 = $6 for Laude.

Using the equation approach $10M + $6L - $20,160 = 0 (break-even profits)

a. the product mix assumption is: M = 3L

$10(3L) + $6L = $20,160

$30L +$ 6L = $20,160

$36L = $20,160

L = 560 units

M = 3L = 3(560) = 1,680 units

b. the product mix assumption is: L = 3M

$10M +$6(3M) = $20,160

$10M + $18M = $20,160

$28M = $20,160

M = 720 units

L = 3M = 3(720) = 2,160 units

4. Peripheral Storage, Inc.

Required profit before tax = $3,600 ÷ (1 - .40) = $6,000

Using the equation technique:

$(20 - 14)N -$12,000 = $6,000

$6N = $6,000 + $12,000

N = $18,000 ÷ $6 = 3,000 units

Proof:

Sales: $20 x 3,000	$60,000
Less expenses:	
Variable $14 x 3,000	42,000
Fixed	12,000
Income before tax	$ 6,000
Taxes @ 40%	2,400
Income after tax	$ 3,600

CHAPTER 3

Measurement of Cost Behavior

<table>
<tr><td align="center">OVERVIEW</td></tr>
</table>

OVERVIEW

Previously, we identified two mutually exclusive patterns of cost behavior: strictly fixed and strictly variable. Now we introduce some variations of these cost behaviors. The objective of this chapter is to expand your understanding of cost behavior and introduce you to methods for measuring cost behavior. Your learning objectives are to:

I. Explain step- and mixed-cost behavior

II. Explain management influences on cost behavior

III. Measure and mathematically express cost functions and use them to predict costs

IV. Describe the importance of activity analysis for measuring cost functions

V. Measure cost behavior using the engineering analysis, account analysis, high-low, visual-fit, and least-squares regression methods

REVIEW OF KEY CONCEPTS

I.   Explain step- and mixed-cost behavior

Understanding how cost drivers affect cost behavior is fundamental to planning and controlling costs. Some costs have multiple cost drivers, but in practice it is more common to use a single cost driver for any cost. Note that different costs may have different (single) cost drivers. The major types of cost functions in addition to fixed and variable costs, which have already been defined, are:

A.   **Step-costs** are costs with abrupt breaks in the pattern of total cost as activity volume shifts from one range to another.

> 1.   Sometimes the breaks are small enough that the step cost can be approximated by a variable cost with little error.
>
> 2.   A step cost is just a fixed cost with multiple relevant ranges—switching to a higher relevant range causes a step increase in fixed costs.

> **Stop and Review**
>
> See textbook Exhibits 3-1 and 3-2

B.   **Mixed costs** are a combination of variable and fixed costs.

> 1.   Examples of mixed costs include repairs, power, and the rental of a truck at a fixed monthly rate plus a mileage rate.
>
> 2.   A mixed cost is just a variable cost on top of a fixed cost.

> **Stop and Review**
>
> See textbook Exhibit 3-3

> **Study Tip:** *Before you go on to the next section, be sure that you understand how step and mixed costs behave with respect to cost-driver activity.*

II.   Explain management influences on cost behavior

Management decisions about *product and service attributes* such as quality, performance options, colors, finishes, and so on have a great influence on cost. Planning for costs must account for these cost effects.

A.   **Capacity costs** originate from fixed outlays for assets, people, and programs. These outlays measure a company's cost of providing a particular capacity for such activities as production, sales, administration, and research.

B.   **Committed fixed costs** are incurred because of a company's basic organization and the ownership of such long-term assets as land, buildings, machinery, and equipment.

> 1.   Examples are certain administrative salaries, insurance, property taxes, rent, depreciation, and long-term lease payments.
>
> 2.   Committed fixed costs cannot be decreased without changing contractual agreements and/or jeopardizing a company's ability to meet its long-range goals.
>
> 3.   Thus capital expenditures, which lay the foundation for many fixed costs, must be planned very carefully (covered in Chapters 11 and 12).

C.   **Discretionary fixed costs,** also called *managed* or *programmed costs*, arise from periodic budget appropriation decisions to implement top management policies.

        a.   Examples include the costs of advertising, sales promotion, employee training programs, and research and development.

        b.   Discretionary fixed costs usually do not depend directly on the volume of activity but are determined in advance by management for the budget period.

        c.   In contrast to committed fixed costs, discretionary fixed costs could be drastically reduced if necessary in the short run, but this may affect the ability of the organization to meet its long-run goals.

D.   Decisions about the *technology* used for manufacturing, customer service, and information systems will have dramatic effects on cost behavior. Usually, improved technology trades off lower variable costs for higher fixed costs. Thus, decisions about capacity are critical to technology decisions.

E.   *Cost control incentives* should affect decisions that managers, engineers, product designers, and sales personnel make about products and services. Incentives should be designed to promote both quality and cost control—this is not an easy task.

> **Study Tip:** *Before going on, can you explain how management decisions can affect product and service costs?*

III.   **Measure and mathematically express cost functions and use them to predict costs**

Cost functions are mathematical representations of cost behavior.

A.   Simple, linear cost behavior can be represented by the following equation:

$$Y = F + VX$$

        1.   Y is the *cost*; for example, power cost.

        2.   X is the *cost driver*; for example, machine hours.

        3.   F is the periodic *fixed cost* (the intercept or value of **Y** when **X** is zero).

        4.   V is the variable cost per unit of cost-driver activity (the slope of the line, the amount of increase in Y for each unit of increase in X).

B.   Measuring cost behavior is quantifying the relationship of Y to X by giving values to F and V.

C.   Two principal criteria are used for accepting and using a particular cost function:

        1.   **Economic plausibility.**   The relationship must seem reasonable. Does a believable cause-and-effect relationship exist between the cost and the proposed cost driver?

        2.   **Reliability.**   Reliability can be measured with "goodness of fit." How well does the cost function predict actual costs?

        3.   Note that the cost-benefit criterion also applies—do not spend more time, effort, and money measuring cost behavior than the organization will benefit through improved decision making. But also note that some firms are spending considerable resources improving their measures of cost behavior because of intense competition.

IV.   Describe the importance of activity analysis for measuring cost functions

Many organizations use *activity analysis* to choose plausible and reliable cost drivers.

Activity analysis finds the most appropriate cost driver for each cost by looking for the underlying activities in the organization that cause costs.

A.   Costs that are caused by a single, volume-related cost driver are the easiest to measure because the association of cost and cost driver is observable.

B.   In contrast, costs that are related to multiple, non-volume cost drivers can be difficult to measure because the association may not be readily observable.

C.   In practice many firms have used a single volume-related cost driver (e.g., units produced or direct labor hours) for all their costs. Because of increasing competition and changing technology, this practice has led to many incorrect cost predictions.

D.   Global competition and rapidly changing technology are two of the reasons why activity analysis is currently a vital management accounting issue.

> **Study Tip:** *Do you know the meaning of the term "cost function," and can you explain each of its elements? Why should cost functions be plausible and reliable? Could you explain why activity analysis is important?*

V.   Measure cost behavior using the engineering analysis, account analysis, high-low, visual-fit, and least-squares regression methods

Cost analysts have developed feasible methods for measuring cost functions by making trade-offs between accuracy, cost, and timeliness.

A.   **Engineering analysis** measures what costs *should be* based on technical plans, prior experience, and product or service prototypes.

    1.   This method is widely used but is costly and not timely.

    2.   It is especially valuable for predicting the costs of new products or services.

B.   **Account analysis** requires only limited past data to analyze what costs *have been*.

    1.   This method is quick and easy to use.

    2.   However, the cost measures may not be valid because only limited data are used.

C.   The **high-low** method is a simple way to measure a cost function between two past levels of cost and cost-driver activity. It also may be unreliable, however, because the choice of the two points is arbitrary and ignores other cost data.

    1.   First, choose a high and a low level of activity--they should be representative of operations and not from unusual time periods.

    2.   Next, measure the variable cost per unit as the change in cost divided by the change in activity.

3. At either the high or the low point, the fixed-cost measure is total cost less total variable cost.

Example: Measure the power-cost function using machine hours as the appropriate cost driver.

Month	Power cost	Machine hours
High: July	$12,000	2,000
Low: November	7,000	1,000
Difference	5,000	1,000

V = Change in cost ÷ Change in machine hours = $5,000 ÷ 1,000

V = $5/machine hour

F = $12,000 – ($5 x 2,000) = $2,000 per month (at the high point)

F = $7,000 – ($5 x 1,000) = $2,000 per month (at the low point)

The cost function is: Y = $2,000 per month + $5 X

> **Stop and Review**
>
> See textbook Exhibit 3-4

D. The **visual-fit** method fits a line through cost and cost-driver levels plotted on a graph.

1. This method is not used in practice, but it is a good introduction to what least-squares regression accomplishes with statistics.

2. The intent is to place a line through the data that captures the general tendency of total cost to vary directly with cost-driver activity.

3. The visual-fit method uses all data points instead of only the two used by the high-low method.

> **Stop and Review**
>
> See textbook Exhibit 3-5

E. The **least-squares method** is a mathematical approach that uses all available data in a more objective way than the visual-fit method.

1. All regression analysis in practice is done using a computer. If not for computers, very little regression would be performed in practice; there are too many calculations necessary.

2. This method also provides statistics to show how well the regression line fits the data. For example, R^2 measures how much of the fluctuation of a cost is explained by changes in cost-driver activity. It is a common statistical measure of reliability or goodness of fit.

> **Stop and Review**
>
> See textbook Exhibit 3-6

3. Regression requires considerable past data and a fair amount of statistical knowledge to interpret the results.

F. In summary, some form of engineering analysis is the most commonly used method for measuring cost functions, though regression analysis is gaining usage as more cost analysts become familiar with it and as accounting systems track costs and cost drivers more consistently.

> **Study Tip:** *Before leaving this section be, sure that you can describe the strengths and weaknesses of the different methods for measuring cost behavior. Do you understand the numerical example of the high-low method?*

G. (Appendix 3) Regression analysis is nearly effortless on the computer. It is dangerous for that reason, though. Without statistical training you may not be able to interpret the regression results properly. If you are serious about cost analysis, you should take at least an introductory regression class and learn to use statistical software. A full treatment of statistical cost analysis obviously is beyond the scope of this text and study guide.

   1. Computer software is very powerful.

      a. Everyone should know how to use spreadsheets, but the statistical output is very limited.

      b. Serious statistical analysis is easiest with serious statistical software; many good statistical software packages are available at most schools and large companies.

      c. The effects of multiple cost drivers can be assessed with regression analysis.

   2. Entering data without error is a critical first step.

      a. Be sure that the cost and cost-driver data are from the same time periods and that there are no recording errors.

      b. Often accounting systems have not recorded cost or cost-driver data in the way you would like. Resist the temptation to "fudge" the data to make it fit your desired analysis.

      c. If you cannot get valid data, then you should not be using regression analysis. Use one of the other techniques until better data are available.

   3. Plotting the cost data against each cost driver is a good idea because the graph will indicate obvious linear relationships and may highlight data errors.

   4. Interpreting most regression output requires statistical training, but some of the output is interpretable by novices.

      a. The most important items to look for are the intercept or constant (F, fixed cost) and the X-coefficient(s) [V, variable cost(s)]. Use these to construct your cost function.

      b. Low values of R^2 (which ranges from 0 to 1) indicate that the cost driver does not explain cost behavior. A high value of R^2 obtained with plausible cost drivers is the desired outcome.

PRACTICE TEST QUESTIONS AND PROBLEMS
True or False Statements

Determine whether each of the following statements is True (T) or False (F), and enter your answer in the space provided.

_____1.   Explanation of accounting cost behavior requires only one cost driver.

_____2.   Costs that vary with respect to cost drivers vary linearly.

_____3.   Step costs and mixed costs are fundamentally different from fixed and variable costs.

_____4.   Committed costs often involve legal, contractual payment obligations.

_____5.   Engineering analysis can be used only to measure what costs should be in manufacturing companies where engineering plans are available.

_____6.   Account analysis is the most objective cost measurement method because it relies on the accounting system for data.

_____7.   The high-low method can be unreliable because the choice of data points is arbitrary.

_____8.   Because it is the most objective method, regression analysis should be used to measure nearly all cost functions.

_____9.   Using activity analysis to select cost drivers results in appropriate cost functions.

_____10.   (Appendix 3) Spreadsheet software is most appropriate for statistically measuring cost functions.

Multiple-Choice Questions

For each of the following multiple-choice questions, select the best answer(s), and enter their identification letters in the space provided.

_____1.   Examples of committed fixed costs could include: (a) direct labor wages, (b) bond interest expense, (c) building depreciation, (d) management training costs.

_____2.   Examples of step-function costs could include: (a) salaries of billing clerks, (b) equipment rentals, (c) direct materials used, (d) research and development costs.

_____3.   Examples of discretionary fixed costs could include: (a) sales commissions, (b) fire insurance on factory building, (c) salaries of payroll clerks, (d) annual factory picnic and holiday party.

_____4.   Examples of strictly variable costs could include: (a) plant manager's salary, (b) wages of maintenance personnel, (c) heating and air conditioning costs, (d) office supplies.

_____5.   Cost prediction methods that use all relevant data points include: (a) least-squares method, (b) visual-fit method, (c) account analysis, (d) high-low method.

_____6. In contrast to discretionary fixed costs, committed fixed costs are: (a) more difficult to measure and evaluate in terms of their outputs, (b) less easily influenced by management on a short-term basis, (c) both of these, (d) neither of these.

_____7. Costs that are most likely to behave as variable costs are: (a) advertising, (b) direct labor, (c) research and development, (d) direct materials.

_____8. The budgeted annual cost of operating a post office truck is $4,400 plus $.20 per mile. In 20X2 the truck was to be driven 24,000 miles uniformly to deliver various mail items throughout the year. Two employees are needed for each truck. If these data were reflected in a linear equation to represent the cost function, the cost driver would be: (a) number of letters and packages delivered, (b) miles driven, (c) weight of mail delivered, (d) number of postal employees per truck.

_____9. See the preceding test item. The total annual variable cost of operating a truck is (a) $.20 per mile, (b) $9,200 per year, (c) $4,800 per year, (d) $400 per month.

_____10. See test item 8 above. The total cost of operating a truck would be (a) $24,000 per year, (b) $9,200 per year, (c) $.38 per mile, (d) $177 per week.

Completion

Complete each of the following statements by filling in the blanks.

1. Measuring cost behavior is _____ and _____ how activities affect levels of costs.

2. Linear cost behavior occurs when a cost changes _____with _____.

3. The two major types of cost behavior are _____and _____ costs.

4. Variable costs that may fluctuate with sales merely because management has allocated in advance certain proportions of dollar sales are really _____ costs.

5. Mixed costs are a combination of _____ and _____.

6. Step costs can be treated as _____costs when the _____ shifts.

7. Changing committed fixed costs can _____ and can _____ long-run goals.

8. The slope and intercept of a straight line correspond to the _____ and _____ of a cost function.

9. _____ and _____ are two essential features of cost functions.

10. One danger of regression analysis is that by the time _____ are collected the _____ may be _____.

Problems

1. Solari Instruments, Inc. uses a cost function for predicting the annual cost of operating its delivery trucks: $Y = \$28,000 + \$.20\ X$. Identify or determine the symbol or amount that represents each of the following ideas or amounts:

    (a) The cost to be explained

    (b) The cost driver

    (c) The slope of the regression line $

    (d) The total cost if X is 200,000 $

    (e) The mathematical value of the cost $
        when the cost driver is zero

    (f) Is (e) the expected cost at zero activity? Why or why not?

2. Given for a mixed materials support cost of Spicer Company that accountants believe varies directly with direct labor (DL) hours:

Volume of activity in direct labor hours per month	June	July	August	September	October
	50,000	60,000	70,000	80,000	90,000
Total cost per month	$14,000	$16,900	$18,000	$21,000	$22,800

    a.   Using the high-low method, compute the variable overhead cost per direct labor hour.

    b.   Compute the indicated fixed cost per month.

    c.   Express the cost behavior as a cost function.

3. Consider the facts in problem 2 above. Activity analysis reveals that in fact materials support costs vary directly with the weight of material shipped, not direct labor hours.

    a.   Discuss why managers may have looked for other cost drivers.

    b.   How might activity analysis have discovered the relationship between materials support cost and weight of materials moved?

    c.   Materials support cost expressed as function of weight of materials moved is:

        $Y = \$1,000/\text{month} + (\$0.17 \times \text{Weight of material moved in kilograms})$

Compare and comment on predicted materials support costs using each cost driver for the following months:

	November	December	January
Direct labor hours	50,000	70,000	90,000
Predicted cost			
Weight moved, kg	90,000	100,000	80,000
Predicted cost			
Difference			

d. Actual material support costs in November, January, and December were: $16,000, $18,200, and $15,000, respectively. Which cost function is more reliable? Why?

Exercises

1. **Predicting Costs:** Given the following four cost behaviors and expected levels of cost-driver activity, predict the total costs:

    a. Fuel costs for a charter bus per month, $ .40 per mile, driven 20,000 miles per month

    b. Equipment rental cost, $1,500 per piece of equipment per month for seven pieces for three months

    c. Ambulance and EMT personnel cost for a basketball tournament, $800 for each 200 tournament participants; the tournament is expecting 1,100 participants

    d. Purchasing department cost in one month, $8,000 per month plus $6 per material order processed at 3,500 orders in one month

2. Identifying Discretionary and Committed Fixed Costs: Identify and compute total discretionary fixed and committed fixed costs from the following list prepared by the accounting supervisor for Monarch Fitness Corp.:

Advertising	$28,000
Depreciation	44,000
Company health insurance	13,000
Management salaries	90,000
Payment on long-term debt	60,000
Property tax	29,000
Grounds maintenance	8,000
Research and development	35,000

3. Cost Effects of Technology: Cloud Nine, an athletic apparel retailer, is considering making it possible for its customers to order on the World Wide Web (WWW). Use the estimated costs of two alternative approaches below to answer the questions:

	Current	WWW
Annual fixed cost	$150,000	$300,000
Variable cost per order	$5	$2.50
Expected number of orders	70,000	70,000

a. Which approach has a lower cost?

b. What is the "break-even" level of orders?

c. What is the meaning of this level of orders?

CHAPTER 3 SOLUTIONS TO PRACTICE TEST QUESTIONS AND PROBLEMS

True or False Statements

1. False   Accountants often assume that this is true, but it probably never is true. The costs of finding and using "true" cost behavior which might involve multiple cost drivers, however, may exceed the benefits. Thus, single cost drivers are most common in accounting cost functions.

2. False   Again, we often assume that variable cost behavior is linear, but it may not be. Economic theory, for example, predicts that variable or marginal costs are not linear. Within the relevant range, however, a linear cost function may be an acceptable approximation.

3. False   Mixed costs are combinations of fixed and variable costs. Step costs are fixed costs that shift as activity shifts from one relevant range to another.

4. True   Committed costs do not have to be the result of legal obligations, though. Such costs as depreciation and research costs may be set by organizations that have made firm commitments to capacity or research activity as part of long-run strategy.

5. False   Engineering analysis can be appropriate in any organization where inputs can be related to outputs.

6. False   Account analysis typically relies on very few data points, which may not be representative of typical operations. Thus, the cost function that results may not be reliable.

7. True   The high-low method uses only two data points which are arbitrarily chosen to represent high and low levels of activity. Other data are ignored.

8. False   Regression analysis is the most objective method when sufficient relevant data are available and when the analyst understands the limitations of regression. Otherwise, another method may be more appropriate.

9. True   This *should* result, but of course an analyst can do a poor job of screening cost drivers for plausibility and reliability and may select inappropriate cost drivers.

10. False   Spreadsheet software is good for "quick and dirty" cost analysis, but more specialized statistical software is generally more appropriate.

Multiple-Choice Questions

1. b, c   Both of these are more typical committed fixed costs. Direct labor wages may be relatively fixed in some countries and in some companies that have permanent employment policies, however.

2. a, b   These two costs typically come in "chunks" as activity such as billing increases by a relatively large amount. Direct materials cost is typically variable. Research and development costs are typically discretionary fixed costs.

3. c, d   Sales commissions are typically variable costs. Fire insurance may be committed if, for example, a mortgage-holder requires insurance on the property.

4. c, d   A manager's salary is usually fixed. Likewise, maintenance personnel costs may be incurred as part of a preventive maintenance program. This may have an element of variable cost in it, however, so it would be a mixed cost. Heating and air conditioning costs are at least partially variable with respect to ambient temperatures (i.e., degree-days). Office supplies are probably variable with respect to staffing levels and office activity.

5. a, b   The other methods use only a few data points. It may be, though, that account analysis after the first time period of experience with a product or service uses the only relevant data point—last period's.

6. b   The effects of discretionary and committed fixed costs are equally difficult to evaluate. Committed fixed costs are less easily changed in the short run.

7. d   Advertising and research and development may be planned as if they were variable (e.g., as a percentage of sales), but they really are discretionary fixed costs. Direct labor may be "sticky," that is, due to policy not very responsive to changes in activity. Usage of direct materials is usually directly variable with regard to measures of productive activity.

8. b   The cost driver is expressed as the number of miles driven.

9. c   Total annual variable cost is predicted to be $.20 x 24,000 miles = $4,800. This is $400 on a monthly basis if mileage is uniform over the year.

10. b, c, d   Total annual operating cost at 24,000 miles is $4,400 + $4,800 = $9,200. Total cost per mile at 24,000 miles is $9,200 ÷ 24,000 = $.38/mile. Total cost per week at 24,000 miles is $9,200 ÷ 52 = $177.

Completion

1.   understanding, quantifying
2.   proportionately, cost-driver activity
3.   variable, fixed
4.   discretionary fixed costs
5.   variable, fixed costs
6.   fixed, relevant range
7.   be difficult, prevent attaining
8.   variable cost per unit, fixed cost per period
9.   plausibility, reliability
10.   sufficient data, data, obsolete

Problems

1. (a) Y; (b) X; (c) $.20; (d) $28,000 + ($.20 x 200,000) = $68,000; (e) $28,000; (f) No, because a cost-driver level of 0 is probably outside the relevant range for which the fixed cost measure is valid.

2. June and October are the low and high months for cost-driver activity. They seem representative.

   a. V = ($22,800 - $14,000) ÷ (90,000 - 50,000) = $8,800 ÷ 40,000 = $.22/ DL hour

   b. F = $22,800 – ($.22 x 90,000) = $3,000 per month, also

   F = $14,000 – ($.22 x 50,000) = $3,000 per month

   c. Y = $3,000 per month + ($.22 x DL hours)

3. a. Managers may have found that actual costs did not correspond to predicted costs using DL hours as the cost driver. The errors may have been sufficiently large to adversely affect decision making, prompting the application of activity analysis.

   b. Activity analysis can be based on direct observation of costs and activities, interviews with relevant personnel, and statistical analysis of past data. These efforts may have found that weight of materials moved explained past materials support costs better than other possible cost drivers and, more important, is expected to predict future materials support costs well.

c.	November	December	January
Direct labor hours	50,000	70,000	90,000
Predicted cost	$3,000 + $.22(50,000) = $14,000	$3,000 + $.22(70,000) = $18,400	$3,000 + $.22(90,000) = $22,800
Weight moved, kg	90,000	100,000	80,000
Predicted cost	$1,000 + $.17(90,000) = $16,300	$1,000 + $.17(100,000) = $18,000	$1,000 + $.17(80,000) = $14,600
Difference (new compared to old)	$2,300 more	$400 less	$8,200 less

The two cost drivers do not seem to be positively correlated (as one goes up, the other goes up, too), so they are probably quite different measures of activity. If weight of materials is the more appropriate cost driver, then using DL hours results in inaccurate cost predictions.

d. Computing average errors of actual from predicted costs using each cost driver gives each cost driver a goodness of fit "score."

Direct labor hours prediction	Actual costs	Error*
$14,000	$16,000	$2,000
18,400	18,200	200
22,800	15,000	7,800
Average error		$3,333

Material moved prediction	Actual costs	Error*
$16,300	$16,000	$300
18,000	18,200	200
14,600	15,000	400
Average error		$300

(*All expressed as positive numbers because an error is undesirable regardless of its direction.)

Based on this limited data, the weight of material moved is obviously the superior cost driver. The average error for the direct labor-hours predictions is nearly nine times as large. As long as it is relatively easy to monitor weight of materials moved each month, it should be the cost driver used for materials support cost. Many firms have found that direct labor hours is not a reliable cost driver for most support costs.

Exercises

1. **Predicting Costs**

   a. $ .40 per mile x 20,000 miles per month = $8,000 total cost

   b. $1,500 per piece of equipment per month x 7 pieces rented x 3 months = $31,500 total cost

   c. (1,100 expected participants ÷ 200 participants) = 5.5 ambulance crews. Round up to 6 x $800 ambulance and AMT personnel cost = $4,800 total cost

   d. $6 per material order x 3,500 orders in one month + $8,000 = $29,000

2. **Identifying Discretionary and Committed Fixed Costs**

   Discretionary fixed costs

Advertising	$28,000
Company health insurance	13,000
Management salaries	90,000
Grounds maintenance	8,000
Research and development	35,000
total	$174,000

Committed fixed costs

Depreciation	$44,000
Payment on long-term debt	60,000
Property tax	29,000
total	$133,000

3. Cost Effects of Technology

a. <u>Current:</u> (70,000 expected orders x $5 variable cost per order) + $150,000 annual fixed cost = $500,000 total cost

<u>WWW:</u> (70,000 expected orders x $2.50 variable cost per order) + $300,000 annual fixed cost = $475,000 total cost

The WWW system is less costly at the expected level of orders.

b. "Break-even" level of orders: equate the two cost functions: $150,000 current annual fixed cost + $5X = $300,000 annual fixed cost with WWW + $2.5X

Solve for X, the number of orders:

$$\$2.5X = \$150,000$$

$$X = 60,000$$

"Break- even" level of orders = 60,000

c. The "break-even" level signifies the number of orders at which the total cost of both alternatives is equal. Because the WWW system has a lower variable cost per order, it is less costly at order levels exceeding 60,000 orders.

Cost Management Systems and Activity-Based Costing

OVERVIEW

The focus of this chapter is how costs are classified, accumulated, and assigned to products, services, and periods. A key concept to learn from this chapter is that though classifications of costs are somewhat arbitrary, the goal of managerial cost systems is to identify and measure all the costs of activities and products and services that generate revenue. After reading this chapter, you should be able to:

I.   Describe the purposes of cost management systems

II.   Explain the relationships among cost, cost object, cost accumulation, and cost assignment

III.   Distinguish between direct, and indirect costs

IV.   Explain the major reasons for allocating costs

V.   Identify the main types of manufacturing costs: direct materials, direct labor, and indirect production costs

VI.   Explain how the financial statements of merchandisers and manufacturers differ because of the types of goods they sell

VII.   Understand the differences between traditional and activity-based costing (ABC) systems and why ABC systems provide value to managers

VIII. Use activity-based management (ABM) to make strategic and operational control decisions

IX.   Describe the steps in designing an activity-based costing system (Appendix 4)

| **I.** | **Describe the purposes of cost management systems** |

A. Cost systems that are designed primarily to aid management decision making (rather than financial reporting) are called **cost management systems**.

   1. A **cost management system** combines cost behavior and decision-making information needs to analyze the costs of cost objects.

      a. Cost management systems rely heavily on activity analysis and ABC (see below).

      b. As discussed in Chapter 1, management accounting serves decision makers best when cost management systems are parallel to the decision-making process.

   2. In many organizations, however, the cost system must serve both decision-making needs and financial reporting requirements. Note that these may not be compatible, and some firms have multiple cost systems—one for financial reporting and one for decision making.

B. Cost management systems must be consistent with the organization's strategy by providing planning and scorekeeping information relevant to the organization's goals and objectives (see Chapter 9 for detailed discussions).

| **II.** | **Explain the relationships among cost, cost object, cost accumulation, and cost assignment** |

A. Any **cost accounting system**, which measures costs for decision making and financial reporting, has two main elements:

   1. The **accumulation** of initial costs by such natural classes as material or labor

   2. The **cost assignment** (also called cost *allocation* or *attribution*) of these costs to cost objectives; for example, to

      a. Evaluate the performance of organizational departments or

      b. Compute costs of outputs (end products and services produced for customers)

> **Stop and Review**
>
> See textbook Exhibit 4-1

B. Understanding cost management systems requires first understanding some basic cost terms and relationships:

   1. **Cost** is the monetary measurement of an exchange of resources for a particular purpose, for example, the dollars paid for printing presses or for typesetting labor by a newspaper publisher. Cost is a measure of the acquisition value of something—for example, what you paid for it. This number is not always obvious for many items.

   2. **Cost objective** (or cost *object*) is any activity for which decision makers need a separate measurement of costs; for example, the cost of operating the credit department or the cost of manufacturing pocket calculators.

| **III.** | **Distinguish between direct and indirect costs** |

A. The terms **direct costs** and **indirect costs** refer to cost relationships to a particular cost objective.

   1. Essentially, the distinction between direct and indirect costs depends on the *economic feasibility of their traceability to the cost object.*

2. **Direct costs** can be identified specifically with a given cost object.

3. **Indirect costs** cannot be identified specifically with a given cost object and are regarded as costs of overall operations. Accountants use cost allocation to assign indirect costs to plausible cost objectives.

4. **Unallocated costs** cannot be assigned to any specific cost objective. Examples of unallocated costs include research and development, process design, information services, and high-level employee salaries.

5. Some costs can be identified as direct costs at a relatively high level in an organization but are indirect costs at lower levels because the cost cannot be more specifically identified to basic activities.

    For example, although a foreman's salary may be direct to the Painting Department that she supervises, it would be indirect to the individual products painted by her department.

6. A major goal of improved cost accounting systems (see activity-based costing below) is to more accurately and thoroughly assign costs to basic activities, products, and services. In concept, most costs could be classified as direct costs at the product level if we understood cost behavior better and if we knew the appropriate cost drivers for each cost. Of course, we must consider the cost-benefit rule.

    > **Study Tip:** *Before going on, be sure that you understand the real, economic reason for the distinction between direct and indirect costs.*

IV. Explain the major reasons for allocating costs

A. Four reasons for allocating costs are:

1. To predict economic effects of control decisions

2. To influence managers to behave in the best interest of the company through feedback and performance evaluation

3. To measure costs for financial reporting

4. To justify costs or obtain reimbursement

V. Identify the main types of manufacturing costs: direct materials, direct labor, and indirect production costs

A. When products or services are the cost objective, the three major categories of costs are:

1. **Direct material cost** is the acquisition cost of materials that are physically identifiable as part of the product and can be traced to the product in an economically feasible way. For example, fabrics, wood, and hardware can be traced to a line of chairs made by a furniture manufacturing company, but it may not be worthwhile to trace glue and fasteners directly to chairs.

2. **Direct labor cost** is the wages of labor that can be identified specifically and exclusively with the product in an economically feasible way. For example, wages of furniture makers can be traced to a line of chairs, but it may not be feasible to directly trace top management salary costs to chairs.

3. **Indirect production (overhead) cost** includes all costs other than direct material and direct labor that are associated with operations. For example, most companies do not try to trace cleaning supplies consumed, custodial labor used, power costs, and depreciation of facilities directly to products or services.

a. These are **indirect** costs in relation to the products manufactured or services provided.

b. Other terms used for *overhead* are **burden, manufacturing overhead, manufacturing expenses,** and **indirect costs.**

c. **Variable overhead** includes supplies, most indirect labor, and other costs that can be shown to vary with some relevant production activity.

d. **Fixed overhead** usually includes supervisory salaries, property taxes, rent, insurance, depreciation, and other support costs that have no discernable (short-run) relationship with any production activities.

4. In many modern factories, direct labor cost is so small compared to other manufacturing costs that firms treat direct labor cost as another overhead item and do not trace it directly to products.

a. This is an application of the cost-benefit rule—tracing direct labor to products would cost more than it is worth.

b. These companies usually maintain two major cost categories: direct material cost and **conversion cost**, which is direct labor plus overhead.

c. A few companies maintain two other major cost categories: **prime cost**, which is direct material and direct labor, and overhead cost.

5. Tracing direct costs in service organizations is more difficult than in manufacturing organizations, but the issues are the same.

a. As discussed in Chapter 2, the output of service organizations is less observable and more labor intensive, making tracing more difficult.

b. Note that many professional lawyers, accountants, and management consultants record their client activities to the minute so that costs of their time can be traced directly to services provided to clients.

> **Study Tip:** *Can you explain the differences among direct materials, direct labor, and overhead costs? Why do some firms treat direct labor as an overhead cost item? Is there a fundamental difference between classifying costs in a service organization and a manufacturing firm?*

B. Cost accounting systems serve the requirements of financial reporting by accumulating costs and assigning them either to *products* and *services* or to *reporting periods*. The primary financial reporting concern is that all costs incurred in a period are allocated to products or time periods.

1. **Product costs** are costs identified with products produced or purchased for resale. These costs are charged against income (i.e., become *product expenses*) when the products are sold. Until products are sold, these costs remain as inventory (unless, for example, the products are obsolete).

a. Product costs for *financial reporting* include direct materials, direct labor, and manufacturing overhead.

b. For income tax reporting only, some sales and administrative costs also are classified as product costs.

c. Note the three stages of inventory flow for a manufacturing company: direct costs plus overhead $\Rightarrow$ work in process $\Rightarrow$ finished goods.

d. For managerial accounting, classification of product costs depends on traceability of costs.

2. **Period costs** are costs that are not assigned to products and are charged against the income of the period (i.e., become *period expenses*).

    a. Period costs of manufacturing firms include most sales and administrative costs.

    b. Note that merchandising and service firms treat all indirect costs as period costs—service firms cannot inventory their output.

    c. Classification of period and product costs also depends on the income measurement method used (see the discussion on the contribution and absorption approaches below).

3. Cost accounting systems for financial reporting may not serve managerial decision making because:

    a. Financial cost accounting assures that all costs of a period are accounted for and is not particularly concerned with how accurately they are assigned across different products and services.

    b. Some major period costs may in fact be traceable to products and services but are not traced.

    c. The primary reason is that the *financial reporting* cost-benefit comparison does not favor improved cost information.

4. According to their traceability, costs may be classified as direct or indirect costs *and* as product or period costs. This may be confusing.

    a. Product costs include direct production costs and some allocation of indirect *production* costs.

    b. Period costs include costs that are indirect to production, but may be direct to different cost objects such as departments. For example, sales costs may be regarded as indirect to products, but as direct to the marketing department, and are period costs for the company.

> **Stop and Review**
>
> See textbook Exhibit 4-4

> **Study Tip:** *Do you understand the potentially overlapping distinctions between direct/indirect and product/period costs for financial reporting? Do you also understand why there is not just one category of cost–direct cost?*

VI. Explain how the financial statements of merchandisers and manufacturers differ because of the types of goods they sell

A. Merchandising companies sell goods without changing their basic form.

    1. Their balance sheets usually carry only one major type of inventory item, merchandise.

    2. Their income statements report the cost of goods sold as the purchase cost of merchandise acquired and resold, including freight charges.

B. Manufacturing companies transform materials into other goods through the use of labor and factory facilities.

1. Their balance sheets usually report three major types of inventory: direct materials, work in process, and finished goods.

2. Their income statements show the manufacturing cost of goods produced and sold.

> **Stop and Review**
>
> Refer again to textbook Exhibit 4-4

C. The three types of manufacturing inventories are affected by movements of resources (transactions) among them:

Change	Direct materials	Work in process	Finished goods
Increase	Purchases of materials	Use of materials, labor, and overhead	Completion of products
Decrease	Use of materials	Completion of products	Sale of products

VII. Understand the main differences between traditional and activity-based costing (ABC) systems and why ABC systems provide value to managers

A. Changes in global competition and manufacturing and information technologies are changing the way cost systems are designed.

B. **Traditional costing systems** *allocate* a large proportion of costs to cost objects. These allocations may be unrelated to the use of resources.

C. **ABC costing systems** seek to find the drivers of costs and use those drivers to directly *trace* costs to cost objects. These traced costs *should be* related to the use of resources.

D. ABC systems may use several stages to trace costs to cost objects. A **two-stage ABC system** uses two stages of allocation to get from the original resource cost to the final product.

> **Stop and Review**
>
> See textbook Exhibits 4-5 and 4-6

E. ABC systems should be evaluated according to costs and benefits.

1. ABC systems provide more detailed information on cost behavior but are expensive to develop and maintain.

2. Many firms are currently implementing ABC systems. See R. Cooper and R. Kaplan, *The Design of Cost Management Systems: Text, Cases, and Readings*, Prentice-Hall, 1999 for a basic treatment of ABC systems.

3. Organizations with rapidly changing technology and strong competitors are most likely to benefit from ABC systems.

VIII. Use activity-based management (ABM) to make strategic and operational control decisions

Perhaps the greatest benefit of activity analysis is improved organizational efficiency through the identification of duplication of effort and *non-value-added activities*. This is called **activity-based management** (ABM)

A. Activity analysis will identify people and groups within an organization that are duplicating the effort of other functions—are they both necessary?

B.   **Value-added activities** enhance the value of the product or service as seen by customers and clients; these activities are why people buy this product or service. These activities should be expanded or improved.

C.   In contrast, **non-value-added activities** do not enhance the value of the product to customers; the customer could care less about these activities. These activities should be eliminated if possible, and resources devoted to these activities should be redeployed to value-added activities.

D.   **Benchmarking** is an example of activity-based management that has become quite common. It is the continuous comparison of a firm's activities to the best industry standards inside and outside of the organization.

> **Study Tip:** *Can you explain activity-based costing and the role of cost management systems? Do you sense that there is tension between decision-making needs of managers and financial reporting requirements?*

IX.   Describe the steps in designing an activity-based costing system (Appendix 4)

A.   Determine the key components of the activity-based cost accounting system, and the goals of the system.

   1.   Key components are: cost objects, key activities, resources, and related cost drivers.

   2.   Goals of the activity-based cost system are: to support strategic decision making, to understand department activities for operational cost control, and to understand key activities and related costs.

B.   Determine relationships among cost objects, activities, and resources.

   1.   Relationships among key activities are determined through a careful study of operations.

   2.   ABC systems improve the accuracy of product and service costs.

> **Stop and Review**
> See textbook Exhibits 4-9 and 4-10

C.   Collect data concerning costs and physical flow of cost driver units among resources and activities.

   1.   Data sources can include accounting records, special studies, and input from managers.

> **Stop and Review**
> See textbook Exhibit 4-11

D.   Calculate and interpret the new activity-based cost information.

> **Stop and Review**
> See textbook Exhibits 4-12 and 4-13

PRACTICE TEST QUESTIONS AND PROBLEMS WITH SOLUTIONS

True or False Statements

Determine whether each of the following statements is True (T) or False (F), and enter your answer in the space provided.

_____1.   A particular cost may be simultaneously both direct and indirect.

_____2.   If products are the cost objectives, examples of direct material cost would include fuel for machinery and abrasives for shaping products.

_____3.   Product costs of a floor-covering manufacturer would include direct material cost and variable factory overhead.

_____4.   For financial reporting, indirect product costs are inventoried and eventually become expenses.

_____5.   Period costs would usually include depreciation of both factory equipment and sales equipment.

_____6.   The purpose of activity-based costing is to provide more accurate product costs for financial reporting.

_____7.   Fixed factory overhead should be treated as a period cost in an ABC system.

_____8.   Unlike activity-based costing systems, cost management systems are focused on management decision-making needs.

_____9.   One goal of ABM is to improve the efficiency of administrative functions.

____10.   Multistage ABC systems are more costly than two-stage ABC systems.

Multiple-Choice Questions

For the following multiple-choice questions, select the best answer(s) and enter the identification letter(s) in the spaces provided:

_____1.   The usual basis for distinguishing between direct and indirect product costs is the economic feasibility of their tracing to a given: (a) product unit, (b) time span, (c) manufacturing department, (d) cost objective.

_____2.   When products are the cost objects, typically the three *major* categories of manufacturing costs are direct labor, direct materials, and: (a) indirect manufacturing costs, (b) indirect materials, (c) indirect labor, (d) manufacturing overhead costs.

_____3.   If products are the cost objectives, examples of direct labor cost for a manufacturer of oil well drilling tools would include: (a) salary of the plant superintendent, (b) salary of the sales manager, (c) wages of a secretary in the plant office, (d) wages of a machinist in the plant.

_____4.   If products are the cost objectives, examples of factory overhead cost would typically include: (a) wages of an assembly worker, (b) salary of the plant manager, (c) sales distribution costs, (d) cleaning supplies.

_____5.   If products are the cost objectives, the wages of factory janitors and maintenance personnel would usually be classified as: (a) factory overhead cost, (b) direct labor cost, (c) product cost, (d) period cost.

_____6. These amounts are included in the operating statement of a company: direct material costs, $40,000; selling expenses, $25,000; factory overhead, $43,000; interest expense, $6,000; direct labor, $55,000; work-in-process inventory, $13,000. The conversion cost is: (a) $138,000, (b) $98,000, (c) $169,000, (d) $95,000, (e) $109,000.

_____7. These amounts appear in the income statement of a company: depreciation of factory building, $4,200; advertising, $2,000; fire insurance on work-in-process, $2,500; lubricants used in manufacturing operations, $3,500; distribution costs, $3,000. The total product costs included above are: (a) $6,000, (b) $10,200, (c) $13,200, (d) $6,500, (e) $7,200.

_____8. See the preceding test item. The total *period* costs included are: (a) $2,000, (b) $5,000, (c) $6,000 (d) $3,000.

_____9. Given for Wye Co. (in thousands): sales, $80; direct material, $12; direct labor, $22; selling and administrative expenses, $15 (two-thirds fixed); factory overhead, $24 (three-fourths fixed); inventories negligible. Compute amount of gross profit: (a) $7, (b) $28, (c) $35, (d) $22.

_____10. Activity analysis of indirect costs identified the following costs and rates:

Materials handling: $0.50 per kilogram

Engineering: $500 per engineering change

Utilities: $0.40 per kilowatt-hour

Distribution: $18 per unit shipped

Order #77, shipped to the customer, consisted of 15 units of finished product and consumed 200 kilograms of material and 300 kilowatt-hours of power. There were five engineering changes to the order before it was completed. The indirect cost of Order #77 was: (a) $490, (b) $2,870, (c) $2,990, (d) $2,720.

Completion

Complete each of the following statements by filling in the blanks:

1. Minor materials that become a physical part of a manufactured product but are difficult to trace to specific product units are classified as _____.

2. Conversion cost is _____ plus _____.

3. The four steps for implementing activity-based costing are:

   _____

   _____

   _____

   _____

4. Activity-based costing applies _____ and _____ to measure accurate _____.

5. Activity-based costing systems provide _____ but are _____.

6. Cost accounting systems _____ and _____ costs for both _____ and _____ needs.

7. What distinguishes a direct cost from an indirect cost is _____.

8.   What distinguishes a period cost from a product cost is _____ and the

_____ .

9.   Multistage ABC systems offer improvements over two-stage ABC systems by using

_____ , _____ , and _____ .

10. Classify each of these costs of Vogon Construction Company as a product cost or period cost, assuming use of the absorption approach (for simplicity, assume all projects are started and finished in a single period). Place an X in the proper column.

		Product cost	Period cost
Fire insurance on equipment building	a.		
Sales commissions	b.		
Salary of company controller	c.		
Concrete used on projects	d.		
Costs of a general management training program	e.		
Property taxes on construction machinery	f.		
Freight on materials purchased	g.		
Supervisory salaries, materials storeroom	h.		
Power for maintenance equipment	i.		
Depreciation of sales office furniture	j.		

Problems

1. The income statement of Corbett-Oxford Corporation, a manufacturing company, included these items (in thousands):

Sales	$1,800
Selling expenses (all variable)	320
Direct labor cost	420
General administrative expenses (all fixed)	180
Direct materials used	340
Fixed factory overhead costs	220
Variable factory overhead costs	100
Interest expense (fixed)	40
All inventories	negligible

Compute:

Prime cost	
Conversion cost	
Total product costs	
Gross margin	
Total period costs	
Net income	

2. Rocky Mountain Motorworks previously used a manufacturing cost system that allocated all indirect manufacturing costs to products based on 440% of direct labor cost. The company has just implemented an ABC system that traces indirect costs to products based on consumption of major activities as indicated below.

a. Compare the total indirect costs of Product Q using both the old labor-based and the new ABC systems.

Activity center	Annual cost driver quantity	Traceable Cost	Cost driver rate (?)	Product Q cost driver consumption
Labor	$300,000	$30,000		$2,000
Machining	20,000 hours	$500,000		800 hours
Setup	10,000 hours	$100,000		100 hours
Production order	2,000 orders	$200,000		12 orders
Material handling	1,000 requisitions	$20,000		5 requisitions
Parts administration	12,000 parts	$480,000		18 parts

b. Explain why the assigned costs may be different and where the costs allocated using the old system have "disappeared."

Exercises

1. Classification of Manufacturing Costs: Classify each of the following as direct or indirect (D or I) with respect to product and as variable or fixed (V or F) with respect to whether the cost fluctuates in total as activity or volume changes over wide ranges of activity. You will have two answers, D or I and V or F.

___1. Supervisor training program

___2. Abrasives (sandpaper etc.)

___3. Cutting bits in a machinery department

___4. Food for a factory cafeteria

___5. Factory rent

___6. Salary for a factory storeroom clerk

___7. Workers' compensation insurance in a factory

___8. Cement for a road builder

___9. Steel scrap for a blast furnace

__10. Paper towels for a factory washroom

2. Variable Costs and Fixed Costs; Manufacturing and Other Costs: For each of the numbered items, choose the appropriate classifications for a manufacturing company. If in doubt about whether the cost behavior is basically variable or fixed, decide on the basis of whether the total cost will fluctuate substantially over a wide range of volume. Most items have two answers among the following possibilities with respect to the cost of a particular job:

a. Variable cost

b. Fixed cost

c. General and administrative cost

d. Selling cost

e. Manufacturing costs, direct

f. Manufacturing costs, indirect

g. Other (specify)

Sample Answers:

Direct material	a, e
President's salary	b, c
Bond interest expense	b, g (interest expense)

___1. Factory power for machines

___2. Salesperson's commissions

___3. Salesperson's salary

___4. Welding supplies

___5. Fire loss

___6. Sandpaper

___7. Supervisory salaries, production control

___8. Supervisory salaries, assembly department

___9. Company picnic costs

___10. Overtime premium, punch press

___11. Idle time, assembly

___12. Freight out

___13. Property taxes

___14. Paint for finished products

___15. Heat and air conditioning, factory

___16. Material-handling labor, punch press

___17. Straight line depreciation, salespersons' automobiles

CHAPTER 4 SOLUTIONS TO PRACTICE TEST QUESTIONS AND PROBLEMS

True or False Statements

1. True — Whether a cost is indirect or direct may depend on the referenced cost object. For example, supervisory salaries are direct to a department but are probably indirect to products made in the department.

2. False — These items are probably difficult to trace to products, so they would be classified as indirect product costs—overhead.

3. True — These are identifiable product costs. Variable overhead would be an indirect product cost, however.

4. True — Both direct and indirect product costs are inventoried and expensed when items are sold.

5. False — Depreciation of factory equipment is a product cost. Depreciation of sales equipment is a period cost, however.

6. False — The primary purpose of ABC is to improve internal decision making. It may not affect the "bottom-line" numbers reported because many effects will be across products and services. That is, total costs are the same, but how they are assigned to products and services may vary significantly.

7. False — All fixed factory costs are treated as product costs in ABC systems. Proponents of ABC think it is incorrect not to try to trace fixed product costs to products.

8. False — ABC is generally part of a cost management system that is focused on management decision making.

9. True — A goal of ABM is to eliminate non-value-added activities in all areas of an organization, including administrative functions.

10. True — Multistage ABC systems are more costly to design and implement than two-stage ABC systems. However, the benefits of more accurate information can exceed the greater costs.

Multiple-Choice Questions

1. d — It may not be feasible (given current technology and cost-benefit considerations) to trace the cost of every resource to each product that uses the resource. The costs for which specific tracing is infeasible are called indirect costs; these costs are assigned to products using some allocation method.

2. a, d — These terms are synonymous. Indirect materials and indirect labor are part of manufacturing overhead.

3. d — Machinist wages should be directly traceable to products. The labor costs of the plant superintendent and secretary would be classified as indirect product costs. In most systems, the salary of the sales manager would be classified as a period cost.

4. a, b, d — Most systems treat sales distribution costs as period costs. Some ABC systems, however, would trace distribution costs to products.

5. a, c — Wages of these employees are classified as factory overhead, which is a product cost.

6. b — Conversion cost is direct labor plus factory overhead = $55,000 + $43,000 = $98,000. Prime cost is direct material plus direct labor = $40,000 + $55,000 = $95,000.

7. b — Product costs include all factory overhead costs, which in part are: $4,200 + $2,500 + $3,500 = $10,200.

8. b   Non-manufacturing, period costs are $2,000 + $3,000 = $5,000.

9. d   Gross profit equals sales less all product costs = $(80 - 12 - 22 - 24) = $22.

10. c   The indirect cost traced to order #77 = (15 units x $18/unit) + (200 kg x $0.50/kg) + (300 kwh x $0.40/kwh) + (5 ECs x $500/EC) = $2,990

Completion

1. indirect materials or overhead

2. direct labor cost plus manufacturing overhead cost

3. (1) determine cost objectives, activities, resources, cost drivers, (2) develop process-based map, (3) collect relevant data, (4) calculate and interpret information

4. cost behavior, activity analysis, product and service costs

5. superior information, expensive to develop and maintain

6. accumulate, allocate, financial reporting, managerial decision making

7. traceability

8. traceability, approach to net income (absorption or contribution margin)

9. more than two stages, cost behavior of resources, more operational information

10.

		Product cost	Period cost
Fire insurance on equipment building	a.	x	
Sales commissions	b.		x
Salary of company controller	c.		x
Concrete used on projects	d.	x	
Costs of a general management training program	e.		x
Property taxes on construction machinery	f.	x	
Freight on materials purchased	g.	x	
Supervisory salaries, materials storeroom	h.	x	
Power for maintenance equipment	i.	x	
Depreciation of sales office furniture	j.		x

1. Corbett-Oxford Corporation:

a.

Prime cost	$420 + $340 = $760
Conversion cost	$420 + $220 + $100 = $740
Total product costs	$420 + $340 + $220 + $100 = $1,080
Gross margin	$1,800 - $1,080 = $720
Total period costs	$320 + $180 + $40 = $540
Net income	$720 - $320 - $180 - $40 = $180, or $720 - $540 = $180

2. Comparative indirect costs of Product Q

a.

Cost System	Cost driver rate	Cost driver consump.	Cost assignment
Labor-based system	440%	$10,000	$44,000
ABC system			
Labor...................	$30,000÷$300,000 = 10%	$2,000	$ 200
Machining............	$500,000÷20,000hr = $25/hr	800 hrs	20,000
Setup...................	$100,000÷10,000hr = $10/hr	100 hrs	1,000
Prod. Orders...........	$200,000÷2,000 = $100/order	12 orders	1,200
Mat'l handling.........	$20,000÷1,000 = $20/requisition	5 requis.	100
Parts admin............	$480,000÷12,000 = $40/part	18 parts	720
Total			$23,220
Difference			$20,780

b. The costs differ because the ABC system more carefully traces the use of indirect resources to products. The $20,780 cost no longer assigned to Product Q did not disappear, but (if the ABC system is accurate) was reassigned to other products that use the indirect resources more intensively. The incorrect costing implied by traditional systems is called "cost distortion" – some products will receive too much cost and others too little.

Exercises

1. Classification of Manufacturing Costs:

1.	Supervisor training program	I, F
2.	Abrasives (sandpaper etc.)	I,V
3.	Cutting bits in a machinery department	I,V
4.	Food for a factory cafeteria	D,V
5.	Factory rent	I,F
6.	Salary for a factory storeroom clerk	I, F
7.	Workers' compensation insurance in a factory	I, V or F
8.	Cement for a road builder	D, V
9.	Steel scrap for a blast furnace	D, V
10.	Paper towels for a factory washroom	D or I, V

2. Variable Costs and Fixed Costs; Manufacturing and Other Costs

1. Factory power for machines	a, f	10. Overtime premium, punch press	a, f
2. Salesperson's commissions	a, d	11. Idle time, assembly	a, f
3. Salesperson's salary	b, d	12. Freight out	a, d
4. Welding supplies	a, f	13. Property taxes	b, c
5. Fire loss	b, g (extraordinary)	14. Paint for finished products	a, e
6. Sandpaper	a, f	15. Heat and air conditioning, factory	a, f
7. Supervisory salaries, production control	b, f	16. Material-handling labor, punch press	a, f
8. Supervisory salaries, assembly department	b, f	17. Straight line depreciation, salespersons'	
9. Company picnic costs	b, c	automobiles	b,d

CHAPTER 5

Relevant Information and Decision Making with a Focus on Pricing Decisions

---

OVERVIEW

OVERVIEW

This entire chapter is based upon a single critical step in decision making: identifying and using relevant information. Only the costs and revenues that are expected in the future and that differ among alternative actions are relevant costs and revenues for choosing among alternative courses of action. Each decision setting appears different, yet the relevant information is the same—what costs and revenues will change as a result of choosing each alternative? After completing this chapter you should be able to:

I. Discriminate between relevant and irrelevant information for making decisions

II. Apply the decision process to make business decisions

III. Construct absorption and contribution-margin income statements, and identify their relevance for decision making

IV. Decide to accept or reject a special order using the contribution-margin technique

V. Explain why pricing decisions depend on the characteristics of the market

VI. Identify the factors that influence pricing decisions in practice

VII. Compute a target sales price by various approaches, and compare the advantages and disadvantages of these approaches

VIII. Use target costing to decide whether to add a new product

I. Discriminate between relevant and irrelevant information for making decisions

The basis of management planning is selecting the best course of action from all the feasible alternatives.

A. Each possible decision can have different future effects. For example, the choice of whether a firm should locate a new plant in Michigan or in Tennessee may have significant impacts on productivity, distribution costs, and profitability.

B. Therefore, making decisions always involves making and analyzing predictions about the future consequences of current alternative choices.

C. **Relevant data for managerial decision making** are predicted costs and revenues associated with each of the feasible alternative actions.

1. Though there is no harm in identifying *all* the costs and revenues of alternative choices, really the *relevant data* are the expected future costs and revenues that will *differ among alternatives*. As a simple example, if two products are being considered for future sale, and expected sales prices and quantities are equal, only predicted *costs* are relevant to choosing between them. Sales prices and quantities, because they are the same for both, are irrelevant to choosing between the products.

2. The only valid role for historical data is in predicting future consequences. What happened in the past has passed. This seems obvious, but some managers are unwilling to let the past go, and they worry about abandoning costs that they have already spent but that are irrelevant to future courses of action. For example, it really does not matter if you spent $10,000 for a piece of equipment just a year ago if the best course of action is to replace it now. Its current disposal value is probably relevant, though.

3. Decision makers and information systems trade off accuracy and relevance. The best circumstance would be to have both accurate and relevant information—that is the goal of activity-based costing, for example, discussed in Chapters 3 and 4.

4. In general, it is better to have somewhat inaccurate but relevant data than to have accurate but irrelevant data. For example, activity-based costs that are not precise are *probably* more useful than costs from financial reports that account for all costs to the penny but which use completely inappropriate cost drivers to do so.

> **Study Tip:** *Can you define relevant information for managerial decision making? What is the role of past costs?*

II. Apply the decision process to make business decisions

There is a basic structure that all business decisions should follow. Complex decisions require the use of the **decision-making process**. These are the steps of the decision making-process:

Step 1: Historical data as well as any other information that may aid in making the decision are compiled.

Step 2: Using the compiled data, predictions are formulated. (Although historical data aids in the decision-making process, it is irrelevant to the decision itself.)

Step 3: Predictions are used to create a *decision model;* a **decision model** is any method for making a choice. Some decision models are very complex, and require elaborate quantitative procedures such as numerous mathematical calculations, while others are as simple as choosing the more affordable of two building materials.

Step 4: Make the decision.

> **Stop and Review**
>
> See textbook Exhibit 5-1

III. Construct absorption and contribution-marginincome statements, and identify their relevance to decision making

There are two important forms of the income statement:

A.   The **absorption approach** is also called *absorption costing, full costing, traditional costing,* or *functional costing.*

1.   All manufacturing costs, *including fixed factory overhead,* are considered to be inventoriable or product costs that do not become expenses until sales take place.

2.   Note that the absorption approach makes a primary classification of costs according to *manufacturing versus non-manufacturing functions,* emphasizing the *gross profit margin* available to cover selling and administrative expenses.

> **Stop and Review**
>
> See textbook Exhibit 5-4

B.   The **contribution approach** is also called *variable costing, direct costing,* or *marginal costing.*

1.   Only variable manufacturing costs *(excluding fixed factory overhead)* are considered to be inventoriable or product costs.

2.   Note that the contribution approach makes a primary classification of costs into *variable versus fixed costs,* emphasizing the *contribution margin* available to cover the fixed costs.

> **Stop and Review**
>
> See textbook Exhibit 5-5

C.   To summarize the difference between these two models of the income statement, the primary classification of costs is:

1.   The absorption approach is classification of costs by management functions and is required by financial reporting.

2.   The contribution approach is classification of costs by cost behavior, parallels cost-volume-profit analysis, and is consistent with management planning and control.

3.   The contribution approach should be used for scorekeeping and attention directing, but the absorption approach is often used internally because of the added cost of the additional contribution margin information.

IV. Decide to accept or reject a special order using the contribution-margin technique

There are situations when *accepting special, reduced-price sales orders* is beneficial. A careful manager would consider several issues before agreeing to sell a product at lower than the customary price:

A.   Is there excess productive capacity? If not, the special order would displace current activity at regular, full prices, and you should probably reject the order.

B.   Would the lower price of the special order adversely affect the current and future sales of the company?

1.   If other customers learn that you are willing to sell at reduced prices, everyone may expect discounted prices.

2.   Do you want to be a discount supplier?

3.   If not, and you fear that the special order will erode future prices, you should probably reject the order.

C.   If there is excess capacity, *and* if future prices will not be adversely affected, what is the other relevant information for choosing whether to accept the special order?

1.   In such a case, the average overall unit costs based on data from the absorption cost-based income statement would *not* serve as an appropriate basis for evaluating these orders.

2.   Absorption costs contain some allocation of fixed costs that probably will not increase in the future as a result of the special order.

3.   The only costs that usually would change in the future are the variable costs affected by accepting the special sales orders. These costs can be more clearly identified from the *contribution-margin-based* income statement.

4.   Ordinarily fixed costs would not change as a result of the decision because with excess capacity no additional capacity (and related fixed costs) would be necessary. However, special orders might affect certain fixed costs, which would be relevant to the decision.

> **Stop and Review**
>
> See textbook Exhibit 5-6

D.   Note in Exhibit 5-6 that there is a $200,000 advantage in accepting 100,000 units of a special order at a $26 selling price despite the fact that this is $4 less than the average absorption cost of ($24,000,000 + $6,000,000) ÷ 1,000,000 units = $30 per unit.

E.   Thus, on the basis of a relevant-cost approach, it might be a good idea to use excess capacity and accept some special orders at selling prices *below* average unit costs that include all fixed and variable costs.

F.   The important point is that such decisions should depend primarily on the revenues and costs expected to change.

G.   You should beware of the misleading effects of *unitizing fixed costs* because this could create the false impression that these are variable costs.

1.   Furthermore, *spreading* fixed costs over more units does not reduce the total amount of fixed cost.

2.   This is why, though, one can omit some fixed costs from analyses because they do not differ across alternatives, it is safer to be sure that all costs, fixed and variable, are explicitly considered. If some fixed costs are the same across alternatives, fine—they will not affect the analysis—but including them may keep you from forgetting a fixed cost that does change.

H.   Because many costs have multiple cost drivers, relevant costs of special orders may be caused by more than just the number of units in the special order.

    1.   For example, any differences in complexity (features, capabilities, etc.) could result in variable costs that are different from usual.

    2.   Product differences also may result in additional fixed or step costs (e.g., setup costs).

> **Study Tip:** *Before going on to the next decision setting, are you sure that you understand what costs and revenues are relevant to analyzing special orders? What if capacity is limited? What if future sales will be affected by the special order?*

V.   Explain why pricing decisions depend on the characteristics of the market

An extremely important management decision is *setting regular selling prices*. Basically, four major factors may influence pricing decisions: *market competition, legal restrictions, customers, and costs*.

A.   The level of market competition may either:

    1.   Dictate what the price of a product or service is. At the extreme, this is **perfect competition** where a firm can sell all of a product it wants at the market price.

    2.   Allow a firm to affect price by choosing sales quantities. This is **imperfect competition**—total sales depends on the price charged.

B.   In economic theory, the firm chooses the sales level that maximizes profits.

    1.   In *perfect competition*, the firm would sell products up to the point where the **marginal cost** (the incremental cost of producing one more unit of product) equals the market sales price. Cost does not determine price at all, but does determine how much product the firm should produce.

    2.   In *imperfect competition*, managers produce up to the point where marginal cost is just equal to **marginal revenue**, the additional revenue earned from an additional sale. Thus, costs determine price indirectly by identifying how much product the firm should produce.

    3.   Managers predict **price elasticity**—the change in sales resulting from a change in price, to determine marginal revenue.

> **Stop and Review**
>
> See textbook Exhibits 5-7 and 5-8

    4.   In practice, however, marginal cost is difficult to observe, so managers use variable cost as an estimate.

    5.   As we have seen, within the relevant range, a constant variable cost is a reasonable estimate of the incremental effects of producing and selling additional units.

    6.   Many of the concepts of economic theory are difficult to observe in practice. However, firms should be very aware of their competition's pricing practices, because customers shop around.

VI.	Identify the factors that influence pricing decisions in practice

A.   Pricing of goods is subject to certain U.S. and international laws that prohibit predatory and discriminatory pricing.

    1.   **Predatory pricing** is designed to unfairly drive out competition. Courts have ruled that prices below variable cost are predatory.

    2.   **Discriminatory pricing** is charging different prices to different customers for the same product or service. This practice is legally defensible only if the firm can demonstrate that differences in cost-driver activity across customers lead to different costs.

    3.   Thus, knowledge of cost behavior is good not only for planning and control, but it is also essential for the legal environment of business.

B.   Often managers claim to set prices with "cost-plus" pricing. They compute average cost and then add a **markup** to reach a desired return on investment.

    1.   Even when managers say that they set prices by adding a **markup** to their costs, they admit that these *markups are adjusted for market conditions*.

    2.   Costs are important for pricing, but markets are more important.

    3.   As we have seen above, costs are extremely important for the production decision— given the price, should we produce this product? How much?

VII.	Compute a target sales price by various approaches, and compare the advantages and disadvantages of these approaches

A.   Many U.S. managers compute their target prices on the basis of certain costs, called **cost-plus pricing** or **target pricing**.

    1.   Essentially, this method adds a "markup" to some cost figure to obtain a selling price that will generate an adequate return on investment. Commonly used cost bases include:

        a.   *Total variable costs:* variable manufacturing cost plus variable selling and administrative cost

        b.   *Absorption cost:* variable manufacturing cost plus fixed manufacturing cost

        c.   *Full cost* (also called fully allocated or fully distributed cost): absorption cost plus total selling and administrative costs

> **Stop and Review**
>
> See textbook Exhibit 5-10

    2.   Many firms use absorption cost or full cost as the base for target prices because these costs indicate the levels of costs that must be recovered in the long run to remain in business.

    3.   Regardless of the cost base used to set initial target prices, one can arrive at the same target price by using different percentage markups. Remember, in most cases these markups are adjusted for market conditions anyway. If customers will not pay target prices, firms will adjust prices or costs (to allow price adjustments) or will not produce the product—just as predicted by economic theory.

4. Some industries, though, set prices directly on costs. These are *rate-regulated industries* that governments have granted some form of monopoly (imperfect competition) power. Markups are generally prescribed by law or by regulation. Therefore, determining the cost base of these industries is critical to both the firm and to regulators, and the rate-paying public.

B. Regardless of the cost base used to set target prices, the contribution-margin approach to measuring income offers some advantages over the absorption-costing approach:

1. More detailed information is available regarding changing levels of variable and fixed costs at different levels of production.

2. The contribution approach provides insights that help management weigh the short-term benefits of cutting prices against possible long-term disadvantages of price cutting and undermining the price structure of an industry.

3. As in the other decision-making settings discussed in this chapter, the pricing decision should consider effects of capacity and what revenues and costs will change as a result of choosing alternative prices.

4. The only difference in this setting is the consideration of external regulation on pricing and the effects of competitors' prices and customers' actions on revenues.

VIII. Use target costing to decide whether to add a new product

---

A. Knowledge of customers' requirements and willingness to pay are essential to competing in markets for products and services.

1. **Target costing** is a relatively new product design approach that works backward from the market price to a target production cost of a product that both meets customer needs and offers a required return on sales. This approach is common among Japanese firms, who argue that they are more market oriented than most U.S. firms.

2. *Target cost = Market price - required return on sales.*

3. As in the theory of perfect competition, if the product cannot be produced at the target cost, the company either will redesign the product or production process or will drop the product.

> **Stop and Review**
>
> See textbook Exhibit 5-13

B. If costs are too great to rationalize the addition of a new product, there are ways to reduce production costs to target level.

1. **Value engineering** is a cost-reduction technique used during design that uses information from all value chain functions to lower costs to a target level.

C. Japanese firms use **kaizen costing**, a term for the continuous improvement during the manufacturing process.

> **Study Tip:** *Before going on to the practice test, be sure that you understand the external influences on pricing (competitive and legal) and the role of costs in determining prices (theoretically and practically).*

PRACTICE TEST QUESTIONS AND PROBLEMS

True or False Statements

Determine whether each of the following statements is True (T) or False (F), and enter your answer in the space provided.

_____1. Pueblo Corp. must choose between two alternative future actions. If a certain predicted variable cost per unit is the same for each action, that cost is not relevant to the decision.

_____2. Past costs are never relevant to decisions about the future.

_____3. The relevant-information approach to evaluating reduced-price special orders implies that future fixed costs are always irrelevant.

_____4. The relevant data for pricing a special sales order that can be filled from idle plant capacity would include expected future unit costs of variable production costs and fixed production costs.

_____5. If firms can affect sales prices, they can charge any price they want and customers have no choice but to pay the prices.

_____6. Target costing works backwards from sales price to determine acceptable product or service costs.

_____7. Absorption costs are commonly used as bases for pricing because this base might prevent managers from accepting marginal orders.

_____8. Variable factory overhead is inventoriable in both the absorption approach and the contribution approach to measuring income.

Multiple-Choice Questions

For the following multiple-choice questions, select the best answer(s), and enter the identification letter(s) in the spaces provided.

_____1. In imperfect competition, price is: (a) set by regulators, (b) set by market conditions, (c) set by equating marginal cost to marginal revenue, (d) set by marking up product cost.

_____2. Each month Winn Co. makes 400 units of Product C at a $40 variable cost per unit and $1,200 of total fixed costs. If a special order for 50 units from a customer is offered at a price of $42 and requiring a $100 special set-up cost, Winn Co. will have: (a) a $100 contribution, (b) a $2-per-unit contribution, (c) an $.88-per-unit contribution, (d) no financial incentive to accept.

_____3. See the preceding test item. Of the following prices, which is the lowest acceptable unit selling price for this order? (a) $42, (b) $40, (c) $23, (d) $15.

_____4. Contribution margin for pricing is equal to sales revenue minus: (a) variable manufacturing expenses, (b) all manufacturing costs, (c) all variable expenses, (d) all fixed and variable expenses.

_____5. Absorption cost for pricing is equal to: (a) total manufacturing cost, (b) manufacturing cost plus selling and administrative cost, (c) full cost, (d) fully allocated cost.

_____6. The contribution approach to pricing makes a basic distinction between: (a) relevant and irrelevant costs, (b) past and future costs, (c) fixed and variable costs, (d) manufacturing and non-manufacturing costs.

_____7. Cost-plus pricing adds a markup to cost to reach a total that is: (a) profit, (b) return on investment, (c) selling price, (d) full cost.

_____8. Each month, a company incurs for a certain product $60,000 of total manufacturing costs (half fixed, half variable) and $20,000 of non-manufacturing costs (half fixed and half variable). Its monthly sales revenues are $100,000. The markup percentage on full cost to arrive at the existing (target) selling price is: (a) 25%, (b) 12.5%, (c) 20%, (d) 10%.

_____9. See the preceding test item. The markup percentage on absorption cost to arrive at the existing (target) selling price is: (a) 33%, (b) 67%, (c) 40%, (d) 50%.

_____10. See item 8 above. The markup percentage on total variable cost to arrive at the existing (target) selling price is: (a) 60%, (b) 150%, (c) 250%, (d) 40%.

_____11. These amounts appear in the *absorption* income statement of a company: depreciation of factory building, $4,200; fire insurance on manufacturing equipment, $2,500; variable overhead used in manufacturing operations, $3,500; variable distribution costs, $3,000. The total product costs included above are: (a) $6,000, (b) $10,200, (c) $13,200, (d) $6,500, (e) $7,200.

_____12. See the preceding test item. The total costs that would be included in contribution margin are: (a) $4,200, (b) $6,500, (c) $6,000 (d) $3,000.

Completion

Complete each of the following statements by filling in the blanks.

1. The costs that are relevant to managerial decision making include only the costs that _____ for each alternative course of action.

2. _____ costs are themselves _____ to _____ but may be relevant to the prediction of future costs.

3. When a multiple-product plant is being operated at capacity, the criterion for attaining maximum profits is the largest contribution _____.

4. The accountant's role in managerial decision making is _____.

5. The danger of using unit costs for decision making is that unit costs treat _____ costs as if they were _____.

6. As activity levels increase, fixed cost in total _____, and fixed cost per unit _____.

7. The decision to accept a special order should consider _____, _____, additional _____ and additional _____.

8. The pricing decision should consider _____ actions, _____ willingness to pay, and additional _____ and _____.

9. Absorption costing treats all _____ costs as period costs.

10. The contribution-margin approach to income measurement includes all _____ costs as part of contribution margin.

Problems

1. The Real Time Products Company has a monthly plant capacity of 1,500 product units. Its predicted operations for the year are:

Sales (1,000 units)	$51,500
Manufacturing costs:	
Fixed	$18,000
Variable	$ 17 per unit
Selling and administrative expenses:	
Fixed	$4,500
Variable (sales commissions)	$ 3 per unit

If the company accepts a special order from a customer for 200 units at a selling price of $18 each, how would the total predicted net income for the month be affected, assuming no effect on regular sales at regular prices? No sales commissions would be required by the special order, but an extra delivery cost of $350 would be required. Indicate the amount and whether it is an increase or a decrease. Ignore income taxes. Complete the following two equivalent analyses:

a.

Item	Company as a whole without special order	Special order	Company with special order
Sales			
Less variable expenses			
Variable manufacturing			
Variable sales and admin			
Contribution margin			
Less fixed expenses			
Fixed manufacturing			
Fixed sales and admin			
Net income			

b.   Additional revenues: _____

Additional variable costs: _____

Additional fixed costs: _____

Net effect of special order: _____

2. Given for Krikkit Company's operations for the year ending December 31:

Sales	$160,000
Direct material	25,000
Direct labor	32,000
Indirect manufacturing costs:	
Variable	$ 5,000
Fixed	25,000
Total	$30,000
Selling expenses:	
Variable	$16,000
Fixed	23,000
Total	$39,000
Administrative expenses:	
Variable	$ 2,000
Fixed	12,000
Total	$14,000

a. Prepare an income statement in the absorption form (omit statement heading).

b. Prepare an income statement in the contribution form (omit heading).

Exercises

1. **Straightforward Special-order Decision:** The Pierce Sport Shop makes game jerseys for athletic teams. The Williams Peak Softball Club has offered to buy 100 jerseys for teams in its league for $14 per jersey. The team price for the jerseys is normally $18, an 80% markup over Pierce's cost of $10 per jersey. Pierce buys blank jerseys for $5 each and adds a name and number to each jersey at a variable cost of $2 per jersey. The annual fixed cost of equipment used in the printing process is $4,000 and other fixed costs allocated to jerseys are $2,000. Pierce makes about 2,000 jerseys a year, making the fixed cost $3 per jersey. The equipment is used only for printing jerseys and stands idle 75% of the usable time.

 a. Compute the amount by which the operating income of Pierce Sport Shop would change if the Williams Peak Softball Club's offer was accepted, with names and numbers on each jersey.

 b. Suppose that you were the manager of Pierce Sport Shop. Would you accept the offer? In addition to considering the quantitative impact computed in the above question, list two qualitative considerations that would influence your decision. Give one qualitative factor supporting acceptance of the offer and one supporting rejection.

2. **Target costing.** CompuStor Electronics, Inc., produces a pocket calculator and presents the following summary of per unit data (100,000 units):

	Total	Fixed	Variable
Manufacturing costs	$ 8.40	$2.80	$5.60
Non-manufacturing costs	$ 5.60	$1.40	$4.20
Target sales price	$15.00		

CompuStor requires a 20% return on sales for its products.

 a. What is the currently projected return on sales percentage?

 b. By how much would cost per unit have to change to meet required return on sales?

 c. What is the break-even sales level in units at projected costs and sales price?

3.   **Straightforward absorption and contribution statement:** J. K. Howard
Company had the following data (in millions) for a recent period. Fill in the blanks.
There were no beginning or ending inventories.

a.	Sales	$920
b.	Direct materials used	350
c.	Direct labor	210
	Factory overhead	
d.	Variable	100
e.	Fixed	50
f.	Variable manufacturing cost of goods sold	___
g.	Manufacturing costs of goods sold	___
	Selling and administrative expenses	
h.	Variable	90
i.	Fixed	80
j.	Gross profit	___
k.	Contribution margin	___
l.	Prime costs	___
m.	Conversion costs	___
n.	Operating income	___

True or False Statements

1. True   Because that cost will not differ between the alternatives, it is irrelevant to the choice between the alternatives. There is no harm, though, in including that cost as long as costs that differ are identified.

2. False   Though past costs cannot differ among future alternatives, past costs may help predict future costs.

3. False   Some fixed costs may change as a result of current decisions. These fixed costs would be relevant to decision making.

4. False   Only those costs that will vary as a result of taking a special order are relevant. Variable costs are relevant, but fixed costs per unit generally are not relevant because fixed costs in total are usually not affected.

5. False   Customers can always choose to not buy the product at all or to find a substitute at a better price. So firms might try to charge a very high price, but customers may not buy.

6. True   The sequence is: determine what customers will pay for a product with given characteristics, and subtract the required return on sales (or profit margin or markup) to determine the target cost.

7. True   If managers feel that they generally should generate sufficient contribution to cover fixed costs, then absorption cost or full cost-based target prices might reinforce that policy. Problems arise with special orders and other "one-time" projects where the temptation to use idle capacity might outweigh pricing guidelines.

8. True   Fixed factory overhead, however, is not. Only in the absorption approach is fixed factory overhead inventoriable.

Multiple-Choice Questions

1. a, b, c, d   Each of these may be true. Regulators may influence prices of rate-regulated companies that the public has granted some monopoly power. Market conditions include prices of other, substitute goods to which customers may switch. Ideally, the firm will produce up to the point where marginal cost equals marginal revenue. Firms may not know what marginal revenue could be at different sales levels, so they may approximate marginal revenue by marking up product cost.

2. a, d   The contribution margin per unit is $2; however, the total contribution of the special order is [$(42 - 40) x 50] - $100 = 0. Thus, there is no obvious incentive to accepting the special order at that price.

3. a   The lowest acceptable unit price for this special order is the variable cost, $40, plus $2 per unit to cover the setup cost ($100/50).

4. c   The definition of contribution margin is unchanged from previous discussions.

5. a   Likewise, the definition of absorption cost is unchanged. Fully allocated cost would include selling and administrative cost.

6. a, c   The costs relevant to pricing using the contribution margin approach are variable costs.

7. c   Cost plus the markup equals price. The amount of the markup may be based on a required return on investment.

8. a   The total amount of the markup (in thousands) is $(100 - 60 - 20) = $20. As a percentage, the markup over full cost is $20/$80 = 25%.

9. b — The markup over absorption cost is $\$(100 - 60) = \$40$. As a percentage markup over absorption cost, the markup is $\$40/\$60 = 67\%$.

10. b — The markup over variable cost is $\$(100 - 30 - 10) = \$60$. As a percentage markup over variable cost, the markup is $\$60/\$40 = 150\%$.

11. b — Product costs include all factory overhead costs, which in part are: $\$4,200 + \$2,500 + \$3,500 = \$10,200$.

12. b — Only variable costs are included in contribution margin. These include variable overhead and variable distribution $(\$3,500 + \$3,000 = \$6,500)$.

Completion

1. will change or will differ

2. Past or historical, irrelevant, decisions

3. margin per unit of constrained or limited capacity

4. to understand and communicate relevant information

5. fixed costs, variable costs

6. is unchanged within the relevant range, decreases

7. whether there is excess capacity, effects on current and future sales, revenues, costs

8. competitors', customers', revenues, costs

9. non-manufacturing

10. variable

Problems

1. Real Time Products Company

a.

Item	Company as a whole without special order	Special order	Company with special order
Sales	$51,500	200 x $18.= $3,600	$55,100
Less variable expenses			
Variable manufacturing	1,000 x $17 = $17,000	200 x $17.= $3,400	$20,400
Variable sales and admin	1,000 x $3 = 3,000		3,000
Contribution margin	$31,500	$200	$31,700
Less fixed expenses			
Fixed manufacturing	$18,000		$18,000
Fixed sales and admin	$ 4,500	350	4,850
Net income	$ 9,000	$(150)	$8,850

b. Additional revenues: 200 x $18.= $3,600

    Additional variable costs 200 x $17.= $3,400

    Additional fixed costs   350

    Net effect of special order $(150)

Because the special order reduces income by $150, the company has no financial incentive to accept the order.

2. Krikket Company

a.

Absorption Income Statement

Sales		$160,000
Less manufacturing cost of goods sold:		
Direct material	$25,000	
Direct labor	32,000	
Indirect manufacturing costs	30,000	87,000
Gross profit		$73,000
Less non-manufacturing costs:		
Selling expenses	$39,000	
Administrative expenses	14,000	53,000
Operating income		$20,000

b.

Contribution Income Statement

Sales		$160,000
Less variable expenses:		
Direct material	$25,000	
Direct labor	32,000	
Variable indirect manufacturing costs	5,000	
Total variable manufacturing cost of goods sold	$62,000	
Variable selling expenses	16,000	
Variable administrative expenses	2,000	
Total variable expenses		$ 80,000
Contribution margin		$ 80,000
Less fixed expenses:		
Manufacturing	$25,000	
Selling	23,000	
Administrative	12,000	
Total fixed expenses		$ 60,000
Operating income		$ 20,000

Exercises

1. **Straightforward Special-order Decision:**

   a. Special-order price   = $14

        Variable cost   = $7

        Contribution margin per jersey   = $7

        Number of jerseys   = 100

        Increase in income   = $7 x 100 = <u>$700</u>

   b. Accepting the offer depends both on the expected increase in income of $700 and also qualitative factors. These factors include the possibility of generating more business from the new customer, but also the danger of alienating existing customers who have paid higher prices.

2. **Target costing:**

a. The currently projected return on sales percentage is $(15 - \$14) \div \$15 = 6.7\%$

b. Cost per unit to meet the 20% required return on sales at projected sales levels must change as follows:

$$0.20 = \$[15 - (14 - X)] \div \$15$$

$$0.20 = \$(1 + X) \div \$15$$

$$(0.20)(\$15) = \$1 + \$X$$

$$\$3 - \$1 = \$2 = X$$

Therefore, manufacturing and/or non-manufacturing cost per unit would have to drop by $2 to meet required return on sales.

c. The break-even level of sales is computed by equating total revenues to total costs:

$$\$15\ X = (100,000)\ (\$4.20) + \$9.80\ X$$

$$\$15\ X = \$420,000 + \$9.80\ X$$

$$\$5.20\ X = \$420,000$$

$$X = 80,769\ \text{units}$$

3. **Straightforward Absorption and Contribution Statement:**

a.	Sales		$920
b.	Direct materials used		350
c.	Direct labor		210
	Factory overhead		
d.	Variable		100
e.	Fixed		50
f.	Variable manufacturing cost of goods sold = 350+210+100		660
g.	Manufacturing costs of goods sold = 350+210+100+50		710
	Selling and administrative expenses		
h.	Variable		90
i.	Fixed		80
j.	Gross profit = 920 - 710		210
k.	Contribution margin = 920 − 660 - 90		170
l.	Prime costs = 350+210		560
m.	Conversion costs = 210+100+50		370
n.	Operating income = 920 −710 −90 - 80		40

Relevant Information and Decision Making with a Focus on Operational Decisions

OVERVIEW
This chapter extends the application of relevant-information analysis for decision-making. Remember that relevant costs and revenues consist of: *estimated future costs and revenues that differ between alternative courses of action.* After finishing this chapter you should be able to:

I.   Use a differential analysis to examine income effects across alternatives and show that an opportunity cost analysis yields identical results

II.   Decide whether to make or to buy certain parts or products

III.   Choose whether to add or delete a product line using relevant information

IV.   Compute optimal product mix when production is constrained by a scarce resource

V.   Decide whether a joint product should be produced beyond its split-off point

VI.   Decide whether to keep or replace equipment

VII. Identify irrelevant and misspecified costs

VIII. Discuss how performance measures can affect decision making

I.	**Use a differential analysis to examine income effects across alternatives and show that an opportunity cost analysis yields identical results**

Managers often have to choose between two or more alternative courses of action. Differential analysis is used to determine the financial difference in costs and revenues between alternatives.

A. **Differential cost** is the difference in total cost between two alternatives.

B. **Differential revenue** is the difference in total revenue between two alternatives.

C. **Incremental analysis** measures the additional costs and benefits of an alternative course of action.

D. **Incremental benefits** are the additional revenues or reduced costs created by an alternative course of action.

E. **Incremental costs** are the additional costs or reduced benefits created by an alternative course of action.

F. **Outlay costs** are costs that require future cash disbursement such as materials and labor.

When managers choose an alternative course of action that prevents taking other alternatives as well, they should consider the *opportunity cost* of the exclusive decision.

A. Scarce resources are facts of life. You cannot pursue every profitable or worthwhile opportunity. By choosing only what appear to be the best opportunities, you are giving up the others.

B. **Opportunity cost** *is the highest contribution to profit that you must give up because selecting one alternative prevents you from also selecting another.*

C. Opportunity cost is as real a cost as the expected costs of raw materials for a proposed product.

   1. You expect to pay out-of-pocket costs for materials, and you likewise expect to give up the contribution from the next-best project you are unable to pursue because resources are limited.

   2. Opportunity costs, however, do not show up in accounting systems because opportunity costs are predicted costs, not the result of actual accounting transactions.

D. An example of opportunity cost is the current income a full-time college student gives up in order to attend school.

   1. That forgone income is as real a cost to the student as the money paid for tuition, fees, and books.

   2. On purely economic grounds, the student must expect that increased future income earned after college will more than offset the income forgone during college plus other costs of college.

E. When comparing the costs and revenues of each feasible alternative, one is implicitly comparing opportunity costs.

   1. Using the preceding example, the prospective college student could prepare an analysis of expected income levels from two alternatives: (1) begin a career after high school or (2) begin a career after college.

   2. The net value of the alternative chosen (career after high school or after college) is its income over time less the opportunity cost (forgone income) of the other career not chosen.

II.   Decide whether to make or to buy certain parts or products

Managers often consider whether to make or buy product components or subassemblies or whether the company should operate its own support activities such as accounting, information systems, and legal services. These are called **make-or-buy** or *sourcing* decisions. ("insourcing" is making; "outsourcing" is buying.)

A.   These decisions may depend greatly on *qualitative factors* such as maintaining good, long-term business relationships with suppliers or controlling the quality and timeliness of products and services.

B.   However, the decision may depend partly on the *quantitative measurement* of the difference in future costs between the alternatives.

   1.   Understanding relevant fixed and variable cost behavior is crucial.

   2.   Identifying and using appropriate cost drivers to predict variable costs also is critical, because inappropriate cost drivers will yield inaccurate cost predictions.

C.   As in the decisions considered in Chapter 5, make-or-buy decisions should always first consider the company's productive capacity.

   1.   If there is idle capacity, some fixed costs will not change in the future as a result of the make-or-buy decision.

   2.   Conversely, if capacity is currently fully used, the make-or-buy decision may affect future fixed costs because making the part or component will require more capacity and capacity-related fixed costs.

D.   **Relevant costs** of the make-or-buy decision are, as in the decisions in Chapter 5, those costs that will change in the future as a result of the decision. Relevant costs include future variable costs and *separable* or *avoidable* fixed costs.

E.   Generally, the make-or-buy decision compares the costs of alternative uses of productive capacity:

   1.   Use the facilities to make a given component or product.

   2.   Buy the component or product, and leave the facilities idle.

   3.   Buy the component or product, and rent out the unused facilities.

   4.   Buy the component or product, and use the facilities to make other components or products.

   5.   If all qualitative factors are equal (and, therefore, irrelevant to the decision), the lowest cost source of the component or product is the preferred alternative.

   6.   Again, **differential cost** is the difference in cost between two alternatives (e.g., making or buying).

III. Choose whether to add or delete a product line using relevant information

Another important management decision deals with the *deletion* or *addition of products* or *departments.*

A. As with the special order decisions, consider effects on capacity first.

1. If a product or department is added, is there currently sufficient capacity to accommodate it? If not, additional capacity costs will be necessary.

2. If a product or department is dropped, what, if any, are the alternative uses of the freed-up capacity?

B. In addition to capacity costs, other relevant data are revenues and fixed and variable costs that will change as a result of adding or dropping products or departments.

1. Of course, adding or dropping operations will add or drop the revenues of the specific product or department. In addition to these, determine whether the change will affect sales of other products or departments.

2. **Avoidable costs** (sometimes called *separable* costs) are those costs that will not continue by changing or deleting an ongoing operation. Conversely, adding a product or department adds those costs.

3. **Unavoidable costs** are those costs that will continue even after dropping a product or department. These are ***common*** costs of facilities and services shared by several departments or product lines that come in large, indivisible "chunks."

C. The text demonstrates a useful way to analyze product/department additions/deletions. This method lists the changes in revenues and costs of each change and then adds or subtracts these changes from the total to obtain the net effect. You should study this method.

> **Stop and Review**
>
> See the textbook example on product/department changes

> **Study Tip:** *Do you understand that the information relevant to adding or dropping products or departments is fundamentally the same as in the case of special orders? Future costs and revenues that will change as a result of each decision are relevant.*

IV. Compute the optimal product mix when production is constrained by a scarce resource

A basic management decision is *determining the best use of the capacity of a multiple-product or service facility.*

A. So far, we have not considered that productive capacity is limited. If capacity were unlimited, then any product or service with a positive contribution margin is a desirable use of capacity.

1. Capacity is rarely if ever unconstrained, so managers must be careful to use capacity wisely.

2. In general, there are multiple dimensions of capacity, each of which is limited. For example, machining capacity, computing capacity, limited skilled labor, limited capital, and so on.

B. Because fixed costs and target profits must be covered, managers must choose products and services that generate the most contribution margin possible from limited capacity. This suggests a straightforward approach:

1. Measure the contribution margin of each product or service.

2. Divide each contribution margin by the amount of capacity needed to produce each unit of product. This is the *contribution margin per unit of limited or constrained capacity*. For example, if a product's unit contribution margin is $10, and each unit of product requires 2 hours of limited machining time, the contribution margin per unit of constrained capacity is $5 contribution per machine hour.

3. Rank all products by their contribution per unit of constrained capacity.

4. Choose the alternative products or services that offer the highest contribution margin per unit of limited capacity first. If you cannot sell all of the highest-ranked product that you could produce, work your way down the ranking until all the constrained capacity is budgeted.

5. This is the mix of alternative products or services that offers the highest total contribution margin from fully using limited capacity.

6. One could begin by looking at the total contribution margins from producing only each of the alternative products, but this is more cumbersome, especially if there are sales limits.

> **Stop and Review**
>
> See textbook Exhibit 6-2

C. Looking merely at product or service unit contribution margins is not sufficient.

1. Product A may have a relatively high contribution margin and may look attractive, but it may consume too much capacity.

2. The facility may be able to produce so many more of product B, which has a lower unit contribution margin but uses much less capacity per unit of B, that total contribution margin is greater making B.

D. This decision appears different from those in objectives II and III, but consider:

1. Capacity is constrained, and fixed costs will not change as a result of which products or services are selected.

2. The revenues and costs that will change as a result of choosing alternative products are reflected in the contribution margins (per unit of constrained capacity or in total).

3. Computing the contribution margin per unit of constrained capacity is an intuitive shortcut in this type of decision.

> **Study Tip:** *Before going on to the next decision setting, can you explain the similarities among all of the three preceding decisions? What are the differences? Only the settings differ.*

V. Determine whether a joint product should be produced beyond the split-off point

When two or more products of relatively significant sales values are produced simultaneously by a single process (or a series of linked processes), they are called **joint products.**

A. The decision-making problem is whether to either sell joint products at the *point of split-off* or process the joint products further before sale.

B. Once again, the only relevant costs are the costs that will change as a result of this decision. This section analyzes which costs are relevant.

C. **The split-off point** is the stage of production at which the different joint products appear:

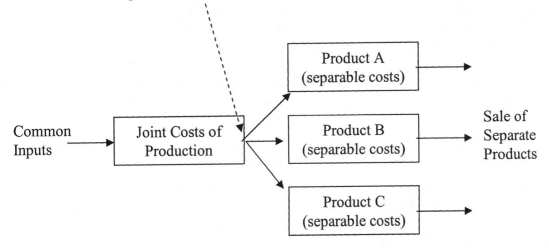

D. The only costs that are relevant to decisions whether to sell each joint product at split-off or after further processing are the *separable costs incurred after the split-off point.*

1. **Separable costs** are *avoidable* costs of further processing, and are, therefore, relevant to the further-processing decision.

2. Compare the contributions of each alternative: sales value at split-off *versus* sales value after further processing less separable (avoidable processing) costs.

3. Alternatively, it is profitable to process an individual product beyond the split-off point if the separable costs are exceeded by the increase in revenue produced by such processing.

E. **Joint costs** include all material and production costs of common inputs incurred *prior* to the split-off point.

1. *Joint costs* are *unavoidable* costs of operating the joint process.

2. Joint costs should not affect the decision to sell products at split-off or to process them further, but joint cost allocations may interfere with proper decision making.

3. Allocation of joint costs to different products is customary for the purposes of costing inventory and goods sold for financial reporting (this is the same concept as allocating fixed factory overhead to products). However, joint cost and joint-cost allocations are *completely irrelevant* to the question of whether the individual joint products should be sold at the split-off point or processed further before being sold.

4. Joint costs will not change as a result of decisions to sell products at split-off or after further processing; therefore, joint costs are irrelevant for decision making, regardless of how they might be allocated to products. Allocations of joint costs can only confuse decision making by altering contributions to profit.

> **Stop and Review**
>
> See textbook Exhibit 6-3

5. Both an analysis of the total joint process and a differential analysis produce the same analysis, and either may be used to aid decision making.

> **Study Tip:** *Do you recognize that decisions about joint products are fundamentally no different from those about accepting special orders, dropping or adding products, or make-or-buy decisions? In each case, determine the revenues and costs that will change.*

VI. Decide whether to keep or replace equipment

A. The *book value* of old equipment is a past, sunk, or historical cost and is, therefore, irrelevant to *making replacement decisions*.

   1. However, the *disposal value* of old equipment is relevant because it is an expected future inflow that would usually differ among alternative replacement decisions.

   2. The gain or loss on disposal (the difference between book value and disposal value) is a combination of relevant and irrelevant costs and it is not useful for making replacement decisions.

   3. The cost of new equipment is relevant, of course, because it is an expected future cost that will differ among alternative replacement decisions.

> **Stop and Review**
>
> See textbook Exhibits 6-4 and
> 6-5

B. That said, net book value of assets might be relevant to predicting future cash inflows that depend upon the *income tax effects* of the disposal of the assets.

   1. Disposing of assets at a loss often results in tax savings, which are counted as a contribution of the disposal alternative.

   2. Also relevant would be the tax benefits of continued depreciation of equipment that is not replaced.

C. A serious incentive problem can exist when decision making using expected costs interacts with scorekeeping (performance evaluation) that uses past costs.

   1. Consider the equipment-replacement case in textbook Exhibit 6-5.

   2. The analysis indicates a $2,500 total advantage of replacement during a four-year period.

   Question: Why might a manager nevertheless decide not to replace the equipment?

   Answer: Because he might fear a poor performance evaluation when the $1,500 loss on disposal is *reported in the first year*.

   3. Thus, an organization could be denied a long-term benefit from replacing the equipment.

   4. *This faulty decision is the result of using mismatched planning and scorekeeping information.*

   5. The decision to replace the equipment affects multiple years, yet the performance evaluation is based on a single year, in this case the year when the loss is recognized and before significant benefits are realized.

   6. This mismatching is a common problem in practice and may cause serious under-investment in new equipment.

   7. In many countries (especially in the U.S., some say) this problem has no easy solution because managers move often and are evaluated for their next positions on the basis of short-term results.

VII.	Identify irrelevant and misspecified costs

One should be wary of unit fixed costs. Total cost should be used instead. Some of the problems with using unit costs are:

A.   The most common problem in make-or-buy decisions is that managers may compare the absorption or unit cost of products made in-house with prices offered by suppliers.

B.   Absorption costs contain allocations of fixed costs, some of which are probably *unavoidable* fixed costs that are irrelevant to the decision.

C.   Another danger of using unit costs is that the fixed cost portion of the unit cost depends on the level of activity used to allocate fixed cost. Making or buying components or parts will affect activity levels and fixed cost allocations.

D.   It is better to remove all allocations of fixed costs from absorption costs because only variable costs per unit and *total avoidable* fixed costs are relevant to the make-or-buy decision.

VIII.	Discuss how performance measures can affect decision making

You should know how to make good decisions based on relevant data. However, knowing how to make these decisions and actually making them are quite different. On occasion, managers may make poor decisions if the performance measures in place will reward them for that particular decision. A good example of this is found in a manager's decision of whether to keep or replace machinery:

A.   If the machine is kept, the first year performance may be better, but after several years it may have been cheaper to replace the machine. Managers want to maximize performance, so they will lean toward keeping the machine.

B.   The conflict between performance measures and decision making can become more severe if managers are moved from one position to another. A manager who is aware of a future move will be more inclined to go for the immediate benefits of keeping the machine rather than saving the company in the long run.

C.   Replacing machinery earlier than planned can reveal flaws in the original purchase decision. Managers often spread the extra cost of keeping the machinery over the future by calling it "depreciation" rather than "loss on disposal."

D.   Evaluating performance decision by decision is a costly procedure. Combined measures are most commonly used. An income statement shows the results of several decisions at once.

PRACTICE TEST QUESTIONS AND PROBLEMS

True or False Statements

Determine whether each of the following statements is True (T) or False (F), and enter your answer in the space provided.

_____1.   In general, all expected future fixed costs are irrelevant to planning decisions.

_____2.   Costs that are relevant to decisions to make or buy a critical component might include the cost of components currently in inventory.

_____3.   An example of opportunity costs could be the interest revenue that would have been received by us if we invested in savings bonds rather than in shares of stock.

_____4.   Opportunity costs do not require dollar outlays and are not ordinarily entered in the accounting records.

_____5.   Joint products are defined as two or more products that are combined to make another product.

_____6.   Determining whether to sell or to process beyond split-off point requires knowing each product's share of joint costs.

_____7.   The past production cost of inventories on hand is irrelevant for choosing among alternatives for disposing of inventories, whether the inventory is obsolete or not.

_____8.   Amounts that could be relevant to choosing among alternative uses of certain materials on hand include their salvage value.

_____9.   The decision to process joint products individually beyond the split-off point should depend partly upon total joint processing costs.

Multiple-Choice Questions

For each of the following multiple-choice questions, select the best answer(s), and enter the identification letter(s) in the space provided.

_____1.   R. T. Jones presently earns an annual salary of $40,000 as an electrician. She accepts an invitation to join an electrical contracting partnership that promises an annual profit of $48,000 to Jones before the deduction of her $5,000 annual share of overhead costs. The opportunity cost of Jones's decision to join the partnership would be: (a) $5,000, (b) $8,000, (c) $40,000, (d) $43,000.

_____2.   See the preceding test item. The opportunity cost of Jones's decision to *not* join the partnership would be: (a) $5,000, (b) $8,000, (c) $40,000, (d) $43,000.

_____3.   Three products emerge from a joint process at a joint cost of $6,000, to be allocated equally to the three products. Product C can either be sold for $5,000 after further processing costs of $7,000 or disposed of after split-off at a cost of $3,000. Amounts relevant to the decision about Product C include: (a) $6,000 joint cost, (b) $2,000 share of joint cost, (c) further processing cost of $7,000, (d) disposal cost of $3,000.

_____4.   Obsolete inventory that cost $50,000 is on hand, but its scrap value is only $15,000. The inventory could be sold for $60,000 if converted into another form at an additional cost of $48,000. The *overall result* of converting and selling the inventory would be: (a) profit of $12,000, (b) profit of $27,000, (c) loss of $3,000, (d) profit of $15,000.

_____5.   See the preceding item. The decision should be: (a) do nothing, (b) sell the inventory for the $15,000 scrap value, (c) convert the inventory into another form and sell it for the $60,000, (d) hold the inventory at its $50,000 cost.

_____6.   An old machine has a net book value of $20,000 and a current salvage value of $7,000. It could be used for ten more years at an annual cash operating cost of $8,000, or it could be sold now and replaced by a new machine priced at $35,000 with a ten-year life and an annual cash operating cost of $5,000. Neither machine would have a salvage value in ten years. *Ignore income taxes and the time value of money.* Amounts that would be relevant to the replacement decision include: (a) $5,000, (b) $7,000, (c) $8,000, (d) $35,000.

_____7.   See item 6 above. If the old machine is replaced, there would be: (a) a gain of $7,000 on the sale, (b) a loss of $13,000 on the sale, (c) an overall benefit of $2,000, (d) an overall benefit of $30,000.

_____8.   See item 6. A manager who was planning to change positions within the next year would most likely be inclined to: (a) replace the machine, (b) reduce the amount of time that the machine operated each year, (c) keep the old machine.

Completion

Complete each of the following statements by filling in the blanks.

1.   Future costs that are relevant to decisions can properly include both _____ and _____ types of costs if they are expected to change and differ among the alternative actions.

2.   Relevant to equipment-replacement decisions is the old equipment's _____ value, but not its _____ value.

3.   It is usually not profitable to process a joint product beyond the split-off point if the _____ exceeds the _____.

4.   Relevant to decisions about the disposition of joint products is any _____ cost but not _____.

5.   Decisions about the disposition of inventory on-hand depend on _____ and effects on future sales, but not _____.

6.   The dangers of using unit costs for decision making are _____ and _____.

Problems

1. Universal Products, Inc. incurs the following costs in making the basket element for its "Sun-Fun" line of picnic accessories:

	Total Cost for 20,000 Units	Cost per Unit
Direct materials	$100,000	$ 5
Direct labor	120,000	6
Variable factory overhead	40,000	2
Fixed factory overhead	140,000	7
Total costs	$400,000	$20

Another manufacturer offers to sell Universal the same basket for $17 per unit for 20,000 units. Determine whether Universal should make or buy the basket, assuming the capacity now used to make the basket would become idle if it were purchased and that $60,000 of the fixed overhead could be avoided by not making the basket.

2. Midwest Corp. owns and operates 713 retail stores. Expected annual operating results for one of these stores are as follows:

Sales revenues	$520,000
Cost of goods sold and other direct cash operating expenses	490,000

Use the opportunity-cost concept in deciding whether to continue operations of this store or to lease the store building to a non-competing retailer for $4,000 per month. Building ownership costs are $19,000 per year.

3. Nature's Way, Inc. annually produces non-toxic cleaning products T and W from a joint production process costing $195,000 per year. Each product can be sold at the split-off point or further processed before being sold:

Selling Prices per Unit

Product	Quantity	At Split-Off	At Completion	Separable Processing Costs after Split-off
T	20,000	$6	$9	$52,000
W	40,000	4	5	47,000

Analyze whether the individual products should be processed beyond the split-off point.

Exercises

Celestial Tea Company presents the following data for a machine it owns:

Net book value	$32,000
Present scrap value	$12,000
Estimated remaining useful life	8 yrs
Predicted scrap value at end of useful life	none
Annual cash operating costs	$11,000

A new machine with the same productive capacity is available as follows:

Purchase price	$43,000
Estimated useful life	8 yrs
Predicted scrap value at end of useful life	none
Annual cash operating costs	$ 6,000

1. Ignoring income taxes and the time value of money, make computations on a *total cost basis* to determine which of the two alternatives the company should select: keep the old machine or replace it with the new machine.

	Eight Years Together	
	Keep	Replace
Cash operating costs:	$	$
Add:		
Total costs	$	$

Conclusion:

2. Use the differential cost approach to reach the same conclusions determined by the total-cost approach.

CHAPTER 6 SOLUTIONS TO PRACTICE TEST QUESTIONS AND PROBLEMS

True or False Statements

1. False   Some future costs may be separable or avoidable and, therefore, would be relevant to planning decisions. Unavoidable fixed costs are not relevant to planning decisions.

2. False   The cost of components in inventory is irrelevant to the make-or-buy decision. Past production costs, however, may be useful for predicting future production costs that are relevant to the "make" option.

3. True   If investing in savings bonds is our highest yielding alternative investment opportunity, forgone savings bond interest is the opportunity cost of investing in stocks. The stock investment must return at least as much as savings bonds to be attractive.

4. True   Opportunity costs are expected costs, but are real nonetheless. To turn the old adage around: "A penny not saved is a penny not earned."

5. False   Joint products are two or more products that are produced simultaneously from a common or joint process.

6. False   Neither the share of joint processing costs nor the total joint processing costs are relevant to the further processing decision. Of course, total joint processing costs are relevant to the decision to continue operating the joint process.

7. True   The past costs are sunk and cannot change or affect future costs of disposal. As in the special-order decision in Chapter 5, however, sales of current inventory below normal sales prices might affect future sales.

8. True   Salvage values are future effects of alternative disposal decisions and are relevant to the decisions.

9. False   Neither the total nor the shares of joint processing costs are relevant to further processing decisions.

Multiple-Choice Questions

1. c   By joining the partnership, Jones forgoes the $40,000 salary, which we assume is her highest-paying alternative. She expects to be $3,000 per year better off as a result.

2. d   The same reasoning applies. She gives up the $43,000 expected profit. She expects to earn $3,000 less by forgoing the $43,000 profit. Perhaps she is willing to give up the $3,000 as the price of security.

3. c, d   Both the further processing cost of $7,000 and the disposal cost of $3,000 are relevant to the disposition of product C. The joint process cost is irrelevant in total or allocated. Incidentally, note that the product would be processed further since the loss of $2,000 is less than the cost of disposal after split-off.

4. c   Sale of the converted inventory would contribute $12,000 to profit, but the opportunity cost of this decision is the contribution forgone by not scrapping the inventory for $15,000. The overall effect is a loss of $3,000, though this figure would never show up on any accounting records.

5. b   Selling the inventory for scrap has the higher contribution to profit by $3,000.

6. a, b, c, d   The annual cash operating costs of $5,000 or $8,000 are relevant since they differ between the alternatives. The $7,000 salvage value of the old equipment also is relevant, for the same reasons. The $35,000 purchase price of the new equipment is a future cost and is relevant. The $20,000 book value of the old equipment is irrelevant because it is a sunk cost and will not change.

7. b, c   The loss on the sale of the old equipment is the salvage value less the book value, $7,000 - $20,000 = -$13,000. Ignoring the time value of money and taxes, the net benefit is $2,000: the $7,000 salvage value of the old equipment plus ten years of $3,000 operating cost savings less the $35,000 purchase price.

8. c   A manager who is aware of a future move will be more inclined to go for the immediate benefits of keeping the machine rather than saving the company in the long-run. Ignoring taxes and depreciation, the first-year effect would be a $10,000 decrease in income: the $13,000 loss on the sale of old equipment plus the $3,000 savings in annual operating costs.

Completion

1.   fixed, variable

2.   salvage, book

3.   separable cost, sales value

4.   separable, joint processing cost

5.   revenues and costs of disposition, past production or purchase cost

6.   including unavoidable costs, comparing inaccurate allocated costs

Problems

1. Universal Products, Inc.

The relevant figures to compare with the $17 purchase price are:

Direct materials	$100,000
Direct labor	120,000
Variable factory overhead	40,000
Avoidable fixed factory overhead	60,000
Total	$320,000

The total cost of purchasing = (20,000)x($17) = $340,000, which is $20,000 more than making the product.

Note that the unavoidable fixed overhead ($140,000 - $60,000 = $80,000) has been excluded from this analysis as being irrelevant to the decision, because it is not an expected future cost that will differ between the alternatives of making or buying the basket.

2. Midwest Corp.

Sales revenues	$520,000
Less costs:	
Cost of goods sold and other direct cash expenses	490,000
Operating profits	$ 30,000
Opportunity cost of leasing: 4,000 x 12=	48,000
Difference in favor of leasing building to non-competing retailer	$ 18,000

(Building ownership costs are not relevant because they would be the same under each alternative.)

3. There are at least two equivalent solutions to Nature's Way, Inc.'s decisions:

(a)   Differential analysis:

T: $52,000 - 20,000 x ($9 - $6) = $52,000 - $60,000 = $8,000 excess of expected benefit over related costs, *decision:* further process.

W: $47,000 - 40,000 x ($5 - $4) = $47,000 - $40,000 = ($7,000) excess of expected costs over related benefit, *decision:* sell at split-off point.

(b)   Opportunity-cost analysis:

T: (20,000 x $9) - (20,000 x $6) - $52,000

$180,000 - $120,000 - $52,000

$8,000, as above.

W: (40,000 x $5) - (40,000 x $4) - $47,000

$200,000 - $160,000 - $47,000

($7,000), as above.

Note that the $195,000 joint costs are irrelevant under both of these approaches.

Exercises

Celestial Tea Company

1. Total cost approach:

	Keep	Replace
Cash operating costs: $11,000 x 8 yrs	$88,000	-
$ 6, 000 x 8 yrs	-	$ 48,000
Disposal value of old machine		(12,000)
Purchase price of new machine	-	43,000
Total costs for 8 years	$88,000	$79,000

2. Differential cost approach (Keep vs. Replace):

Cash operating cost difference:	
($11,000 - $ 6, 000) x 8 yrs	$40,000
Net purchase price of new machine	
$43,000 - $12,000	31,000
Total cost difference for 8 years	$ 9,000

Note that the net book value of the old machine is irrelevant to the decision in either approach.

Conclusion: Replace old machine, because total costs are $9,000 lower for 8 years.

Introduction to Budgets and Preparing the Master Budget

<table>
<tr><td colspan="2" align="center">OVERVIEW</td></tr>
<tr><td colspan="2">The keystone of successful planning and control systems is budgeting. We focus on the master budget, a coordinated set of detailed operating plans for all parts of an organization. This chapter is one of the most detailed so far and requires a basic understanding of financial statements. After finishing this chapter you should be able to:</td></tr>
<tr><td>I.</td><td>Explain how budgets facilitate planning and coordination</td></tr>
<tr><td>II.</td><td>Anticipate possible human relations problems caused by budgets</td></tr>
<tr><td>III.</td><td>Explain potentially dysfunctional incentives in the budget process</td></tr>
<tr><td>IV.</td><td>Understand difficulties of sales forecasting</td></tr>
<tr><td>V.</td><td>Explain the major features and advantages of a master budget</td></tr>
<tr><td>VI.</td><td>Follow principal steps in preparing the master budget</td></tr>
<tr><td>VII.</td><td>Prepare the operating budgets and the supporting schedules</td></tr>
<tr><td>VIII.</td><td>Prepare the financial budget</td></tr>
<tr><td>IX.</td><td>Use a spreadsheet to develop a budget (Appendix 7)</td></tr>
</table>

I. Explain how budgets facilitate planning and coordination

Budgets are quantitative plans for future operations and financial position targets.

A. Budgets are used to evaluate business activities and can be used as a tool for planning potential future decisions.

    1. Some firms assume that activities in a new budget period will be the same as in the previous budget period. Other firms use a **zero-base budget** in which the budget for every activity starts at zero. This means managers must justify all expenditures in each new budget.

B. When preparing a budget managers set goals and form plans to achieve these goals. The budgeting process forces firms to prepare for the future.

C. Managers use budgets to communicate the goals of the company to its employees at all levels. Lower-level managers provide feedback on these goals and objectives. Budgeting also forces managers of different departments to coordinate their activities.

D. Budgets are an effective tool for performance evaluation. Contrasting actual performance with budgeted goals is more useful than comparison with past performance.

II. Anticipate possible human relations problems caused by budgets

The budgeting process may seem to be mechanical, but it requires considerable human input to be successful.

A. Individuals realize that budgets serve as both planning tools and benchmarks for their own evaluations.

    1. Individuals may have incentives to disguise their true beliefs in order to make budgets easier to attain.

    2. Organizations, therefore, must design incentives to reinforce good planning, and effective and efficient implementation of budgets. (This important topic is explored further in Chapter 9.)

    3. Problems are acute where budgets are used primarily to limit spending as in many government agencies.

B. It is believed that individuals will accept budgeting better and will set challenging objectives for themselves when they are permitted an active role in the budgeting process (called **participative budgeting**).

III. Explain potentially dysfunctional incentives in the budget process

When used effectively, budgeting provides useful information that can help companies achieve their goals and objectives. Unfortunately, budgets can have the adverse effect of giving managers incentives to lie and cheat.

A. Managers may create biased budgets to increase resources allocated to their departments. Increased resources can make it easier for a department to reach targeted outputs often resulting in rewards for managers.

B. **Budgetary slack** or **budget padding** is another way unethical managers can misuse budgeting systems. By overstating budgeted cost or understating budgeted revenue, these managers create budgeted goals that are easier to achieve.

C.   Organizations can avoid creating incentives to lie and cheat by rewarding good budget forecasts and good performance against the budget.

IV.   Explain difficulties of sales forecasting

Sales forecasting is a difficult and critical step in the master budgeting process.

A.   A **sales forecast** is a prediction of sales under specified conditions (general economic trends, competitors' actions, advertising levels, and so on). As the underlying conditions change, sales forecasts will change.

    1.   Nonprofit and government organizations would forecast demands for services, which would drive their budgets.

    2.   Sales forecasts are generated using information from a wide variety of sources:

- Past sales patterns
- Sales force estimates
- General economic conditions
- Market research studies
- Competitors' actions
- Pricing alternatives
- Product mix alternatives
- Advertising and sales promotion alternatives

B.   A **sales budget** is the forecast that the organization accepts as a target. This sales budget or target then determines the conditions that the organization can control—the operating budget.

V.   Explain the major features and advantages of a master budget

A.   As we saw in Chapter 2, organizations may target certain levels of profit.

    1.   Organizations may also target certain levels of cash flow or asset position.

    2.   The important issue covered in this chapter is how organizations plan resources in order to achieve those targets.

    3.   Most organizations that are successful in meeting their targets do so with the help of the formal planning mechanism called the *master budget*.

    4.   This chapter discusses the organizational role, the components, and the preparation of the master budget.

B.   Budgets quantitatively express the organization's plans to achieve targets over various time periods.

    1.   **Strategic plans** set overall, long-run goals and objectives of the organization.

    2.   **Long-range plans** set specific financial targets for a 5- or 10-year horizon.

    3.   **Capital budgets** detail capacity-related spending required by long-range plans.

    4.   **Master budgets** summarize the organization's planned activities in the form of *operating budgets* and *financial budgets* for periods of one year or less.

5. **Operating budgets** are plans for the basic activities of the organization necessary to support financial or other outcome targets.

6. **Financial budgets** are forecasted financial statements that demonstrate the planned achievement of financial objectives (also called **pro forma financial statements**).

7. **Continuous** or **rolling budgets** are annual master budgets expressed as 12 monthly targets, wherein as one month ends, another month is added to the budget. For example, the master budget may run from the beginning of June 20X2 to the end of May 20X3. As June 20X2 ends, the first month of the continuous master budget becomes *July* 20X2, and *June* 20X3 is added as the last month of the 12-month continuous master budget.

C. The **operating budget** consists of supporting plans for the activities of the organization that may include (depending on the nature of the organization):

1. Sales budget (and other cost-driver budgets as necessary), which details the levels of basic activities necessary to meet financial objectives

2. Purchases budget, which plans resources to be acquired to support basic activities through cash outlays or credit purchases

3. Cost of goods or services sold budget, which computes the cost of goods sold expenses to be *recognized*

4. Operating expenses budget, which details all the operating expenses to be *recognized*

5. Budgeted income statement, which reflects the effects of sales and other basic activities on income performance for the budget period (In a sense, this is a proof that successful implementation of the preceding plans will result in the targeted income.)

D. The **financial budget** includes budgets that demonstrate the effects of implementing the operating budget and the capital budget on cash and on financial position. The financial budget includes:

1. Capital budget

2. Cash budget, showing sources and uses of cash and ending cash balance

3. Budgeted balance sheet, showing the period's ending financial position

> **Stop and Review**
>
> See textbook Exhibit 7-2

E. Advantages of budgets to organizations and individuals include:

1. Budgets force managers to face the task of planning, to anticipate changing conditions, and to formulate and implement organizational policies to deal with expected changes.

2. Budgets force managers to translate plans into explicit terms for evaluating actual performance in the future. Expectations are the best benchmark for evaluating actual performance.

3. Budgets force managers to communicate management plans, coordinate plans, and help carry them out.

VI. Follow the principal steps in preparing a master budget

The principal steps in preparing the master budget are:

Basic Data

1. Using the data given, prepare the following detailed schedules for each of the months of the planning horizon:

    Schedule a. Sales budget

    Schedule b. Cash collections from customers

    Schedule c. Purchases and cost-of-goods-sold budget

    Schedule d. Cash disbursements for purchases

    Schedule e. Operating expense budget

    Schedule f. Cash disbursements for operating expenses

Operating Budget

2. Using the schedules, prepare a budgeted income statement for the four months ending July 31, 20X1 (Exhibit 7-4).

Financial Budget

3. Using the data given and the supporting schedules, prepare the following forecasted financial statements:

    a. Capital budget

    b. Cash budget, including details of borrowings, repayments, and interest for each month of the planning horizon (Exhibit 7-5)

    c. Budgeted balance sheet as of July 31, 20X1 (Exhibit 7-6)

VII. Prepare the operating budget and the supporting schedules

Preparation of the master budget includes the following steps:

A. *The starting point is the ending balance sheet for the prior budget period.* Usually this, too, is a forecasted balance sheet because budgeting for the next period would not wait for the actual end of the current period—which would be too late.

   1. The beginning balance sheet shows the organization's resources at the beginning of the period (cash, materials, work in process, finished goods, plant and equipment, and so on).

   2. To meet the period's objectives, these beginning balances may not be sufficient, so subsequent parts of the operating budget detail which additional resources the organization must acquire.

B. Other *essential data* for beginning the master budget are the various *operating and financial characteristics and policies* of the organization. Among others these include:

   1. Sales collection and bad debt expectations, including credit terms granted to customers

   2. Payment policies for purchases, acquired services, and operating expenses, including credit terms granted by suppliers

   3. Inventory policies, including required cash balance

   4. Sources and terms of short-term financing

   5. Planned additions or retirements of long-term assets and debt

C.   Given the starting position and conditions, the *sales forecast and forecasts of other basic activities drive the rest of the master budget*.

   1.   These forecasts lead to sales budgets and other cost-driver budgets. The sales budget identifies the expected pattern of sales during the budget period(s).

> **Stop and Review**
>
> See textbook steps 1a and 1b

   2.   The sales and cost-driver budgets then lead to purchases and disbursements (payments) for purchase budgets for materials and for labor and services.

   3.   Each part of the operating budget is linked to the previous part by the organization's policies and by simple budget relationships of the form:

   Start   Desired ending balance of inventoried resource (skip for non-inventoriable resources such as labor and acquired services)

   Plus   Resources required for sales or cost-driver activity

   Equals Total resources needed on hand during the period

   Less   Beginning balance of inventoried resource (skip for non-inventoriable resources)

   Equals Total resources to be acquired for the period (equals total resources needed on hand during the period for non-inventoriable resources)

> **Stop and Review**
>
> See textbook steps 1c and 1d

   4.   Purchases budgets and cost-driver activity budgets then lead to operating expense budgets, which *match* costs of resources used to planned sales.

   Note: Not all expenses are cash outlays of the period. Some, such as depreciation, are matching of past cash outlays to sales of the current period.

> **Stop and Review**
>
> See textbook steps 1e and 1f

   5.   Combining the sales budgets with operating expense budgets generates the budgeted income statement.

> **Stop and Review**
>
> See textbook step 2

   6.   The cash budget analyzes the period's cash flow and generates the ending cash balance by combining the following components:

   The beginning cash balance

   The cash portions of the operating budget

   The capital budget and plans for long-term debt and equity (not covered here)

   Short-term financing policies

> **Stop and Review**
>
> See textbook step 3a

7. The final step of the master budget is to combine the beginning balance sheet, the operating budget, and the cash budget to generate the ending or budgeted balance sheet of the period.

Note: Some companies do not prepare budgeted balance sheets due to the size and complexity of the task. Omitting this final step can be a mistake because forcing total assets to equal total liabilities and equities forces your budget assumptions to be consistent. For example, the assistant controller of General Motors stated at a 1992 meeting that GM did not prepare budgeted balance sheets, because to do so was too difficult. But GM would have caught a several hundred million dollar budgeting error before the bills came due if it had. One of the assistant controller's new tasks was to figure out how GM could prepare budgeted balance sheets.

> **Study Tip:** *Do you understand the* linked *steps of the master budget process? If you are not sure, review the textbook example again.*

VIII. Prepare the financial budget

The financial budget includes the *capital budget (covered in Chapter 11), cash budget, and budgeted ending balance sheet.*

A. The **cash budget** combines the beginning cash balance, cash receipts, and cash disbursements to determine whether there is an excess or deficiency of cash.

B. The **budgeted balance sheet** adjusts the beginning balance sheet accounts for each change in the gain or use of resources indicated from all the previous schedules.

> **Study Tip:** *Look at Exhibit 7-6 and see that every balance sheet account can be computed by this simple formula: ending balance = beginning balance + increases − decreases.*

C. So far, we have discussed what can be called **functional budgeting,** or budgeting processes that focus on preparing budgets for various functions of the firm such as production and sales.

D. Organizations that use activity-based cost accounting systems often use **activity-based budgets,** or budgets that focus on the budgeted cost of activities required to produce and sell products and services.

> **Stop and Review**
>
> See textbook Exhibit 7-8

E. Properly made master budgets that consider all aspects of a company's operations provide the basis for an effective **financial planning model**. A financial planning model is a mathematical model of the master budget that can react to any set of assumptions about sales, costs, or product mix.

IX. Use a spreadsheet to develop a budget (Appendix 7)

A. Financial planning models are algebraic representations of an organization's value chain.

1. These models would not be possible without computer software.

2. Some organizations are implementing activity-based budgets and financial planning models, which combine knowledge of ABC and modeling methods.

B. Appendix 7 introduces the use of spreadsheet software for building financial planning models.

1. You should learn how to use this software. Virtually any PC-based spreadsheet software will do. Powerful software also is available for mainframe computers (one popular program is IFPS).

2. If possible, you should try to solve your homework problems or the practice test problems in this study guide with spreadsheet software and test the sensitivity to different sales assumptions. *Note*: this may be time consuming, but it is valuable practice.

> **Study Tip:** *Before going on to the practice test, be sure that you can explain some of the difficulties of sales forecasting and human participation in the budgeting process. If it is possible, you should try to apply Appendix 7 to its example, to your homework, or to this practice test. Spreadsheet software is extremely important in today's environment—learn to use it if you can.*

PRACTICE TEST QUESTIONS AND PROBLEMS

True or False Statements

Determine whether each of the following statements is True (T) or False (F), and enter your answer in the space provided.

_____1. Pro forma statements are prepared for comparison with actual financial statements at the conclusion of the budget year.

_____2. The financial budget includes the budgeted balance sheet and the budgeted income statement.

_____3. The operating budget includes the cash budget and the production budgets.

_____4. As a general rule, the master budget should be based on the actual operating data for the preceding year or on an average of the data for the two or three most recent years.

_____5. The main goals of budgets include limiting expenditures and identifying poor performance.

_____6. Expected performance is generally considered to be a better basis for judging actual operating results than past performance.

_____7. Cash collections from customers are composed of cash sales and (eventually) collections on all credit sales.

_____8. The budget for disbursements for operating expenses plans for outlays such as materials, labor, and depreciation.

_____9. Budgeted income statements combine sales budgets and operating expense budgets.

_____10. Individuals are more likely to accept the discipline of budgeting if they have an active part in budget participation.

Multiple-Choice Questions

For each of the following multiple-choice questions, select the best answer(s), and enter the identification letter(s) in the space provided:

_____1.   Budgets for individual projects requiring an extended period of years for completion are called: (a) rolling budgets, (b) operating budgets, (c) master budgets, (d) capital budgets.

_____2.   Budgets that plan a year's basic activities and the needed resources are called: (a) financial budgets, (b) operating budgets, (c) master budgets, (d) capital budgets.

_____3.   Budgets that plan the organization's ending financial position are called: (a) financial budgets, (b) operating budgets, (c) master budgets, (d) capital budgets.

_____4.   A company had sales last month of $60,000 and expects sales this month of $90,000. One-third of all sales are cash sales. Two-thirds of all sales are collected in the month following the sale. The company should expect total cash collections from sales this month to equal: (a) $60,000, (b) $70,000, (c) $80,000, (d) $90,000.

_____5.   A merchandising company has $64,000 of accounts receivable at April 30. In May it expects to collect 75% of these receivables and 30% of the May sales on account. Its budgeted credit sales for May are $70,000. The budgeted accounts receivable at May 31 would be: (a) $69,000, (b) $65,000, (c) $37,000, (d) $97,000.

_____6.   The pattern of collections of accounts receivable for a company is 20% in the month of sale, 50% in the following month, and 30% in the month after that. Sales on account were $80,000 for January and $60,000 for February. Budgeted sales for March are $70,000. Compute the budgeted *cash collections* in March: (a) $74,000, (b) $70,000, (c) $68,000, (d) $72,000.

_____7.   See the preceding test item. Compute the budgeted accounts receivable balance on April 1: (a) $56,000, (b) $74,000, (c) $68,000, (d) $80,000.

_____8.   A merchandising company forecasts $150,000 of sales for September. Its gross profit rate is 40% of sales, and its August 31 merchandise inventory is $112,000. Compute the budgeted purchases for September if the company wishes to budget an inventory of $112,000 for the end of September: (a) $90,000, (b) $70,000, (c) $80,000, (d) $100,000.

_____9.   See the preceding item and assume that all data are the same except that the company is moving to a JIT system and budgets an inventory of $12,000 for the end of September. The budgeted purchases for September would be: (a) $10,000, (b) $20,000, (c) $2,000, (d) zero.

_____10.   A company has a $7,200 cash balance at June 1. The budgeted cash transactions for June are receipts of $53,800 and disbursements of $67,500. If the company's minimum June 30 cash balance is $5,000, what is the budgeted amount to be borrowed during June? (a) $11,500, (b) $13,700, (c) $18,700, (d) $16,500.

Completion

Complete each of the following statements by filling in the blanks.

1.   A budget that is regularly updated to show a one-year forecast by adding a month or quarter in the future as the month or quarter just ended is dropped is called a _____ budget.

2.   The advantages to an organization of the budgeting process include: _____, _____, and _____.

3.   In general, it is usually best to start with forecasts of _____ or _____ plus the company's _____ in constructing a master budget.

4.   The operating budget usually consists of: the _____, _____, _____, _____, and the _____ .

5.   The budgeted ending cash balance is generally _____ when borrowing is required.

Problems

1. Given for Maxim Co. (in thousands):

	April Actual	May Actual	June Budgeted	July Budgeted
Cash sales	$ 80	$ 50	$ 60	$ 80
Sales on account	320	200	300	280

Compute the budgeted cash receipts for June and July, assuming credit sales are collected as follows: 15% in month of sale, 60% in the following month, and 25% in the month after that:

2. Given for Boxes, Inc.:

	April	July
Beginning merchandise inventory	$ 15,400	$ 33,900
Expected sales	160,000	180,000
Desired ending merchandise inventory	21,000	30,000
Expected gross profit rate on sales	30%	40%

Find the budgeted purchases for each month:

$	$

3. Given the data below for Floor Veneer Products, complete the parts of the cash budget necessary to compute "borrowing" or "available for repayments":

	September	November
Beginning cash balance	$16,100	$15,600
Expected cash receipts	62,900	71,600
Expected cash disbursements	45,200	77,300
Minimum ending cash balance desired	12,000	14,000

a. Borrowing	$	$
b. Available for repayments	$	$

Exercise

1. The Four-Sight Lens Company presented the following balance sheet at March 31, 20X5, the beginning of a budget period:

ASSETS		LIABILITIES AND OWNERS' EQUITY	
Current assets:		Current liabilities:	
Cash	$ 9,500	Accounts payable	$ 27,700
Accounts receivable	33,300	Accrued taxes payable	4,200
Merchandise inventory	66,600	Total current liabilities	$ 31,900
Total current assets	$109,400	Owners' equity	104,500
Plant and equipment	$45,000	Total liabilities and owners' equity	$136,400
Less accumulated depreciation	18,000		
Net plant and equipment	27,000		
Total assets	$136,400		

The company's budgeted operations for the month of April 20X5 are shown as follows:

Cash receipts:		Other transactions and information:	
From cash sales	$14,800	Sales of merchandise on account	$25,000
From collections of accounts receivable	20,100	Purchases of merchandise (all on account)	18,500
Total	$34,900	Depreciation of plant and equipment	300
Cash disbursements:		Additional accrued taxes	1,200
For operating expenses	$14,500	Cost of goods sold	22,300
For payments on accounts payable	17,000	Minimum ending cash balance desired	9,000
Total	$31,500	Interest rate on borrowed funds	12%

Please resist the temptation to look at the solution until you have attempted your own solution. Using the forms provided below, prepare the following:

- The detailed budget schedules, (a) through (h), for April 20X5.

- The budgeted income statement for April 20X5.

- Budgeted statement of cash receipts and disbursements for April 20X5.

- The budgeted balance sheet at April 30, 20X5.

Detailed budget schedules:

(a) Sales for April 20X5:

(b) Cash balance at April 30, 20X5:

(c) Accounts receivable at April 30, 20X5:

(d) Merchandise inventory at April 30, 20X5:

(e) Accumulated depreciation at April 30, 20X5:

(f) Accounts payable at April 30, 20X5:

(g) Accrued taxes payable at April 30, 20X5:

(h) Owners' equity at April 30, 20X5:

Budgeted income statement:

Sales (Schedule a)	
Less cost of goods sold	
Gross Margin	
Less operating expenses:	
Total expenses	
Net income	

Budgeted Statement of Cash Receipts and Disbursements

Cash balance, beginning	
Cash receipts:	
Collections from customers	
Total cash available, before financing	
Cash disbursements	
Minimum cash balance	
Total cash needed	
Excess (deficiency)	
Financing:	
Borrowing	
Repayments	
Interest (at 12% per annum)	
Total Cash increase (decrease) from financing	
Cash balance, ending	

Budgeted balance sheet:

Current assets:	
Cash (Schedule b)	
Total current assets	
Plant and equipment	
Less accumulated depreciation (Schedule e)	
Net plant and equipment	
Total assets	
Current liabilities:	
Total current liabilities	
Owners' equity (Schedule h)	
Total liabilities and owners' equity	

CHAPTER 7 SOLUTIONS TO PRACTICE QUESTIONS AND PROBLEMS

True or False Statements

1. True   But this is not the primary reason for preparing the pro forma financial statements. These statements are prepared as part of the master budget process. Planning is the primary purpose of the statements.

2. False   The budgeted balance sheet is part of the financial budget, but, generally, the budgeted income statement is considered part of the operations budget.

3. False   Production budgets are parts of the operating budget, but the cash budget is considered part of the financial budget.

4. False   The master budget should be based on expectations for the coming year. Past operating results are helpful only to the extent that they help the organization understand cost behavior and implementation problems, and help predict future events.

5. False   The main goals of budgets are planning, coordinating and communicating, as well as providing a benchmark for evaluating performance. Limiting expenditures is not a planning function, but in some organizations (particularly governmental), approved budgets are legal constraints on spending.

6. True   Expectations of future performance should be based on the best planning and forecasting that is feasible. Expectations state what should be achieved. Past performance may be completely unrelated to current performance.

7. False   Not all sales are collectible; you must make some allowance for uncollectible sales.

8. False   Materials and labor may require cash outlays, but depreciation is recognition of the use of past outlays.

9. True   The budgeted income statement collects plans for sales and subtracts all operating expenses, but also includes interest expense.

10. True   Or at least this is what most studies have shown, and this conclusion is intuitively appealing. One would especially expect to see benefits from participative budgeting in organizations that are implementing JIT approaches, where employees at all levels must be involved in managing productive processes. Participative budgeting is still controversial, though, because it is unclear whether financial performance increases with participation.

Multiple-Choice Questions

1. d.   Capital budgets analyze the viability of individual, long-term projects. The cash flows from accepted capital budgets are inputs to the cash budgets of each period's master budget.

2. b   Operating budgets plan a year's basic activities and the needed resources. Financial budgets determine the effects of operations and other financing activities on cash and financial position. Master budgets combine operating and financial budgets.

3. c   Financial budgets determine the effects of operations and other financing activities on cash and financial position.

4. b   Cash collections should equal $^1/_3(\$90,000) + {}^2/_3(\$60,000) = \$70,000$.

5. b   The ending accounts receivable balance should equal the beginning balance plus credit sales less collections: $\$64,000 + \$70,000 - (.75 \times \$64,000) - (.30 \times \$70,000) = \$65,000$.

6. c   See the column total under March below.

Collections

Month	Sales	January	February	March	March A/R
January	80,000	16,000	40,000	24,000	
February	60,000	-	12,000	30,000	18,000
March	70,000	-	-	14,000	56,000
				68,000	74,000

7. b   See the column total under March A/R (accounts receivable) above.

8. a   The purchase amount is calculated as follows:

Desired ending balance	$112,000
Required for sales	
$150,000 x 0.6	90,000
Total required	$202,000
Less beginning balance	$112,000
Purchases	$ 90,000

9. d   There is an excess of inventory, so no purchase is necessary, as shown below:

Desired ending balance	$ 12,000
Required for sales	
$150,000 x 0.6	90,000
Total required	$102,000
Less beginning balance	$112,000
Excess inventory	$ 10,000

10. a   The amount of borrowing is the cash available less the cash required: $7,200 + $53,800 - $67,500 - $5,000 = the cash deficiency = $11,500.

Completion

1. continuous or rolling budget

2. formalizing planning, evaluating performance, coordinating efforts

3. sales or sales budgets, other cost-driver activities and policies

4. sales budget, purchases budget, cost of goods sold budget, operating expenses budget, budgeted income statement

5. negative

Problems

1. Maxim Co.

   June: 60 + 15% (300) + 60% (200) + 25% (320) = 60 + 45 + 120 + 80 = 305

   July: 80 + 15% (280) + 60% (300) + 25% (200) = 80 + 42 + 180 + 50 = 352

2. Boxes, Inc.

		April	July
Expected cost of goods sold:	70% (160,000)	$112,000	
	60% (180,000)		$108,000
Add desired ending inventory		21,000	30,000
Total needs		$133,000	$138,000
Less beginning inventory		15,400	33,900
Budgeted merchandise purchases		$117,600	$104,100

3. Floor Veneer Products

	September	November
Beginning cash balance	$ 16,100	$15,600
Add expected cash receipts	62,900	71,600
Total available before current financing (a)	$79,000	$87,200
Expected cash disbursements	$45,200	$77,300
Add minimum ending cash balance desired	12,000	14,000
Total cash needed (b)	$57,200	$91,300
1. Necessary to borrow: (b) - (a)		$4,100
2. Available for repayment of loans and interest: (a) - (b)	$21,800	

Exercise

1. Four-Sight Lens Company

Budget schedules:

(a) Sales for April 20X5:

Cash sales	$14,800
Sales on account	25,000
Total budgeted sales for April 20X5	$39,800

(b) Cash balance at April 30, 20X5:

Cash balance at March 31, 20X5	$ 9,500
Add total budgeted cash receipts for April	34,900
Total	$44,400
Less total budgeted cash disbursements for April	31,500
Budgeted cash balance at April 30, 20X5	12,900

(c) Accounts receivable at April 30, 20X5:

Accounts receivable at March 31, 20X5	$33,300
Add budgeted sales on account for April	25,000
Total	$58,300
Less budgeted cash collections on account for April	20,100
Budgeted accounts receivable at April 30, 20X5	$38,200

(d) Merchandise inventory at April 30, 20X5:

Merchandise inventory at March 31, 20X5	$66,600
Add budgeted purchases for April	18,500
Total	85,100
Less budgeted cost of goods sold for April	22,300
Budgeted merchandise inventory at April 30, 20X5	$62,800

(e) Accumulated depreciation at April 30, 20X5:

Accumulated depreciation at March 31, 20X5	$18,000
Add budgeted depreciation for April	300
Budgeted accumulated depreciation at April 30, 20X5	$18,300

(f) Accounts payable at April 30, 20X5:

Accounts payable at March 31, 20X5	$27,700
Add budgeted merchandise purchases on account for April	18,500
Total	$46,200
Less budgeted payments on accounts payable for April	17,000
Budgeted accounts payable at April 30, 20X5	$29,200

(g) Accrued taxes payable at April 30, 20X5:

Accrued taxes payable at March 31, 20X5	$ 4,200
Add additional accrued taxes budgeted for April	1,200
Budgeted accrued taxes payable at April 30, 20X5	5,400

(h) Owners' equity at April 30, 20X5:

Owners' equity at March 31, 20X5	$104,500
Add budgeted net income for April	
(from budgeted income statement for April)	1,500
Budgeted owners' equity at April 30, 20X5	$106,000

Budgeted income statement:

Sales (Schedule a)	$ 39,800
Less cost of goods sold	22,300
Gross margin on sales	$ 17,500
Less expenses:	
Operating expenses	$ 14,500
Depreciation	300
Taxes	1,200
Total expenses	$16,000
Net income	$ 1,500

Budgeted Statement of Cash Receipts and Disbursements:

Cash balance, beginning	$ 9,500
Cash receipts:	
Collections from customers	34,900
Total cash available, before financing	$44,400
Cash disbursements	31,500
Minimum cash balance	9,000
Total cash needed	$40,500
Excess (deficiency)	$ 3,900
Financing:	
Borrowing	0
Repayments	0
Interest (at 12% per annum)	0
Total cash increase (decrease) from financing	0
Cash balance, ending ($44,400 - $31,500)	$ 12,900

Budgeted balance sheet

Current assets:

Cash (Schedule b)	$ 12,900
Accounts receivable (Schedule c)	38,200
Merchandise inventory (Schedule d)	62,800
Total current assets	$113,900
Plant and equipment	$ 45,000
Less accumulated depreciation (Schedule e)	18,300
Net plant and equipment	26,700
Total assets	$140,600

Current liabilities:

Accounts payable (Schedule f)	$29,200
Accrued taxes payable (Schedule g)	5,400
Total current liabilities	$ 34,600
Owners' equity (Schedule h)	106,000
Total liabilities and owners' equity	$140,600

CHAPTER 8

Flexible Budgets and Variance Analysis

OVERVIEW

This chapter develops budgeting systems for performance evaluation by utilizing the underlying activities that drive master budgets. By reformatting the master budget using actual driving activities that differ from budgeted activities, one creates a flexible budget that is a more informative benchmark for actual performance than the original master budget. Your learning objectives are to:

I.   Distinguish between flexible and static budgets

II.   Use flexible-budget formulas to construct a flexible budget based on the volume of sales

III.   Prepare an activity-based flexible budget

IV.   Explain the performance evaluation relationship between static budgets, flexible budgets, and actual results

V.   Compute activity-level variances and flexible-budget variances

VI.   Compute and interpret price and quantity variances for inputs based on cost-driver activity

VII.   Compute variable overhead spending and efficiency variances

VIII. Compute the fixed overhead spending variance

I.	**Distinguish between flexible and static budgets**

A. Master budgets are **static**, that is they do not change even if the underlying sales and other cost-driver activities do change.

1. One of the major roles of the master budget is to provide a benchmark for evaluating actual performance.

   a. Recall from Chapter 1 the common form of the performance report:

   Actual result - Expected result = Variance

   b. When the "expected result" is the master budget, say the budgeted income statement, the performance report variance is called the **master-budget variance**.

   c. When a variance has an increasing effect on income (such as higher-than-budgeted revenue or lower-than-budgeted expense), it is labeled "favorable." A variance that decreases income is labeled "unfavorable."

Stop and Review

See textbook Exhibit 8-1

---

   d. The shortcoming of the master-budget variance is that it is the net result of at least two underlying causes:

   • Differences in underlying sales and other cost-driver activities that cause total costs and revenue to differ from the master budget

   • Differences in revenue and costs per unit of activity that cause costs and revenue in total to differ from the master budget

   e. From the master-budget variance alone, managers cannot determine why actual results differed from the master budget. Since each cause has different control implications, it would be useful to separate their effects.

   f. The *flexible budget* is used to attribute part of the master budget to different activity levels and the other part to differences in revenue and costs per unit of activity.

Study Tip: *Before going on to the next section, be sure that you understand that we have re-introduced the concept of a variance from Chapter 1 and have applied it to the master budget from Chapter 7. Can you explain two possible causes of a master-budget variance?*

B. The **flexible budget** is part or all of a master budget that is prepared for the actual (or any) levels of sales and other cost-driver activities.

1. Contrast with a master budget, which is tied to a single level of underlying activities.

2. Obviously, use of a computerized financial planning model makes preparation of flexible budgets relatively easy because the model contains the quantitative relationships between activity levels and revenues or expenses, but flexible budgets can be prepared manually, too.

C. Actual revenues and expenses rarely equal budgeted expenses. Differences between budgeted amounts and actual amounts result in either a *favorable* or *unfavorable* variance.

1. Actual revenues that exceed budgeted revenues result in **favorable revenue variances**. Actual revenues that fall short of budgeted revenues result in **unfavorable revenue variances**.

2. Actual costs that are below budgeted costs result in **favorable cost variances**. Actual costs that exceed budgeted costs result in **unfavorable cost variances**.

II. Use flexible-budget formulas to construct a flexible budget based on the volume of sales

The relationships between activities and costs and revenues can be called *flexible-budget formulas*, but they are just the revenue and cost *functions* developed and used in previous chapters.

1. Recall for *strictly variable costs*, this formula is the *cost per unit of cost-driver activity*, as shown in the upper part of Exhibit 8-2.

> **Stop and Review**
>
> See textbook Exhibit 8-2

2. For *fixed and step costs*, the flexible-budget formula is simply the total budgeted amounts per budget period, as illustrated in the lower part of Exhibit 8-2.

3. The relationship between these two formulas is identical to the relationships discussed in Chapters 2 and 3.

> **Stop and Review**
>
> See textbook Exhibit 8-3

> **Study Tip:** *Before going on to the next section be sure that you understand that by introducing the flexible budget we are combining concepts of CVP relationships, cost behavior, and the master budget. All the elements of the flexible budget should already be familiar to you.*

III. Prepare an activity-based flexible budget

The master-budget variance can be split into two variances by "inserting the flexible budget between the master budget and actual results."

A. This is an important result because each variance can be attributed to differences in either activity levels or per unit revenues and variable costs and fixed costs per period.

B. For simplicity, the textbook chapter and this study guide chapter *assume that the only relevant activity level is sales activity*.

1. In practice, multiple activity levels can be used for different portions of the master budget and flexible budget.

2. The concept of what follows is applicable to activities other than sales.

3. Note how the flexible budget is "inserted" between the master budget and actual results for a model income statement.

> **Stop and Review**
>
> See textbook Exhibit 8-4

IV. Explain the performance evaluation relationship between static budgets, flexible budgets, and actual results

---

V.   Compute activity-level variances and flexible-budget variances

A.   The **sales-activity variance** is the difference between the master-budget amount and the flexible-budget amount.

    1.   The underlying cause of the sales-activity variance is that actual sales activity was different than expected in the master budget.

    2.   The sales-activity variance is the portion of the master-budget variance attributed to sales activity.

    3.   The sales-activity variance can be split into various contributing causes, but that is beyond the scope of this textbook.

B.   The **flexible-budget variance** is the difference between the flexible-budget amount and the actual result.

    1.   The underlying cause of the flexible-budget variance is that actual fixed costs per period, per unit revenues, or variable costs differed from expectations.

    2.   The flexible-budget variance is the portion of the master-budget variance attributed to cost and revenue control.

    3.   Later we learn to split the flexible-budget variance into several contributing causes.

	Actual results at actual activity level	*Flexible-budget variances*	**Flexible budget for actual activity**	*Activity variances*	**Master budget**
Units	xxx	xx	xxx	xx	xxx
Sales	xxx	xx	xxx	xx	xxx
Variable costs	xxx	xx	xxx	xx	xxx
Contribution margin	xxx	xx	xxx	xx	xxx
Fixed costs	xxx	xx	xxx	xx	xxx
Operating income	xxx	xx	xxx	xx	xxx

Total flexible-budget variances — *Total activity-level variances*

Total master-budget variances

a. The variances are defined below.

b. Another explanation follows:

Master budget	-	Actual result	=	Master-budget variance
(Master budget - Flexible budget)	-	(Actual result - Flexible budget)	=	Master-budget variance
Sales-activity variance	+	*Flexible-budget variance*	=	Master-budget variance

c. Mathematically, the second line above, with the flexible budget inserted, is identical to the first (the flexible budgets "cancel out").

C. Master budgets and flexible budgets are constructed using *expected costs* or *standard costs*:

1. An **expected cost** is the cost that is *most likely to be attained*.

2. A **standard cost** is a carefully predetermined cost that *should be attained* (which may be the same as the expected cost).

3. A **standard cost system** is an inventory valuation and control system that values inventories at standard costs only.

   a. Differences between standard costs and actual costs are charged to income.

   b. *Using standard costs for budgeting does not require using a standard cost system for inventories.*

   c. In practice, some companies use multiple cost systems for multiple purposes. This is because a single cost system that would support all decision making and financial reporting would be too expensive—an application of the cost-benefit criterion.

   d. In this textbook and study guide, we consider only the budgeting and performance evaluation uses of standard costs.

   e. In budgeting and performance evaluation, the terms *expected cost* and *standard cost* are often used interchangeably.

4. **Perfection standards,** also called **ideal standards,** are expressions of the absolutely minimum unit costs possible under the best conceivable conditions, using current specifications and facilities.

   a. These are not widely used for budgeting or performance evaluation.

   b. Perfection standards are thought to have adverse motivational effects because they can never be attained and always result in unfavorable cost variances.

   c. Perfection standards direct attention to inefficiencies in the organization.

5. **Currently attainable standards** represent costs that should be incurred under very efficient operations.

   a. These are widely used for budgeting and evaluation.

   b. These standards do make allowances for normal shrinkage, spoilage, lost time, and equipment breakdowns.

   c. Currently attainable standards usually have a *desirable motivational effect* on employees because, although difficult to reach, they are reasonable goals.

> **Study Tip:** *Can you explain the different types of standards and their advantages and disadvantages? Which are the most widely used for budgeting and performance evaluation? Why?*

6. Managers may trade off variances.

    a. For example, a manager may consider reducing material costs by buying lower quality materials even though this might cause higher labor costs due to more required rework of defective products.

    b. Trading off variances can be beneficial, but it is a dangerous practice because the trade-off may be unfavorable.

    c. If standards or expectations are set carefully, they take into account the most favorable trade-offs of various costs. Usually managers should try to change the standards rather than trying to informally change the trade-offs.

7. Decisions to investigate variances balance the costs of investigating versus the costs of not investigating.

    a. Costs of investigating include managers' and other employees' time and downtime for equipment and processes.

    b. Costs of not investigating include allowing costs to be uncontrolled in the future.

    c. As discussed in Chapter 9, standard cost variances tend not to be very useful for control of operations where quick feedback is necessary—more timely and relevant measures are available (e.g., defects, yields).

    d. Standard cost variances are more useful for periodic performance evaluations. Explanations of large variances serve to inform higher-level managers about the quality of lower-level managers—how problems were resolved.

VI. Compute and interpret the price and quantity variances for inputs based on cost-driver activity

---

A. Flexible-budget cost variances can be split into several effects: *price* of inputs and *quantity* of inputs.

> **Stop and Review**
>
> See textbook Exhibit 8-7

1. We define **price variances** for direct materials, direct labor, and variable overhead items like supplies as:

Price variance = (Actual input) x (Expected price - actual price)

    This is the portion of the flexible-budget variance due to spending a different amount per unit for inputs than expected.

2. We define **quantity variances** for inputs as:

Quantity variance = (Expected price) x (Expected input - actual input)

    a. This is the portion of the flexible-budget variance due to using an amount of input different than expected.

    b. The "expected input" in the above formula is more formally known as the *standard input allowed for the output achieved*.

    c. Quantity variances are also known as *efficiency* variances, but efficiency includes both spending and quantity, so the term efficiency variance is misleading.

3. Flexible-budget variable overhead variances can be split similarly.

B. Another approach to computing price and quantity variances is to split the flexible-budget variance into two complementary effects in much the same way as we split the master-budget variance.

    1. We split the master-budget variance by inserting the flexible budget between the master budget and the actual result.

    2. We can split the flexible-budget variance by inserting a *flexible budget based on actual inputs at expected prices*, between the previous flexible budget (which uses *expected inputs* for the outputs achieved *and expected prices*) and actual results.

> **Stop and Review**
>
> See textbook Exhibits 8-7
>
> and 8-8

    3. For another explanation see below:

Actual result	-	Flexible budget (at expected inputs and expected prices)	=	Flexible-budget variance
(Actual result - Flexible budget at *actual* inputs and *expected* prices)	-	(Flexible budget at expected inputs and expected prices - Flexible budget at *actual* inputs and *expected* prices)	=	Flexible-budget variance
Price variance	+	*Quantity variance*	=	Flexible-budget variance

    a. Note that the two entries for *flexible budget at actual inputs and expected prices* cancel out in the second equation, leaving the first equation.

    b. The only difference between the actual result and the *flexible budget at actual inputs and expected prices* is the difference between actual and expected prices. Thus, the first part of the second equation is the price variance.

    c. The only difference between the two flexible budgets in the second part of the second equation is the difference between actual and expected quantity of inputs. The second part of this equation is the quantity variance.

VII. Compute variable overhead spending and efficiency variances

A. When actual cost-driver activity differs from the standard amount allowed for the actual output achieved, a **variable overhead efficiency variance** occurs. The cause is identical to that for an activity efficiency variance.

B. A variable overhead spending variance is the difference between actual variable overhead and budgeted variable overhead for actual cost driver-activity.

> **Stop and Review**
>
> See textbook Exhibit 8-9

VIII. Compute the fixed overhead spending variance.

A. Fixed overhead is by definition not expected to vary with changes in level of output or inputs.

B. The difference between actual fixed overhead and budgeted fixed overhead is called **fixed overhead spending variance**.

Stop and Review

See textbook Summary
Problem on p. 363

Study Tip: *Before going on to the practice test, be sure that you understand how the flexible-budget variance is split into price and quantity effects. There are several ways to perform this analysis--use the approach that makes the most sense to you -- they are equivalent.*

PRACTICE TEST QUESTIONS AND PROBLEMS
True or False Statements

Determine whether each of the following statements is True (T) or False (F), and enter your answer in the space provided:

_____ 1. Comparisons between the master budget and the actual result obscure the effects of sales activity and efficiency.

_____ 2. Using flexible budgets is really only feasible in large firms with computerized financial planning models.

_____ 3. The sales-activity variance is the difference between the master-budget variance and the flexible-budget variance.

_____ 4. Flexible budgeting is possible only if one assumes that sales activity is the only cost driver.

_____ 5. Flexible-budget variances measure how effective an organization was in achieving its objectives.

_____ 6. Use of standard costs for budgeting and performance evaluation is only feasible in companies that use standard cost systems.

_____ 7. Currently attainable standards have little motivating impact because they require little or no effort to achieve.

_____ 8. Perfection standards tend to have a positive effect on employee motivation because they direct attention to correctable inefficiencies.

_____ 9. Labor-price variances are usually the responsibility of the same manager who is in charge of labor quantity.

_____ 10. Generally, the cost variances that are more subject to immediate management control are quantity variances.

Multiple-Choice Questions

For each of the following multiple-choice questions, determine the best answer(s), and enter the identification letter(s) in the space provided.

_____ 1. The master-budget variance is the difference between: (a) flexible budget and master budget, (b) actual result and flexible budget, (c) master budget and actual result, (d) total costs at actual prices and actual inputs and master budget.

_____ 2. The flexible-budget variance is the difference between: (a) flexible budget and actual results, (b) master budget and flexible budget, (c) actual results and master budget, (d) actual results and the budget at standard prices and standard inputs allowed for the outputs achieved.

_____3.   A summary of performance showed three amounts for variable costs: actual, $180,000; master budget, $185,000; and flexible budget, $170,000. The master-budget variance is (a) $5,000 unfavorable, (b) $5,000 favorable, (c) $10,000 favorable, (d) $15,000 unfavorable.

_____4.   See the preceding test item. The sales-activity variance is: (a) $15,000 favorable, (b) $5,000 favorable, (c) $10,000 unfavorable, (d) $5,000 unfavorable.

_____5.   See item 3. The flexible-budget variance is: (a) $15,000 favorable, (b) $5,000 favorable, (c) $10,000 unfavorable, (d) $5,000 unfavorable.

_____6.   There is no conceptual difference between a budget amount and a standard amount if standards are: (a) ideal standards, (b) perfection standards, (c) currently attainable standards, (d) flexible standards.

_____7.   The main flexible-budget cost variances are: (a) price and rate, (b) quantity and efficiency, (c) quantity and quality, (d) price and quantity.

_____8.   For most effective control, material-price variances should be measured at the time materials are: (a) purchased, (b) used, (c) sold to customers, (d) issued to production.

_____9.   A process has a standard assembly time of 3 hours per component. The process used 800 labor hours to assemble 250 components. The standard wage rate is $9 per hour. The labor-quantity variance is: (a) $800 unfavorable, (b) $800 favorable, (c) $450 unfavorable, (d) $500 unfavorable.

_____10.   See the preceding test item. Wages paid for the assembly process totaled $7,800. The labor-rate variance is: (a) $600 favorable, (b) $562.50 unfavorable, (c) $600 unfavorable, (d) $562.50 favorable.

Completion

Complete each of the following statements by filling in the blanks.

1.   Comparisons of actual results with _____ are not as useful as comparisons with _____ or _____.

2.   The flexible-budget variance is the difference between the _____ and the _____.

3.   The master budget is also called the _____, and the flexible budget is also called the _____.

4.   The difference between a flexible-budget formula and a cost function is _____.

5.   Standard costs that make no allowance for lost time, spoilage, shrinkage, or equipment breakdowns are called _____ standards.

6.   Activity-level variances are due to _____.

7.   The decision to investigate variances is a trade-off between _____ and _____.

8.   Managers may _____ variances because the _____ in one area is linked to the _____ in another.

9.   Material-price variances are the responsibility of either the _____ or _____.

10.   The material-price variance is computed as the difference between actual and standard _____ multiplied by _____.

Problems

1. Principle Co., which uses activity-based costs and a flexible budget, provides the following data for its ordering operations during last month:

Ordering Activity	Traceable costs	Planned cost-driver activity	Cost-driver rate (?)	Actual cost-driver activity	Actual costs
Order preparation	$20,000	1,000 orders		1,200 orders	$22,000
Order data entry	$10,000	20,000 lines		18,000 lines	$ 9,000
Order verification	$12,000	20,000 lines		18,000 lines	$16,000
Order approval	$ 8,000	1,000 orders		1,200 orders	$ 5,000

Show calculation of flexible-budget variances in the format given below. Use F for favorable variances and U for unfavorable variances.

Ordering Activity	Actual cost	Flexible-budget variance	Flexible budget
Totals			

2. Thorton Corporation, which uses standard costs and a flexible budget, provides the following data for its operations during the first week in April:

Finished product units produced	3,000 units
Direct material:	
Purchases	9,000 lb.
Standard price per pound	$8
Actual price per pound	$7
Pounds used in production	7,000 lb.
Standard quantity allowed per product unit	2 lb.

Suppose the company is organized so that the purchasing manager bears the primary responsibility for the acquisition prices of materials, and the production manager bears the primary responsibility for the efficient use of materials but no responsibility for unit prices.

Show computations of direct material costs and variances in the analysis framework given below. Use F for favorable variances and U for unfavorable variances.

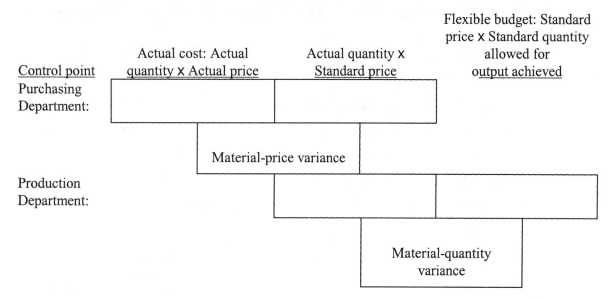

Exercise

1. Data-Bilt, Inc., presents the following data pertaining to its total manufacturing costs for a given month:

Master budget sales for 8,000 units	$800,000
Actual sales of 7,000 units	730,000
Actual variable costs of producing 7,000 units	248,000
Actual fixed costs of producing 7,000 units	220,000
Flexible-budget cost formula:	$200,000 plus $40 per unit

Complete the following analysis:

Use F for favorable variances and U for unfavorable variances.

	Actual results at actual activity level	*Flexible-budget variances*	Flexible budget for actual activity	*Activity variances*	Master budget
Units					
Sales					
Variable costs					
Contribution margin					
Fixed costs					
Operating income					

Total flexible-budget variances	Total activity-level variances

Total master-budget variances

True or False Statements

1. True   The difference between the master budget and the actual result is the master-budget variance, which may be due to either actual activities being different from the master budget or actual efficiency being different from the master budget.

2. False   Effective flexible budgeting existed long before computers were readily available. It is true, however, that computers have made flexible budgeting much easier and much more responsive to managers' inquiries.

3. True   The master-budget variance is the sum of the sales-activity variance and the flexible-budget variance. Therefore, the sales-activity variance is the difference between the (overall) master-budget variance and the flexible-budget variance.

4. False   Different parts of the master budget may have different appropriate cost drivers. Flexible budgeting only requires that the appropriate cost drivers be used to compute the flexible budget, just as the master budget does.

5. False   Flexible-budget variances are due to the efficiency of operations. Activity-level variances (e.g., sales-activity variances) measure effectiveness.

6. False   Standard costs are measures of what costs should be under desired conditions. They may be used for budgeting and performance evaluation even if the company does not use a standard cost system for financial reporting purposes.

7. False   Currently attainable standards may be set at different levels, requiring different levels of effort. These standards can motivate improved performance if incentives are present.

8. False   Most observers of company practice believe that perfection standards are de-motivators because these standards can never be achieved.

9. True   Generally, the manager who schedules the use of labor also controls which laborers, at their particular wage rates, will work. This is not always true, however, because company or union policy may dictate wage rates, leaving only labor quantity under a manager's control.

10. True   In the very short term, prices of inputs may not be as controllable as the quantity of the input. Purchase contracts and union labor agreements may fix per-unit prices for the short term.

Multiple-Choice Questions

1. c, d   The master-budget variance is the difference between the master budget and actual results—the same as the difference between total costs at actual prices and actual inputs, which are actual results, and the master budget. The difference between the flexible budget and master budget is the activity-level variance. The difference between the actual result and flexible budget is the flexible-budget variance.

2. a, d   The flexible-budget variance is the difference between the flexible budget and actual results, or between actual results and the budget at standard prices and standard inputs allowed for the outputs achieved, which is the flexible budget.

3. b   The master-budget variance is the difference between the master budget and actual costs: $185,000 - $180,000 = $5,000 favorable. The variance is labeled favorable because the actual cost is less than the master budget. The meaning is ambiguous because, as the next items show, the master budget variance is composed of sales-activity and flexible-budget variances.

4. a   The sales-activity variance is the difference between the master budget and the flexible budget: $185,000 - $170,000 = $15,000 F. The variance is labeled favorable because the flexible budget is less than the master budget, but it has no cost-control implications because it is due to sales activity.

5. c   The flexible-budget variance is the difference between the flexible budget and the actual result: $170,000 - $180,000 = $10,000 U. The variance is labeled unfavorable because the actual result is greater than the flexible budget. The implication is that productive activity was not efficient.

6. c   Currently attainable standards are expected to be achieved given certain levels of effort; thus, they may be used for budgeting. Ideal or perfection standards cannot be achieved and would not be useful for budgeting. Flexible standards are not standards at all, but are probably just actual results.

7. d   Price and quantity variances are the customary divisions of the flexible-budget variance. The other pairs are synonyms.

8. a   In some cases the person or department that purchases material is different from the person or department that uses the material. If so, it is better to isolate the material-price variance at the time of purchase so that current variances can be associated with current performance.

9. c   The labor-quantity variance is the difference between the standard hours allowed and the actual hours used multiplied by the standard wage rate: [(3 x 250) – 800] x $9 = (750 - 800) x $9 = $450 U. The variance is unfavorable because actual hours used exceeded the standard hours allowed.

10. c   The labor-rate variance is the difference between the actual labor cost and the standard allowed for the number of hours used: $7,800 – ($9 x 800) = 600U. The variance is labeled unfavorable because actual labor cost exceeded the standard allowed. Note that the rate and quantity variances resulted in an overall, unfavorable flexible-budget variance: $450 U + $600 U = $1,050 U, which also equals the difference between the actual cost and the total standard cost: $7,800 – ($9 x 3 x 250).

Completion

1. prior periods' results, the master budget, the flexible budget

2. master budget, flexible budget

3. static budget, variable budget

4. nothing; they are the same

5. perfection or ideal

6. differences between the master budget and the flexible budget, which differ because of differences in planned activity levels

7. costs of investigating, costs of not investigating (or benefits of investigating)

8. trade-off, performance, performance

9. purchasing agent, production manager--depending on responsibilities

10. prices, actual quantity of material used or purchased--depending on the control point

Problems

1. Principle Co.

Ordering Activity	Traceable costs	Planned cost-driver activity	Cost-driver rate (?)	Actual cost-driver activity	Actual costs
Order preparation	$20,000	1,000 orders	$20/order	1,200 orders	$22,000
Order data entry	$10,000	20,000 lines	$0.50/line	18,000 lines	$ 9,000
Order verification	$12,000	20,000 lines	$0.60/line	18,000 lines	$16,000
Order approval	$ 8,000	1,000 orders	$8/order	1,200 orders	$ 5,000

Calculation of flexible-budget variances:

Ordering Activity	Actual cost	Flexible-budget variance	Flexible budget
Order preparation	$22,000	$2,000 F	$20 x 1,200 = $24,000
Order data entry	$ 9,000	0	$0.50 x 18,000 = $9,000
Order verification	$16,000	$5,200 U	$0.60 x 18,000 = $10,800
Order approval	$ 5,000	$4,600 F	$8 x 1,200 = $9,600
Totals	$52,000	$1,400 F	$53,400

2. Thorton Corporation

Control point	Actual cost: Actual quantity x Actual price	Actual quantity x Standard price	Flexible budget: Standard price x Standard quantity allowed for output achieved
Purchasing Department:	9,000 lb. x $7 = $63,000	9,000 lb. x $8 = $72,000	

$63,000 - $72,000 = $9,000 F
Material-price variance

Control point		Actual quantity x Standard price	Flexible budget
Production Department:		7,000 lb. x $8 = $56,000	(2 lb. x 3,000) x $8 = $48,000

$56,000 - $48,000 = $8,000 U
Material-quantity variance

Exercise

1. Data-Bilt, Inc.

	Actual results at actual activity level	Flexible-budget variances	Flexible budget for actual activity	Activity variances	Master budget
Units	7,000	-	7,000	1,000 U	8,000
Sales	$730,000	$30,000 F	$700,000	$100,000 U	$800,000
Variable costs	248,000	32,000 F	280,000	40,000 F	320,000
Contribution margin	$482,000	$62,000 F	$420,000	$60,000 U	$480,000
Fixed costs	220,000	20,000 U	200,000	-	200,000
Operating income	$262,000	$42,000 F	$220,000	$60,000 U	$280,000

$42,000 F	$60,000 U
Total flexible-budget variances	Total activity-level variances

$18,000 U
Total master-budget variances

Management Control Systems and Responsibility Accounting

OVERVIEW
A management control system combines knowledge of the types of key management decisions, cost behavior, budgeting, performance evaluation incentives, and motivation to help decision makers achieve organizational goals. Your learning objectives are to:

I. Describe the relationship of management control systems to organizational goals

II. Use responsibility accounting to define an organizational subunit as a cost center, a profit center, or an investment center

III. Develop performance measures and use them to monitor the achievements of an organization

IV. Explain the importance of evaluating performance and how it impacts motivation, goal congruence, and employee effort

V. Prepare segment income statements for evaluating profit and investment centers using the contribution margin and controllable-cost concepts

VI. Use a balanced scorecard to recognize both financial and nonfinancial measures of performance

VII. Measure performance against quality, cycle time, and productivity objectives

VIII. Describe the difficulties of management control in service and non-profit organizations

---

I.   Describe the relationship of management control systems to organizational goals

---

A **management control system** integrates all the management accounting tools covered so far in this text to aid and coordinate management decision making and to motivate individuals to achieve organizational *goals*.

A.   Information from the accounting system alone usually is not sufficient to support a successful management control system.

    1.   Many management concerns do not show up in the accounting system soon enough to prevent problems (such as warranty expenses and repeat sales).

    2.   Some management concerns may never show up in the accounting system in a way that allows effective control (such as customer satisfaction and quality performance).

B.   Design of the management control system begins with specifying *organizational goals*.

    1.   An organization's **goals** are the purposes for the existence of the organization—generally the goals of the founders, directors, shareholders, or major contributors of the organization.

    2.   Some organizations never build effective management control systems because they either cannot identify goals or do not communicate them.

    3.   Organizations may fail to gain acceptance of goals in the organization; usually this is a symptom of both communication and incentive problems.

C.   Organizational goals are too vague to be helpful in planning, budgeting, and performance evaluation.

    1.   Goals should be translated into observable, attainable objectives such as profit targets, standard costs, and so on. Top managers determine **key success factors** that are necessary to the optimal performance of the organization.

    2.   As shown in earlier chapters, managers can establish plans or budgets to attain these objectives.

    3.   Plans to attain objectives are the best benchmark for evaluating effectiveness and efficiency in actual performance.

    4.   Objectives may be in conflict (e.g., short-term profit versus long-term profit), and balancing them can be the most difficult part of designing a management control system.

D.   Most management control systems are designed for existing organizations.

    1.   Though it may be desirable, it may not be possible to redesign both the system and organization to be more effective and efficient.

    2.   A key concern is that the organization's structure may be relatively fixed.

    3.   Constrained resources may mean that the management control system is revised "piecemeal."

    4.   No system is perfect, but it should be the result of careful weighing of costs and benefits of possible improvements.

Stop and Review

See textbook Exhibits 9-1 and 9-2

E. Because all the factors that affect the design of management control systems can change, system designers must be prepared to redesign the system over time.

　　1. This may mean radical changes in relatively short periods of time.

　　2. Standard cost systems have been around for over 50 years, yet only recently have some companies found that they are obsolete for management control purposes.

　　3. It is likely that today's management control systems will be obsolete in the future but much sooner than 50 years—maybe 10 years at most.

　　4. This means managers, accountants, and system designers must keep ahead of new developments and decision-making needs.

> **Study Tip:** *Before going on to the next section, be sure that you can explain the links among goals, objectives, and management control systems. What is the relationship of management accounting to management control systems?*

II. Use responsibility accounting to define an organizational subunit as a cost center, a profit center, or an investment center

---

A. A **responsibility center** is a set of activities designated to be under the management control of a specific individual or group of individuals within an organization.

　　1. **Responsibility accounting** designs planning, scorekeeping, and attention-directing information that is consistent with the designation of responsibility centers.

　　　　a. Responsibility centers often have multiple objectives (financial and nonfinancial).

　　　　b. The usual form of responsibility center corresponds to *financial responsibility*.

　　2. There are three principal forms of responsibility centers:

　　　　a. **Cost centers**, usually departments that are responsible for efficient use of inputs and for which costs are accumulated and reported

　　　　b. **Profit centers**, usually divisions that are responsible for both revenues and costs and for which income is reported

　　　　c. **Investment centers**, which are responsible for their invested capital as well as for revenues and costs, and for which income relative to the magnitude of the investment is reported (Chapter 10 covers this in more detail)

　　3. In many situations, a manager may have only a little influence over operating results.

　　　　a. Nevertheless, a responsibility accounting system identifies the person with the most day-to-day influence over a particular cost or revenue.

　　　　b. That person will then at least be responsible for explaining deviations of actual results from budgeted results.

B. Measurement of financial performance

　　1. **Responsibility performance reports** provide managers of responsibility centers on each level with data concerning the items they have the authority and ability to influence.

　　2. Many organizations measure performance using the contribution-margin approach because it identifies expected and actual cost behavior more clearly than the absorption approach.

　　3. The contribution-margin approach is also consistent with CVP approaches to planning.

4.   Therefore, such reports often identify or exclude any revenues and costs beyond the control of the manager being evaluated.

> **Study Tip:** *Can you explain the differences between the types of responsibility centers? Between controllable and uncontrollable costs?*

III.   Develop performance measures and use them to monitor the achievements of an organization

Nonfinancial measures of performance provide critical management control information that is not available from the accounting system.

A.   Nonfinancial measures often "lead" financial measures of performance.

B.   Superior, *sustained* financial performance is usually the result of superior non-financial performance.

C.   Paying attention to only financial measures of performance may mean never getting at the root causes of poor financial performance or never appreciating the reasons for superior financial performance.

D.   Important areas of nonfinancial performance include: *quality*, *cycle time*, and *productivity*.

> **Stop and Review**
>
> See textbook Exhibit 9-3

> **Study Tip:** *Why is controlling nonfinancial performance so important?*

IV.   Explain the importance of evaluating performance and describe how it impacts motivation, goal congruence, and employee effort

Motivation of employees to achieve organizational goals may be a difficult task.

A.   **Goal congruence** exists when individuals aim at the same organizational goals.

B.   **Managerial effort** is exertion toward a goal or objective.

C.   **Motivation** is the amount of drive an individual has that creates effort toward meeting an objective. Motivation is a function of the organization's *incentives* and an individual's personal values and desires.

D.   An organization can supply incentives, which link rewards to actions and outcomes, but the individual must supply the desire. That is why hiring-decisions are so critical to an organization's success.

E.   A key distinction in a responsibility accounting system is the *controllability* of an outcome; in particular, we will be concerned with costs.

 1.   A **controllable cost** is a cost that can be influenced by a specific responsibility center for a given period of time.

 2.   An **uncontrollable cost** cannot be affected by a specific responsibility center within a given time period.

 3.   Controllability is a matter of degree. For example, more costs are controllable at higher levels within an organization and/or as the time span increases.

 4.   Uncontrollable revenue may come from changes in sales due to general economic conditions, yet there are arguments for not shielding managers from these uncontrollable forces. How well did the manager react or perform relative to other managers in the same environment?

V.	**Prepare segment income statements for evaluating profit and investment centers using contribution margins and controllable-cost concepts**

The text develops a model income statement by segments at three different segment levels: divisions, product lines, and individual stores.

> **Stop and Review**
>
> See textbook Exhibit 9-4

A. Note how this income statement reports costs by *controllability* as well as by fixed or variable behavior.

B. The **segment contribution margin** (line a in Exhibit 9-4) is the excess of revenues over controllable variable costs.

C. The **contribution controllable by segment managers** (line b in Exhibit 9-4) is computed as the segment contribution margins less the fixed costs controllable by segment managers.

D. The **contribution by segments** (line c in Exhibit 9-4) subtracts the additional fixed costs controllable by others (e.g., top management). This measures the financial performance of the entire segment.

E. **Unallocated costs** (just before line d in Exhibit 9-4) are borne by the entire company and cannot be meaningfully distributed to segments.

> **Study Tip:** *Can you construct a segment performance report and explain the importance of each element?*

VI.	**Use a balanced scorecard to recognize both financial and nonfinancial measures of performance**

A. The **balanced scorecard (BSC)** is a new description of a management control system that includes measures of performance in four areas called **key performance indicators**:

    1. Financial strength – profitability and financial position

    2. Customer satisfaction – customers' views of the value of products and services provided

    3. Business processes – the efficiency and quality of internal processes

    4. Competence – the capabilities of the organization and its employees to innovate and improve

> **Stop and Review**
>
> See textbook Exhibit 9-7

VII.	**Measure performance against quality, cycle time, and productivity objectives**

A. **Quality control** is the effort to insure that products and services meet customer requirements.

    1. Emphasis now is on **total quality management (TQM),** which motivates all members of the organization to satisfy customers and clients.

    2. In order to gauge the quality control efforts, some companies generate **cost of quality reports**.

        a. **Quality costs** include defect prevention, appraisal, internal failure and external failure costs.

     b.   Employees should be able to shift resources from appraisal, internal failure, and external failure (which are non-value-added activities) to prevention.

     c.   Costs of quality draw attention to the financial impact of quality problems.

     d.   If employees can see how costly poor quality is, they can be motivated to improve quality.

   3.   Quality control charts are used to monitor quality on a "real time" basis and provide information much more quickly than a cost-variance report could.

> **Stop and Review**
>
> See textbook Exhibits 9-8 and 9-9

B.   **Cycle time** is the time it takes from beginning to completion of a product or service.

   1.   Improvements in cycle time are possible only with high quality products and processes.

   2.   Reducing cycle time exposes more quality and process problems, which must be solved to obtain further improvements.

   3.   Companies monitor cycle time with flexible-budget-type reports and with control charts.

> **Stop and Review**
>
> See textbook Exhibit 9-10

C.   **Productivity** is a measure of the efficiency of an operation based on ratios of key outputs to related inputs.

   1.   Improved productivity is a key to surviving global competition, and is often due to improvements in quality and cycle time.

   2.   Faulty management control systems have been blamed when companies continue to lag behind their competitors. In recent years, however, many companies have made dramatic improvements in productivity.

   3.   Properly designed productivity measures should help managers by identifying inefficient operations.

   4.   In contrast, poorly thought-out productivity measures may be quite misleading.

> **Stop and Review**
>
> See textbook Exhibit 9-11

VIII. Describe the difficulties of management control in service and non-profit organizations

Management control systems are more difficult to design and implement in service, nonprofit, and government organizations.

A.   Management control in these organizations is critical to all of us because they comprise the large majority of the U.S. economy.

B.   In concept, management control in these organizations is no different from in a manufacturing firm, only more difficult.

C. Management control in service and government organizations is more difficult because:

    1. Goals and objectives are less clear.

    2. Professionals in these organizations are less receptive to control and may have different motivations.

    3. Labor is more important both as a share of total costs and as the point of contact with customers and clients.

    4. There are fewer objective measures of performance (e.g., what is a "good unit of output" in a government organization?).

    5. There is less competitive pressure to improve.

    6. Budgeting may be less planning than negotiating for larger appropriations.

D. In all types of organizations different goals require different objectives and performance measures. It is important to understand how management control systems use accounting information.

    1. Individuals act in their own self-interest.

    2. Accounting-based incentives should be consistent with individual self-interest.

    3   Accounting-based incentives should measure the financial impacts of decisions on the whole value chain.

    4. Modify incentive systems until they achieve the desired objectives.

> **Study Tip:** *Before going on to the practice test, be sure that you can explain the difficulties of designing management control systems in service and nonprofit organizations.*

PRACTICE TEST QUESTIONS AND PROBLEMS

True or False Statements

Determine whether each of the following statements is True (T) or False (F), and enter your answer in the space provided. (Note that concepts in this chapter are especially difficult to classify as true or false— many of the correct answers could be, "True, but..." or "False, but....")

_____1.   A management control system is another name for the master-budget process.

_____2.   There is no practical difference between a profit center and an investment center.

_____3.   Properly designed incentives will motivate employees to achieve organizational goals.

_____4.   Net income before income taxes is the total contribution by segments less unallocated costs.

_____5.   A contribution income statement by segments is aimed at reporting costs by cost behavior and segment controllability.

_____6.   Segment contribution is the complete measure of a segment's achievement of company objectives.

_____7.   Successful management control systems allow managers to balance competing goals as best they can.

_____8.   Measurement of segment contribution is consistent with financial reporting rules.

_____9.   Productivity measures of organizational efficiency relate goods and services sold to customers to the inputs required to produce them.

____10.   There is little sense in studying today's management control systems, such as the balanced scorecard, because they will be obsolete before I graduate from college.

Multiple-Choice Questions

For each of the following multiple-choice questions, select the best answer(s), and enter the identification letter(s) in the space provided.

_____1.   Usually the management control system should incorporate (a) financial reporting rules, (b) organizational goals, (c) short-term objectives, (d) the master budget.

_____2.   A large company's responsibility centers might include: (a) cost centers, (b) profit centers, (c) investment centers, (d) shopping centers.

_____3.   The focus of responsibility accounting is: (a) accounting accuracy, (b) rewarding managers, (c) identifying blame or fault, (d) information-gathering and reporting.

_____4.   Responsibility accounting basically asks, "Who in the organization is in the best position to: (a) control the outcome, (b) explain why the outcome occurred, (c) predict the outcome, (d) take the blame for the outcome."

_____5.   The most basic segment of activity or area of responsibility for which costs are accumulated is called: (a) a mini-center, (b) a profit center, (c) a cost center, (d) an investment center.

_____6.   Managers should focus their attention on the parts of performance reports that do not reflect smoothly running aspects of operations. This is called: (a) exceptional management, (b) management by perception, (c) perceptional management, (d) management by exception.

_____7. The following data (in thousands) appeared for a certain segment of a company in the contribution-approach income statement: Variable expenses, $500; Fixed costs controllable by others, $80; Fixed costs controllable by segment managers, $110; Unallocated costs, $50; Net sales, $690. The segment contribution margin is: (a) zero, (b) -$50, (c) $190, (d) $80.

_____8. See the preceding test item. The contribution controllable by segment managers is: (a) zero, (b) -$50, (c) $190, (d) $80.

_____9. Quality costs may include (a) inspection costs, (b) rework costs, (c) contribution margin from lost sales, (d) redesign of the production process.

____10. Total quality management involves whom in creating customer-oriented quality? (a) top management, (b) middle managers, (c) sales representatives, (d) factory workers.

Completion

Complete each of the following statements by filling in the blanks.

1. Organizational _____ are generally too _____ for operating personnel, so companies express _____ as _____.

2. Because most management control systems are redesigned for existing organizations, a new system often must be consistent with the existing organization _____ and _____.

3. The most common types of responsibility centers in government organizations could be characterized as _____.

4. A segment is a set of activities that _____.

5. The contribution controllable by segment managers is the excess of the _____ margin over the _____.

6. The contribution of segments is the excess of the contribution _____ over the _____.

7. The balanced scorecard usually has _____ in the areas of _____, _____, _____, and _____.

8. The more a manager's evaluation and rewards are linked to _____ the more _____ there is to _____.

9. _____ due to poor product quality may be far greater than _____ costs reported on quality cost reports.

10. Productivity in general is measured by dividing a measure of _____ by _____.

Problems

1. From the following data for Homer Equipment Company (in thousands), prepare a contribution-approach income statement by segments:

	Company Total	Beta Division	Gamma Division
Net sales	$850	$500	$350
Fixed costs:			
Controllable by division managers	140	60	80
Controllable by others	70	10	60
Variable costs:			
Manufacturing cost of sales	450	300	150
Selling and administrative expenses	130	60	70
Unallocated costs	45	-	-

	Company Total	Beta Division	Gamma Division
Net sales			
Less			
Income before taxes			

2. From the following data, evaluate the Burns Company's cost of quality and productivity during April 20X4. The Burns Company could sell all of its output at market prices. Defective units are detected at the end of the manufacturing process.

Master-budgeted production............	4,600 units
Sales revenue..............................	$82,000 @ $20/unit
Total good production....................	3,500 units @ $7 variable cost/unit
Defective units—scrapped...............	500 units
Defective units—reworked..............	600 units (reworked at additional $2 cost/unit)
Sales warranty expense..................	$6,000
Number of employees...................	50
Redesign of product to reduce future defects....................................	$ 5,000
Quality control personnel salaries......	$ 6,000
Operation and depreciation of quality test equipment..........................	$ 8,000
Total fixed manufacturing cost..........	$20,000
Direct labor cost.........................	$ 4,000
Quality training costs for direct labor to detect defects earlier in the future	$10,000

Cost of Quality Report:

Analysis of productivity:

Exercise

1. **Sales Clerk Compensation Plan:** You are the manager of a discount software store. Sales are subject to month-to-month variations, depending on the individual sales clerk's efforts. A new salary-plus-bonus plan has been in effect for four months, and you are reviewing a sales performance report. The plan provides a base salary of $1,000 a month, a $500 bonus if the monthly sales quota is met, and an additional 5% commission of all sales over monthly quota. The quota is set approximately 3% above the previous months' sales to motivate clerks to increase sales (Data are in thousands):

		Sales clerk A	Sales clerk B	Sales clerk C
January:	Quota	$5,000	$2,500	$2,000
	Actual	2,000	2,500	2,500
February:	Quota	$2,060	$2,575	$2,575
	Actual	2,550	2,575	1,000
March:	Quota	$2,627	$2,652	$1,030
	Actual	3,500	2,000	2,500
April:	Quota	$3,605	$2,060	$2,575
	Actual	3,250	2,250	1,000

A. Compute the compensation for each sales clerk for each month.

B. Evaluate the compensation plan. Be specific. What changes would you recommend?

2. **Performance Evaluation:** Benjamin Brothers is a stock brokerage firm that evaluates its employees on sales activity generated. Recently the firm also began evaluating its stockbrokers on the number of new accounts generated. Discuss how these two performance measures are consistent and how they may conflict. Do you believe that these measures are appropriate for the long-term goal of profitability?

CHAPTER 9 SOLUTIONS TO PRACTICE TEST QUESTIONS AND PROBLEMS

True or False Statements

1. False   The master-budget process is *part* of a successful management control system. However, in some companies, it may be the only part.

2. False   In many cases, however, this is true due to sloppy terminology. An investment center has responsibility and authority over the investment in plant, equipment, and other long-term assets, whereas a profit center does not have authority over its investment.

3. False   If only it were that easy (and even that is difficult). External incentives are part of motivation, but individuals may be motivated by other, internal desires that conflict with the organization's objectives. Incentives that are sufficient to overcome most base desires (e.g., effort-aversion) plus hiring internally motivated employees may result in motivated workers.

4. True   Total contribution by segments includes contribution margin, less fixed costs controllable by managers, less fixed costs controllable by others. All that remains is unallocated costs.

5. True   By combining cost behavior (contribution-margin approach) and responsibility (by segment), this approach provides useful feedback information for both performance evaluation and planning.

6. False   Segment contribution measures only the past period's financial performance. Nonfinancial performance is an important component of segment performance not captured by the income statement by segments. Nonfinancial performance may be reflected in future financial performance measures such as future segment contribution.

7. False   In general, the more guidance (possibly through incentives) given to managers about the organization's desired trade-offs, the more likely it is that managers will achieve organizational goals. Some argue that the performance of profit centers should be based on the "bottom line" only and that good managers will figure out how to improve that number, to the benefit of the organization as a whole. This assumes, however, that managers will be in place long enough to experience the long-term effects of their actions.

8. False   The revenue portions of segment contribution are probably consistent with financial reporting, but the cost or expense portions need not be. Financial reporting measures expenses by operational function, whereas segment contribution measures expenses by cost behavior. Because of the effects of inventories, there may be sizable differences in expenses between the two approaches.

9. True   But this is an incomplete definition. Many measures of productivity are possible before goods and services are sold to customers.

10. False   Though current management controls may be obsolete in only a few years, there are principles of management control that will be valid for many years. Though it is helpful to be aware of current practice, be sure that you are learning basic principles.

Multiple-Choice Questions

1. b, c, d   The management control system includes these items (and others) but is not bound by financial reporting rules. In some organizations, however, the financial reporting system is a major part of the management control system. Some critics of accounting practice believe that this causes serious decision-making errors.

2. a,b,c,d   Of course, the first three are responsibility centers. The inclusion of "shopping center" may seem like a feeble joke, but a real-estate holding company, for example, could own a shopping center that it operates as a profit or investment center.

3. d   Accounting accuracy is desirable, but not as desirable as relevance. Rewarding managers for excellent performance may be an outcome of using responsibility accounting, but management bonuses are the responsibility of top management or the board of directors. Identifying blame or fault may occur as a result of investigating poor performance highlighted by responsibility accounting, but information-gathering and reporting is the primary function of responsibility accounting.

4. a, b, c   The most general assignment is the ability to explain outcomes. However, the one who explains works closest with the operations of the responsibility center and may also be in the best position to control and/or predict outcomes.

5. c   A cost center is the most basic level of financial responsibility, but this does not mean that all cost centers are small or their operations simple. The U.S. Department of Defense is essentially a cost center, and it certainly is neither small nor simple.

6. d   Management by exception is facilitated by well-designed reports that direct attention to unusual outcomes.

7. a   The segment contribution margin is contribution after all but unallocated costs: $690 - $500 - $110 - $80 = 0.

8. d   The contribution margin controllable by managers is the contribution margin less controllable fixed costs: $690 - $500 - $110 = $80.

9. a,b,c,d   Quality costs include all of these, and more. Inspection costs are classified as appraisal costs. Rework costs are internal failure costs. Lost sales are external failure costs. And redesign of the production process is a prevention cost.

10. a,b,c,d   For total quality management to succeed, all employees must be involved in creating customer-oriented quality.

Completion

1.   goals, vague, goals, tangible objectives

2.   goals, structure (other possibilities: culture, information system, management)

3.   cost centers

4.   has been designated the responsibility of an individual or group

5.   contribution margin, fixed costs controllable by managers

6.   margin controllable by managers, fixed costs controllable by others

7.   performance measures, organizational learning, business processes, customer value, financial strength

8.   objectives, incentive, attain objectives

9.   Contribution margin from lost sales, external failure

10.   output, a measure of input

Problems

1. Homer Equipment Company

	Company Total	Beta Division	Gamma Division
Net sales	$850	$500	$350
Less variable costs			
Manufacturing cost of sales	$450	$300	$150
Variable selling and admin. expenses	130	60	70
Total variable costs	$580	$360	$220
Contribution margin	$270	$140	$130
Less fixed costs controllable by managers	140	60	80
Contribution controllable by managers	$130	$ 80	$ 50
Less fixed costs controllable by others	70	10	60
Contribution by segments	$ 60	$ 70	$(10)
Less unallocated costs	45		
Income before taxes	$ 15		

2. The Burns Company

Cost of Quality

Prevention cost			
Product redesign		$ 5,000	
Employee training		10,000	$15,000
Appraisal cost			
Quality control salaries		6,000	
Test equipment operation		8,000	14,000
Internal failure cost			
Scrapped units	500 x $7	3,500	
Reworked units	600 x $2	1,200	$ 4,700
External failure cost			
Warranty expense		6,000	
Lost sales contribution*	500 x $13	6,500	12,500
Total			$46,200

*Note that other, future sales may have been lost due to defective units.

These are only some of the possible productivity measures:

Non-value-added quality cost as a percentage of sales revenue (all but prevention costs)	($46,200 - $15,000) ÷ $82,000	38%
Sales revenue per employee	$82,000 ÷ 50	$1,640 per employee
Production per employee	(4,600 - 500 - 600) ÷ 50	70 units per employee
Direct labor cost as a percentage of sales revenue	$4,000 ÷ $82,000	4.9%
Direct labor cost as a percentage of manufacturing costs	$4,000 ÷ $[20,000 + (7 x 4,600) + (2 x 600)]	7.5%
Product yield (first-time good units as a percentage of total units)	3,500 ÷ (3,500+500+600)	76%

Note: These are useful only if compared to Burns's competitors or over time for Burns.

Exercise

1. **Sales Clerk's Compensation Plan**

A.

	Sales clerk A	Sales clerk B	Sales clerk C
January:	$1,000 (didn't meet quota)	$1,500 (met quota)	$1,000 + $500 (bonus) + .05 x ($2,500-$2,000) = $1,525
February:	$1,000 + $500 (bonus) + .05 x ($2,550-$2,060) = $1,525 (rounded)	$1,500 (met quota)	$1,000 (didn't meet quota)
March:	$1,000 + $500 (bonus) + .05 x ($3,500-$2,627) = 1,544 (rounded)	$1,000 (didn't meet quota)	$1,000 + $500 (bonus) + .05 x ($2,500-$1,030) = 1,574 (rounded)
April:	1,000 (didn't meet quota)	$1,000 + $500 (bonus) + .05 x ($2,250-$2,060) = 1,510 (rounded)	1,000 (didn't meet quota)

B.   Basing the quota on actual sales from the previous month leads to erratic sales targets and salesclerk compensation. It would probably be better to base quotas on expected sales rather than past actual sales. Also, the $500 bonus is probably too large relative to the bonus percentage. It may be better to have no fixed bonus but a higher bonus percentage. This would motivate sales clerks to generate sales beyond the quota.

C.   The plans are consistent because they focus employees on increasing sales activity from current customers as well as finding new customers for future sales growth. Existing customers can be very profitable if they are satisfied. Therefore, it is important that employees maintain good customer service while they are seeking new customers. Rewards for new customers should not cause employees to ignore existing customers. If these incentives are balanced properly, they should lead to future profitability.

CHAPTER 10

Management Control in Decentralized Organizations

OVERVIEW

To complete the basic description of management control systems, this chapter covers the closely related topics of transfer pricing and alternative measures performance in decentralized organizations. The discussion of transfer prices raises problems common to all organizations with responsibility centers that share outputs. There are a number of transfer pricing policies; each has advantages and disadvantages. This chapter covers transfer pricing based on cost, market prices, and negotiation. The discussion of alternative measures of decentralized performance extends Chapter 9's discussion of evaluating investment centers. This chapter covers return on investment, residual income, and various ways of measuring the components of each. Your learning objectives are to:

I.   Define *decentralization* and identify its expected benefits and costs

II.   Distinguish between responsibility centers and decentralization

III.   Explain how the linking of rewards to responsibility-center performance metrics affects incentives and risk

IV.   Compute ROI, economic profit, and economic value added (EVA) and contrast them as criteria for judging the performance of organization segments

V.   Compare the advantages and disadvantages of various bases for measuring the invested capital used by organization segments

VI.   Define *transfer prices* and identify their purpose

VII.   State the general rule for transfer pricing and use it to assess transfer prices based on total costs, variable costs, and market prices

VIII.   Identify the factors affecting multinational transfer prices

IX.   Explain how controllability and management by objectives (MBO) aid the implementation of management control systems

REVIEW OF KEY CONCEPTS

I.	**Define *decentralization* and identify its benefits and costs**

Decentralization is the delegation of decision-making authority to segment managers.

A. Decentralization implies more **segment autonomy** than merely designating a subunit as a responsibility center.

    1. Decentralized segments are operated more as separate businesses than as just divisions of the larger company.

    2. Decentralization implies the ability to set major policies and make major investment decisions at the segment level.

B. Decentralization seeks to have the better of two worlds:

    1. Decentralized segments must compete with other, autonomous businesses, and so managers must develop competitive practices, products, and services to survive.

    2. Affiliation with the larger company provides access to capital and other business services that may not be available to truly separate businesses, except at much higher cost.

    3. Other benefits of decentralization include:

        • Better and timelier decisions because of managers' closeness to problem areas

        • Improvement of skills in the pool of company managers that will benefit the company as a whole

        • Improved motivation of managers who have enhanced status and who see rewards tied closely to their performance

C. Decentralization has disadvantages as well:

    1. Managers may focus narrowly on their own segment performance.

    2. Managers may be unaware of all relevant information regarding other segments and the company.

    3. Segments may duplicate costly central services.

    4. Overall information costs may rise.

D. As a result of these disadvantages, decentralization tends to be most successful when segments are relatively independent of each other.

    1. An additional criterion for designing and evaluating a successful control system in decentralized organizations is respect for segment autonomy.

    2. This means allowing segment managers to make decisions without interference from top managers.

> **Study Tip:** *Before going on, be sure that you can describe the difference between a decentralized segment and a responsibility center. What are the advantages and disadvantages of decentralization?*

II.	**Distinguish between responsibility centers and decentralization**

Decentralization is not equivalent to the use of profit centers.

A. *Decentralization* is the delegation of the authority to make decisions.

B. *Profit centers* generate revenues and expenses of segments.

C.   Thus, profit centers are designations of the scope of *responsibility*, but not necessarily *authority*.

D.   Some profit centers have far more *decentralized authority and autonomy* than others do, and even some cost centers may have more decentralized authority and autonomy than some profit centers.

III.   Explain how the linking of rewards to responsibility-center performance metrics affects incentives and risk

---

A.   Segment managers make supplying and sourcing decisions regarding other segments of the same company in just the way described in Chapter 5.

      1.   These are special-order and make-or-buy decisions, and the decisions among autonomous segments revolve around *transfer prices*.

      2.   Segments managers who are evaluated on some basis of income will want to charge as much as possible to supply other segments and pay as little as possible when buying from other segments--just as they would if dealing with an outside company.

      3.   The same concerns exist for utilization of capacity within segments.

      4.   Review make-or-buy and special-order decisions if they are not fresh in your memory.

B.   Negotiating transfer prices can consume considerable time and energy, but may resolve an important area of conflict. Further, this conflict-resolution process may carry over into other areas of conflict.

      1.   Conflicts are inevitable, but well-designed incentives will steer managers toward making decisions that benefit the company as a whole.

      2.   Negotiations that stray from what top management would prefer are one of the costs of decentralization.

Stop and Review

See textbook Exhibit 10-1

C.   A company may choose to use different transfer prices for different purposes: motivation, performance measurement, taxation, and domestic and international government regulation.

D.   **Agency theory** describes contractual relations between an organization (the principal) and its employees (the agents). These contractual relations will trade off three factors:

      1.   **Incentives**: Employees act to increase measures related to economic incentives.

      2.   Risk: Employees usually seek to avoid risk, so the organization must compensate them adequately to take risks.

      3.   Costs of measuring or monitoring performance: Measuring performance accurately is expensive, so the organization may accept imperfect measures and the possibility that employees will take actions that maximize the performance measure but may not meet the organization's goals.

IV. Compute ROI, economic profit, and economic value added (EVA) and contrast them as criteria for judging the performance of organization segments

A common goal of profit-seeking organizations is to achieve competitive profits. To give segment managers guidance, this goal is translated into *profit objectives, usually related to capital invested in the segment.* These measures are most appropriate for investment centers:

A.   A widely used measure is the rate of return on investment (ROI).

1.   ROI can be computed as:

$$\text{ROI} = \text{Income} \div \text{Invested capital}$$

2.   An alternative computation is:

$$\text{ROI} = (\text{Income} \div \text{Revenue}) \times (\text{Revenue} \div \text{Invested capital}), \text{ or}$$

$$\text{ROI} = \textbf{Return on sales} \times \textbf{Capital turnover}$$

3.   Subdividing ROI into its basic components as shown helps identify strategies for improving ROI. For example, reducing expenses (which increases income and return on sales) or reducing investment in assets (which increases capital turnover) will improve ROI.

B.   **Economic profit** *(Residual income or RI)* is another measure of performance that relates segment profit to invested capital.

1.   **RI** is the excess of income over the *opportunity cost* of the invested capital.

2.   A segment manager evaluated on RI would expand the segment only if the expansion would earn at least the charge for invested capital (the minimum desired rate of return).

3.   A variation of RI that uses the opportunity cost of capital is known as **economic value added (EVA).** In concept, it is no different than RI but is marketed by consultants as a superior form of RI.

> **Stop and Review**
>
> See the textbook exhibit 10-2

C.   Evaluation of segments based on ROI may lead to managers rejecting projects that promise more than the required rate of return but less than the current ROI.

1.   If managers' performances are compared across the company, a manager would be unwilling to decrease his or her ROI even if the company as a whole would benefit.

2.   In contrast, a manager evaluated on RI would be better off (as would the company) by accepting any project that earned more than the required rate of return.

3.   Most companies, however, use ROI, but add growth and profit objectives.

V. Compare the advantages and disadvantages of various bases for measuring the invested capital used by organization segments

To apply either the ROI or RI approach to measuring segment performance, the company must choose how to measure both income and invested capital.

A.   As discussed in Chapter 9, the contribution-margin approach is the preferred measure of income.

    1.   The contribution-margin approach highlights cost behavior and controllable versus uncontrollable costs.

    2.   Many companies, however, use the absorption approach because it is the method required for financial reporting.

        a.   Segment incomes "roll up" into overall reported income

        b.   Multiple cost systems are not used (though perhaps they should be for decision making)

B.   Different bases can be used for measuring *invested capital.* Alternatives include:

    1.   *Total assets*: the most inclusive measure, appropriate if managers have authority over all assets

    2.   *Total assets employed*: appropriate if managers are required to maintain some unused capacity

    3.   *Total assets less current liabilities*: appropriate if managers control short-term credit policy and bank loans

    4.   *Stockholders' equity*: appropriate only if managers have control of short-term and long-term debt (unlikely)

C.   Expect managers to try to reduce assets counted and increase liabilities deducted. The definition of the asset base should be sure to include only those assets that managers should be able to reduce or expand, likewise with liabilities.

D.   Of crucial importance is the *valuation base* for measuring assets.

    1.   For the routine measurement of assets included in the investment base, the most frequently used valuation is *historical cost* because it is the cheapest measure to obtain—it is already in the accounting system.

    2.   Some argue that *replacement* or *disposal* values are more relevant, but they are more costly to obtain, which makes their use usually not feasible, except for special decisions.

    3.   When historical cost is used as an investment measure, some prefer **net book value** of assets (cost less accumulated depreciation) *because it is consistent with conventional reporting of assets and net income.*

    4.   But others prefer **gross book value** (undepreciated cost) *because it facilitates comparisons among divisions, and because ROI and RI do not increase merely with the passage of time* (as it may with net book value).

    5.   Managers evaluated on a base of gross book value will tend to replace assets sooner than those using net book value (whose asset base declines and ROI and RI increase as assets age).

VI. Define *transfer prices* and identify their purpose

Transfer prices are the amounts charged for the exchanges of goods and services among the decentralized segments of a company.

A. Transfer prices exist to communicate information that promotes goal congruence.

B. If segments are evaluated on some basis of income (as discussed in later sections), then transfer prices charged will influence where and how much managers will pay for goods and services.

C. Transfer pricing and performance evaluation are closely tied together.

D. If transfer prices did not affect evaluations of segments and segment managers, then transfer pricing policies would not cause so many problems in decentralized companies.

VII. State the general rule for transfer pricing and use it a assess transfer prices based on total costs, variable costs, and market prices

A. Organizations have three general transfer pricing policies, each of which may be appropriate under different circumstances:

   1. *Cost-based transfer prices* use some measure of cost—variable cost, full cost, full cost plus markup, and any of these using standard or actual cost.

   2. *Market-based transfer prices* rely on competitive market prices.

   3. *Negotiated transfer prices* rely on negotiations between autonomous segment managers who may consider costs and market prices in their negotiations.

B. *Transfer prices based on total costs* other than strictly variable cost depend heavily on the process of *cost allocation* of fixed costs.

   1. Allocation of fixed costs is arbitrary and, when coupled with transfer pricing, increases opportunities for disagreements among segment managers.

   2. Arguments are over appropriate cost-drivers, cost-driver levels, identification of avoidable versus unavoidable costs, appropriate markups, use of actual or expected costs, and so on.

   3. Suffice to say, cost-based transfer prices cause considerable headaches.

C. Using *market prices* for transfer prices is usually appropriate when decentralized segments are profit centers.

   1. The problems of disagreements, goal congruence, managerial effort, and segment autonomy are minimized when market prices are used.

   2. If market prices do not exist, some organizations try to imitate market prices with "cost-plus-a-profit," but these are just cost-based transfer prices and introduce all their problems.

VIII.　Identify the factors affecting multinational transfer prices

Multinational companies use transfer prices to minimize worldwide income taxes, import duties, and tariffs.

A.　Transferring at a low price from a high-tax country to a low-tax country causes most profit to be earned in the low-tax country.

B.　Transferring at a high price from a low-tax country to a high-tax country also causes most profit to be earned in the low-tax country.

C.　Tax effects, however, can be offset by import duties.

D.　Tax authorities generally have restrictions on allowable transfer prices. Often this means that transfer prices must be similar to market prices.

IX.　Explain how controllability and management by objectives (MBO) aid the implementation of management control systems

A.　When evaluating the performance of a division in an organization it is important that top managers draw the distinction between the performance of the division's manager and the performance of the division as an investment.

　　1.　Managers should be evaluated only on the basis of *controllable performance*. Decisions that were not influenced by that manager should not be used in the evaluation of his performance.

B.　**Management by objectives (MBO)** involves both division managers and their superior managers.

　　1.　A set of attainable goals or objectives and a corresponding budget is agreed on at the beginning of a period and then compared with actual results at the end of the period to evaluate the performance of the manager and her division.

　　2.　MBO eliminates a great deal of disagreement between managers and their superiors because both are involved in creating reasonable goals and budgets.

C.　Using MBO and other methods that use budgets to define goals and judge performance can be quite effective, but it can also encourage managers to behave unethically in order to meet the budget.

> **Study Tip:** *Before going on to the practice test, be sure that you understand the advantages and disadvantages of using MBO.*

PRACTICE TEST QUESTIONS AND PROBLEMS

True or False Statements

Determine whether each of the following statements is True (T) or False (F), and enter your answer in the space provided.

_____1. Decentralization tends to be least successful when the segments of an organization are extremely independent.

_____2. The amount of an organization's decentralization depends on the existence of profit centers within the organization.

_____3. Segment autonomy means the freedom of each organization segment to define its job or function.

_____4. The costs of decentralization can include poorer training for managers and dysfunctional decision making.

_____5. The benefits of decentralization can include improved management motivation and decreased costs of gathering and processing information about market opportunities.

_____6. Disadvantages of transfer prices based on total actual cost include reduction of incentives for managers of supplying divisions to control their costs.

_____7. Transfer pricing is a form of cost allocation.

_____8. It is better to use an arbitrary basis for allocating asset costs to segments than to not allocate asset costs to divisions at all.

_____9. When historical cost is used as an investment measure, it is more appropriate to use gross book value than net book value.

____10. The use of stockholders' equity as an investment base would be just as appropriate for evaluating owners' returns as management performance.

Multiple-Choice Questions

For each of the following multiple-choice questions, select the best answer(s), and enter the identification letter(s) in the space provided.

_____1. Decentralized segments may be: (a) cost centers, (b) profit centers, (c) investment centers, (d) government agencies.

_____2. Defining characteristics of a decentralized segment include: (a) manufacturing capability, (b) profit responsibility, (c) autonomous decision making, (d) physical separation from parent company.

_____3. Costs of decentralization include: (a) the need to use summary performance measures like ROI or EVA, (b) dysfunctional decision making, (c) required measurement of segment profit, (d) duplication of services.

_____4. Transfer prices are most like: (a) consulting fees, (b) cost allocations, (c) transportation charges, (d) interest payments.

_____5. An investment center is a business segment that relates its net income to its: (a) sales, (b) total assets, (c) stockholders' equity, (d) invested capital.

_____6. ROI is return on sales multiplied by: (a) revenue, (b) income, (c) capital turnover, (d) total assets.

_____7. Given for a division of Phaeton Co.: $32,000 operating income, $800,000 revenues, and a capital turnover of five times. Compute ROI: (a) 4%, (b) 5%, (c) 10%, (d) 20%.

_____8.   Astin Corporation turned over its capital six times and earned an operating income of 2.5% of sales. Compute ROI: (a) 6%, (b) .4%, (c) 15%, (d) 10%.

_____9.   Given for a division of Bugatti Co.: 18% ROI, 12 % cost of capital, and $2 million of invested capital. Compute residual income: (a) $360,000, (b) $240,000, (c) $120,000, (d) $0.

_____10.   Other factors remaining the same, the rate of return on investment may be improved by: (a) increasing investment in assets, (b) increasing expenses, (c) reducing sales, (d) decreasing investment in assets.

Completion

Complete each of the following statements by filling in the blanks.

1.   _____ of an organization occurs when sets of activities are designated as _____.

2.   The degree of decentralization should be a function of _____.

3.   Decentralization is more popular in profit-seeking organizations than in nonprofit organizations because _____.

4.   Transfer prices are of three general types:_____, _____, _____.

5.   Managers of segments that are evaluated on the basis of income and that must buy parts from other segments or outside companies consider the transfer-pricing decision in the same way as a _____ decision.

6.   ROI is _____ divided by _____.

7.   Capital turnover is _____ divided by _____.

8.   Residual income is _____ less _____.

9.   The residual income calculation subtracts _____ from net income because _____.

10.   _____ of assets may be better than _____ as a valuation basis for measuring assets included in the investment base because _____ does not increase with just the passage of time.

Problems

1.   Complete the calculations for three divisions of EarthWise Brands Inc.:

	Maritime Division	Farm Division	Industrial Division
Cost of capital	15%	11%	12%
Invested capital	$250,000	$200,000	
Revenues (sales)	$750,000		$450,000
Net income	$ 37,500		$ 13,500
Capital turnover			4.5 times
Income percentage of revenue		5%	
Rate of return on investment		10%	
Residual income			

2. Given for the Ozone Regeneration Division of Mother Earth Company:

Cost of manufacturing 2,000 units of a thraxadyne assembly:

	Total	Per Unit
Variable costs	$120,000	$60
Fixed costs	$ 60,000	$30

Find the total advantage (or disadvantage) to the company if there are at least 2,000 units of idle capacity in the Ozone Division, *and* if the Global Cooling Division of the same company purchases 2,000 units of this assembly from an outside supplier at a market price of:

   a. $63 per unit

   b. $58 per unit

Exercise

1. Given for the real-estate division of the Continental Corporation:

   Capital invested in operating assets $3,000,000

   Net income $ 540,000

   Revenues $2,700,000

   a.   What is the division's ROI? _____

   b.   If Continental can earn 16% (before tax) on other investments, what is the division's residual income (RI)?_____

   c.   A project is available to the division that promises a 17% return on a $200,000 investment. Could it make a difference whether the division manager is evaluated on ROI or RI? Show why._____

   d.   Continental is considering increasing the required rate of return to 20%. If ROI is used, by how much would revenues have to be increased in the real-estate division to meet this new requirement? _____

   Independently, by how much would expenses have to be reduced to meet this new requirement?_____

   Independently, by how much would investment have to be reduced to meet this new requirement?_____

CHAPTER 10 SOLUTIONS TO PRACTICE TEST QUESTIONS AND PROBLEMS

True or False Statements

1. False   Just the opposite is true, because increased independence reduces the likelihood that conflicts among segments will occur.

2. False   Decentralization does not depend on the form of responsibility center, but it does depend on the degree of decision-making authority.

3. False   Decision-making authority usually is constrained to maintain the purpose of the segment.

4. False   Though dysfunctional decision making is a possible cost, managers should receive improved training in a decentralized organization.

5. True   Improved motivation is a benefit of decentralization, but a major motivation is that managers most likely are better able to identify profitable opportunities.

6. True   When transfers are made at actual cost, the supplying division is able to pass on its inefficiencies to the purchasing divisions.

7. True   When transfer prices are based on cost (rather than market prices), one faces the same difficulties as in other cost allocation situations.

8. False   If it is not possible to trace costs to divisions, it is probably better to leave the costs as unallocated costs.

9. True   But opinions vary. On one hand, gross book value remains constant over the life of the asset and does not inflate ROI or RI the way that net book value does. On the other hand, net book value is more consistent with financially reported asset values that are consistent with overall company asset values.

10. False   Stockholders' equity is a measure of the owners' investment in a company, but using it to evaluate a manager's performance confuses the financing of a segment with the operations of a segment.

Multiple Choice-Questions

1. a,b,c,d   A decentralized segment may be any type of responsibility center, even a government agency.

2. c   Of those listed, only autonomous decision making defines a decentralized segment. A segment does not have to be a manufacturer, manage profits, or be physically separated.

3. b, d   Dysfunctional decision making—decisions that work against the benefit of the company as a whole—and duplication of services are possible costs of decentralization. Measurement of profit and use of summary performance measures are common, but not necessary.

4. b   Determining transfer prices based on full costs requires some allocation of fixed or common costs.

5. b, d   Performance is measured as income to invested capital, which may be measured as total assets.

6. c   ROI = return on sales x capital turnover. ROI may be increased by increasing return on sales or capital turnover or both.

7. d   Capital turnover = Revenue/Invested capital

$$5 \text{ times} = \$800,000/\text{Invested capital}$$

$$\text{Invested capital} = \$800,000/5$$

$$\text{Invested capital} = \$160,000$$

$$\text{ROI} = \$32,000/\$160,000 = \underline{20\%}$$

8. c   ROI = return on sales x capital turnover = .025 x 6 = $\underline{15\%}$

9. c   ROI = 0.18 = Net income / invested capital = NI/\$2,000,000

$$\text{NI} = 0.18 \times \$2,000,000 = \$360,000$$

$$\text{RI} = \$360,000 - (0.12 \times \$2,000,000) = \underline{\$120,000}$$

10. d   Decreasing invested capital increases capital turnover and ROI. The other actions will decrease ROI.

Completion

1.   Decentralization, the responsibility of an individual or group

2.   autonomy of decision making

3.   profit-seeking firms have more reliable measures of performance

4.   cost-based, market price, negotiated

5.   make-or-buy

6.   net income, invested capital

7.   revenue, invested capital

8.   net income, imputed interest on invested capital or opportunity cost of capital

9.   imputed interest, that is what the invested capital could be earning if invested elsewhere

10.   Gross book value, net book value of assets, return on investment or residual income

Problems

1.   EarthWise Brands, Inc.

	Maritime Division	Farm Division	Industrial Division
Invested capital	$250,000	$200,000	$450,000 ÷ 4.5 = $100,000
Revenues (sales)	$750,000	$20,000 ÷ 0.05 = $400,000	$450,000
Net income	$37,500	.10 x $200,000 = $20,000	$13,500
Capital turnover	$750,000 ÷ $250,000 = 3 times	$400,000 ÷ $200,000 = 2 times	4.5 times
Income percentage of revenue	$37,500 ÷ $750,000 = 5%	5%	$13,500 ÷ $450,000 = 3%
Rate of return on investment	$37,500 ÷ $250,000 = 15%	10%	$13,500 ÷ $100,000 = 13.5%
Residual income	$37,500 – (0.15 x $250,000) = 0	$20,000 – (0.11 x $200,000) = ($2,000)	$13,500 – (0.12 x $100,000) = $1,500

2.   Ozone Regeneration Division of Mother Earth Company:

	(a)	(b)
Outside market price per unit	63	58
Variable cost per unit	$60	$60
Advantage (disadvantage) per unit	($3)	$2
Multiply by number of units	2,000	2,000
Total advantage (disadvantage) to the company	($6,000)	$4,000

(The fixed costs are irrelevant.)

Exercise

1. Continental Corp.

    Find for the real-estate division:

a. ROI = $540,000 ÷ $3,000,000 = <u>18%</u>

b. RI = $540,000 - .16 x $3,000,000 = <u>$60,000</u>

c. Yes. It would be beneficial to the company as a whole because it earns additional residual income of (0.17 - 0.16) x $200,000 = $2,000. However, the manager would find it unattractive on an ROI basis because overall ROI would decline:

    ROI [new] = [$540,000 + (0.17 x $200,000)] ÷ ($3,000,000 + $200,000)

    ROI [new] = $574,000 ÷ $3,200,000 = <u>17.9%</u>

d. The ROI would have to increase to 20%

    <u>Revenues:</u>

    Current expenses = $2,700,000 - $540,000 = $2,160,000

    ROI [new] = 0.20 = (Revenues [new] - $2,160,000) ÷ $3,000,000

    Revenues [new] = (0.20 x $3,000,000) + $2,160,000 = <u>$2,760,000, an increase of $60,000</u>

    <u>Expenses:</u>

    ROI [new] = 0.20 = ($2,700,000 - Expenses[new]) ÷ $3,000,000

    Expenses [new] = $2,700,000 – (0.20 x $3,000,000) = <u>$2,100,000, a decrease of $60,000</u>

    <u>Investment:</u>

    ROI [new] = 0.20 = $540,000 ÷ Investment[new]

    Investment [new] = $540,000 ÷ 0.20 = <u>$2,700,000, a decrease of $300,000</u>

CHAPTER 11

Capital Budgeting

OVERVIEW

Capital budgeting is the process of arriving at decisions regarding investments in projects covering several years. The leading model for capital-budgeting analysis is discounted cash flow (DCF). This model is based on the concept of time value of money and discounting expected future cash flows. We focus on the two DCF models for selecting and evaluating long-term investments: net present value (NPV) and internal rate of return (IRR). We discuss the limitations and possible benefits of two other models that are sometimes used for analysis of long-term projects: payback period and accounting rate of return. Your learning objectives are to:

I.   Describe capital-budgeting decisions and use the net-present-value (NPV) method to make such decisions

II.   Evaluate projects using sensitivity analysis

III.   Calculate the NPV difference between two projects using both the total project and differential approaches

IV.   Identify the relevant cash flows for NPV analyses

V.   Compute the after-tax net present values of projects

VI.   Explain the after-tax effect on cash of disposing of assets

VII.   Use the payback model and the accounting rate-of-return model and compare them with the NPV model

VIII. Reconcile the conflict between using an NPV model for making a decision and using accounting income for evaluating the related performance.

IX.   Compute the impact of inflation on a capital-budgeting project (Appendix 11)

I. **Describe capital-budgeting decisions and use the net-present-value (NPV) to make such decisions**

A. **Capital budgeting** is the process of selecting and evaluating investments in long-term projects.

   1. There are three steps in preparing a capital budget:

      a. Identifying potential investments

      b. Selecting investments to undertake

      c. Follow up or "postaudit" to compare outcomes with expectations (This is a source of valuable feedback, but, unfortunately, this is the least-followed step in practice.)

   2. Accounting information plays a significant role in the second and third steps, and may play a role in the initial screening step. *This chapter focuses on the second step.*

      a. Note that *capital budgeting is project oriented*, in contrast to the organization-oriented budgeting we have focused on in earlier chapters.

   3. Recall that a segment of an organization can be characterized as a set of activities. Another way of characterizing a segment is a *set of capital projects* under the management of an individual or group. The net-present-value (NPV) model uses a minimum desired rate of return for *discounting* cash outflows and inflows to the present time.

      a. Because future cash flows could be obtained by investing an amount now at some interest rate, we *discount* future cash flows to a present equivalent—what we would have to invest now to have the expected future cash flow.

      b. For example, if we expect a project's future cash inflow will be $110 one year from now, and our opportunity rate is 10%, how much would we have to invest now in our other opportunities to have the same future cash flow? It is easy to tell that $100 invested today at 10% interest would earn $10, and we would have $110 a year from now. Therefore, our project's expected cash flow of $110 a year in the future is equivalent to $100 today. This is the essence of *discounting*.

   4. The conceptually superior approaches to selecting the best projects from those available are **discounted cash flow (DCF)** models because they explicitly and systematically weigh the **time value (or opportunity cost) of money.**

      a. Money that is tied up in particular projects is not available for other productive purposes. DCF models account for the opportunity cost of money tied up over time.

      b. At a minimum, money could be earning interest in the bank, so any project evaluated on financial criteria should do at least as well as money in the bank. In this example, the opportunity cost of capital tied up in projects is at least (expressed as a percentage) the interest rate the money could be earning.

      c. Because any decision is about the future, one could argue that all financial decisions should consider the time value of money. If the time period of a project is short, the time value of money can be ignored (unless interest rates are very high).

      d. The forgone opportunities are *compounded* over time.

e.　Note that DCF models are concerned with cash inflows and outflows, not net income. The reason is that cash could be used (consumed or reinvested), whereas net income may not (e.g., depreciation is an expense but is not a cash outflow).

f.　The initial investment in an asset is typically treated as a single outflow of cash at the start of a project (DCF models easily allow subsequent actual investment).

g.　Therefore, to also deduct periodic depreciation from periodic cash inflows would be a double-counting of this cost over the life of the project and confusing the timing of actual cash outflows.

5.　The major information requirements of the DCF models are:

a.　*Predicted cash flows.* Most models assume that cash inflows and outflows are expected to occur at definite times and amounts. These cash flows are the tangible costs and benefits of investing in the future. Usually benefits are more difficult to measure than costs.

b.　*The minimum desired rate of return.* This is also called the opportunity rate, **required rate of return**, interest rate, cost of capital, hurdle rate, discount rate, or the time value of money. Alternative interest rates abound, but theoretically it is difficult to specify which one is appropriate for a given project.

> **Study Tip:** *Before going on to the next section, be sure that you understand the nature of capital budgeting and are familiar with the theory and mechanics of compound interest.*

B.　Two DCF models are most commonly used in capital budgeting: the *net-present-value* model and the *internal-rate-of-return* model. In most applications, they are equivalent.

Note: In practice, the mathematics of capital budgeting is accomplished with computer programs, particularly spreadsheet software for PCs. The textbook chapter and this study guide discuss manual approaches to capital budgeting because we believe that once you are familiar with the arithmetic involved, you can use computer programs with the assurance that you are providing the correct inputs. The easy part of capital budgeting is the arithmetic, which is performed quickly by computers, eliminating computational effort. The difficult management task, which computers cannot do, is to develop the cash flows and required rate of return. To confidently develop the proper information and interpret the results, you need to know how the models work. It will reinforce your learning if you also work the examples in the text using a spreadsheet, but only after you understand the manual steps

II.　Evaluating projects using sensitivity analysis

A.　Perhaps a better way to model uncertainty is to use *sensitivity analysis*, introduced in Chapter 7. A popular form of sensitivity analysis prepares three possible NPVs or IRRs:

1.　Make and compare three separate sets of predictions for each possible project: *pessimistic, expected,* and *optimistic.*

2.　Determine how much the optimistic and pessimistic NPVs or IRRs differ from the expected NPV or IRR for each project.

3.　*Riskier* projects have a wider range of NPV and IRR from the expected values.

4. By identifying the risk of projects, managers can make trade-offs between the expected NPV or IRR of a project and its risk. For example, a manager may choose a project with a lower IRR if higher IRR projects have unacceptably high risk. This trade-off is a personal one, but, as discussed in Chapter 9, incentive systems may be designed to align managers' goals with owners' goals.

B. Summary of typical concerns in analyzing expected cash flows:

1. *Current* disposal values of old assets are most conveniently handled by offsetting them against the gross cash outlays for new assets at time zero.

2. All initial investments (including receivables, inventories, and intangibles) are typically regarded as cash outflows at time zero, and their *terminal* disposal values (if any) are treated as cash inflows at the end of the project's useful life.

3. Errors in forecasting future disposal values are usually not crucial because the combination of relatively small disposal values and long time periods tends to produce rather small present values.

4. In the relevant-cost analysis of factory overhead, the only pertinent cost is avoidable overhead.

5. A reduction in an operating cash outflow is the same as a cash inflow.

6. Depreciation and book values are ignored because they are cost allocations, not cash flows.

7. When comparing projects with unequal lives, make the projects have equal lives by either imposing the shorter life on both or assuming reinvestment in the shorter-life project.

8. Income taxes and inflation do affect cash flows, but consideration of their effects is postponed until the next chapter.

C. It is important to recognize that not adopting new technology could result in lower future cash flows than were predicted for the current process. The status quo actually may decline from the present course because of the advantages new technology will give to competitors.

> **Study Tip:** *Do you have an appreciation for the difficulties of measuring future cash flows? This is what causes managers and budget analysts the most problems and where subjectivity is the greatest. Sensitivity analysis may be crucial to making good capital-budgeting decisions.*

III. Calculate the NPV difference between two projects using both the total project and differential approaches

The attractiveness of two projects can be compared by two equivalent NPV methods or by comparing IRRs.

A. The **total project approach**:

1. Calculate the NPV of each of the two projects.

2. Find the difference between these NPVs.

B. The **differential approach**:

1. Find the differences between the cash flows of each of two projects in each time period.

2. Calculate the NPV of these differences.

> **Stop and Review**
>
> See textbook Exhibit 11-2

> **Study Tip:** *Before going on to the next section, be sure that you are comfortable with the concepts and the computations of the NPV and the IRR approaches to capital-budgeting analysis.*

IV. Identify the relevant cash flows for NPV analyses

A. The NPV model *discounts* the expected future cash flows of each project to their *present equivalents* or *present values* so that the projects' *net present values* can be compared.

    1. *Net present value is the sum of the present values of the expected future cash inflows and outflows.*

    2. *If the net present value of a project is zero or positive, the project is acceptable. If capital is constrained, choose the projects with the highest net present values first.*

B. The arithmetic of NPV analysis is not difficult, but it pays to be methodical and to be sure that all relevant information is used.

    1. The first step (manual or with spreadsheet software) is to display the relevant cash flows in a diagram. (Just entering cash flows in the cells of a spreadsheet builds a diagram of cash flows.)

> **Stop and Review**
>
> Work through the textbook
> Summary Problem on p. 485

    2. The next step is to compute the present value of each cash flow. The manual approach, which you should try until you are comfortable with NPV analysis, requires looking up appropriate present value factors in the tables of Appendix B. These factors depend on when cash flows are expected and the appropriate discount rate.

C. The internal rate of return (IRR) is the rate of return (discount rate) that makes the net present value of a project equal to zero.

    1. The IRR approach treats the NPV of a project as known (zero) and treats the discount rate as the unknown—the IRR process is just the inverse of the NPV process.

> *For example, what is the IRR of a project that costs $100 now and will have a cash inflow of $110 one year from now? It is easy to see that this project earns $10 or 10% on the investment in one year; that is, its IRR is 10%.*
>
> *What you did in your head, we could prove mathematically by solving the following equation for the unknown IRR:*
>
> $$\$110 = \$100 + \$100 \times IRR$$
>
> $$\$110 = \$100 \times (1 + IRR)$$
>
> $$(1 + IRR) = \$110 \div \$100 = 1.10$$
>
> $$\therefore IRR = 1.10 - 1 = .10 = \underline{10\%}$$

2. As shown in the example above, the essence of the IRR process is conceptually not difficult, but when the pattern of cash flows is complex, the arithmetic can be messy.

3. *If the IRR equals or exceeds the minimum desired rate of return, accept the project; if not, reject the project. If capital is scarce, choose the projects with the highest IRRs first.*

D. The IRR approach to capital budgeting follows these steps:

1. The first step of the IRR approach is identical to the first step of the NPV approach— diagram the pattern of cash flows.

2. The second step is to find the interest rate that makes the NPV of the project equal to zero. The manual approach is to use a *trial-and-error* search (another name for systematically guessing the IRR):

- Choose an interest rate.

- Multiply the expected cash flows by the appropriate discount factors in Appendix B.

- See whether the sum of all the present values (NPV) of the cash flows equals zero.

- If the NPV is positive, you have not discounted enough, so choose a higher interest rate and repeat.

- If the NPV is negative, you have discounted too much, so choose a lower interest rate, and repeat.

- Repeat the process until the NPV is close enough to zero.

3. The best approach in practice is to use a spreadsheet program (or programmable calculator) IRR function, which itself is just a computer program to conduct a trial-and-error search.

4. However, do not use a spreadsheet program to find the IRR until you are comfortable with the arithmetic involved.

E. There is always some *uncertainty* whether cash-flow predictions actually will be realized.

1. One could recognize this uncertainty by becoming more conservative in the measurement of the inputs to the NPV or IRR models:

a. Use higher discount rates when uncertainty is greater.

b. Predict lower cash inflows and higher cash outflows when uncertainty is greater.

c. Reduce expected lives when uncertainty is greater.

V.	Compute the after-tax net and present values of projects

A. *Example 1:* Assume a project initially costs $1,000, has no disposal value, and has an expected life of 4 years. The project promises operating cash savings of $500 per year. The cost of capital is 8%, and the tax rate is 40%: (a) Compute the NPV of the project using straight-line depreciation, (b) compute the NPV of the project using accelerated depreciation.

(a) Straight-line depreciation:

	Present value at 8%	Annual after-tax income:				
		1	2	3	4	total
Cash savings		$500	$500	$500	$500	$2,000
Less depreciation		250	250	250	250	1,000
Income		$250	$250	$250	$250	$1,000
Taxes at 40%		100	100	100	100	400
Income after tax		$150	$150	$150	$150	600
Add back depreciation		250	250	250	250	1,000
After-tax net cash flow	$	$400	$400	$400	$400	$1,600
Discounted cash flows	400 x 3.312 =					$1,325
Less investment cost						(1,000)
Net present value						$ 325

(b) Accelerated depreciation:

	Present value at 8%	Annual after-tax income:				
		1	2	3	4	total
Cash savings		$500	$500	$500	$500	$2,000
Less depreciation		500	250	125	125	1,000
Income		$ 0	$250	$375	$375	$1,000
Taxes at 40%		0	100	150	150	400
Income after tax		$ 0	$150	$225	$225	$600
Add back depreciation		500	250	125	125	1,000
After-tax net cash flow		$500	$400	$350	$350	$1,600
PV factors (from tables in text)		0.926	0.857	0.794	0.735	
Discounted cash flows		$463	$343	$278	$257	$1,341
Less investment cost						(1,000)
Net present value						$ 341

Difference in NPV = $341 - $325 = $16 in favor of accelerated depreciation

Note: (1) Depreciation is added back to net income after tax to obtain net cash flow after tax because though depreciation reduced income, it is not a cash outflow.

(2) The total incomes, depreciations, taxes, and net cash flows are the same over the four-year life, regardless of depreciation method.

(3) *The NPV of the project is higher using accelerated depreciation because the timing of the tax savings is earlier using accelerated depreciation.*

B. *Example 2:* Assume the same facts as the previous example, but compute the present values of the tax savings using either straight-line or accelerated depreciation.

Straight-line depreciation		1	2	3	4	total
Annual depreciation		$250	$250	$250	$250	$1,000
Tax savings at 40%		100	100	100	100	400
Present value of tax savings	$100 x 3.312 = $331					

Accelerated depreciation		1	2	3	4	total
Annual depreciation		$500	$250	$125	$125	$1,000
Tax savings at 40%		200	100	50	50	400
Discount factors		0.926	0.857	0.794	0.735	
Discounted cash flows(rounded)	$348	$185	86	40	37	
Difference	$ 17					

Notes: (1) The difference in the present value of the tax savings is exactly the same as the difference in NPVs using the alternative methods.

(2) Again, though the total depreciation and tax savings are the same over the investment's four-year life, the difference in present values is due to the *timing* of tax savings.

(3) In the U.S., MACRS depreciation is the allowed accelerated method for taxation for most investments. Schedules similar to Exhibit 11-5 are available for MACRS.

VI. Explain the after-tax effect on cash of disposing of assets

When a depreciable asset is sold, the amount of the after-tax cash inflow from the disposal is the sales proceeds:

A. *Minus* the income tax on the gain, or

B. *Plus* the tax savings from the loss on sale.

> **Stop and Review**
>
> See the textbook example of after-tax effects of disposal

VII. Use the payback model and the accounting rate-of-return model and compare them with the NPV model

DCF models are recommended for capital-budgeting decisions, but several other approaches are still used in some businesses:

A. The crisis-response or emergency-persuasion method uses no formal planning but seems to be based mainly on urgency caused by procrastination and neglect (not recommended!).

B. The **payback model** measures the estimated number of years before cash inflows return the initial cash investment.

1. If cash flows are uniform, the initial cash investment is divided by the annual cash inflow; if cash flows are not uniform, a cumulative approach is used.

2. Though this method ignores the profitability of investment, it is a popular way for providing a rough estimate of risk—longer paybacks imply greater risk.

C. The **accounting rate of return (ARR)** is the predicted amount of future average annual net income divided by the initial (sometimes average) amount of the required investment.

1. This model ignores the time value of money.

2. However, it is used because it measures profit by conventional accrual accounting methods, and because it is easy to evaluate the performance of projects by comparing actual accounting income to expected income.

3. It is also used because it is constructed the same way as the return-on-investment (ROI) figure used to evaluate decentralized profit centers as a whole (Chapter 10).

VIII. Reconcile the conflict between using an NPV model for making a decision and using accounting income for evaluating the related performance.

A. Using DCF methods for both capital budgeting and evaluation eliminates the conflict.

B. A **postaudit,** a follow-up evaluation of capital budgeting decisions, helps reduce the conflict. The elements of a postaudit are:

1. Reviewing investment expenditures

2. Comparing actual to predicted cash flows

3. Improving predictions of future cash flows

4. Evaluating whether to continue a project

IX. Compute the impact of inflation on a capital-budgeting project (Appendix 11)

In most cases, DCF models should be adjusted for the effects of price inflation (the decline in the general purchasing power of money).

A. **Inflation** is the condition of eroding purchasing power of money over time; that is, when prices have risen in unison, it costs more to buy the same goods and services now than it did in the past.

1. If inflation is expected, operating expenses (*except depreciation*) should be predicted to rise with inflation.

2. Note that because depreciation is an allocation of a past cost to future periods, tax laws usually do not permit adjusting depreciation expense for the effects of inflation.

3. If inflation is expected, sales revenues also should be expected to rise. A difficult prediction is whether sales prices will increase at the same rate as operating expenses.

4. Because interest rates are the costs of money, they can be expected to rise as well.

5. Even modest rates of inflation can have very large compounded effects after a number of years. Of course, in parts of the world with three- or four-digit inflation rates, the problem is critical.

B.   The **nominal** (or market) discount rate includes an element that is the real rate of interest and another element representing the expected rate of inflation.

1.   If nominal, market rates are used in DCF models, future cash flows must also be adjusted for expected inflation.

2.   If only the real rate of interest is used, then do not adjust future cash flows for expected inflation; use estimates in today's costs.

3.   The key is consistency in either using an inflation element in both the discount rate and the predicted operating cash flows or in neither.

Stop and Review
See the textbook Exhibit 11-9

C.   Operating expenses or revenues are adjusted for expected inflation by multiplying current amounts by an index that measures percentage changes in expected prices.

1.   For example, if an operating cost today is $100, and 10% inflation is expected each year for the next three years, adjusted expenses will be:

now	$100
in 1 year	110
in 2 years	121
in 3 years	133

2.   Note that continued inflation has the same mathematical impact as compound interest.

3.   Many different price indexes that measure past levels and rates of inflation are available for use, but it is not always clear which one to use. In practice, analysts use either a very general (economy-wide) price level index or a very specific (product, region, or industry) index.

PRACTICE TEST QUESTIONS AND PROBLEMS

True or False Statements

Determine whether each of the following statements is True (T) or False (F), and enter your answer in the space provided.

_____1.   If a capital-budgeting project has a zero net present value, this would indicate that the project is acceptable.

_____2.   The main purpose of postaudits of capital-budgeting projects is to verify that the accounting records accurately reflect the actual transactions of the projects.

_____3.   The internal rate of return is the discount rate that produces a zero NPV.

_____4.   If a project has a negative NPV, the IRR would be higher than the discount rate used to compute NPV.

_____5.   A project has a positive NPV using a 15% discount rate. Its IRR would be greater than 15%.

_____6.   The use of the discounted-cash-flow approach requires that periodic depreciation expense be deducted from cash inflows.

_____7.   Discounted-cash-flow techniques are designed to measure the opportunity cost of investments.

_____8.   Generally, in a DCF analysis of replacing equipment, we should ignore book values.

_____9.   The time-value of money is ignored by the accounting-rate-of-return model.

____10.   A follow up or postaudit of a capital-budgeting decision is facilitated by the capital-budgeting use of the accounting-rate-of-return model.

____11.   The gain or loss on the disposal of depreciable equipment is the disposal value less the net book value of the equipment.

____12.   The gain or loss on the disposal of depreciable equipment is a cash flow in the year of disposal.

____13.   A World Bank budget analyst uses the pure rate of interest to evaluate the acceptability of a 50-year dam project in an underdeveloped country. Because inflation rates have been, and are expected to be, nearly 100% per year for the foreseeable future, the analyst must adjust future cash flows for the enormous expected inflation.

____14.   The expected future cash flows caused by income tax savings from depreciation should be adjusted by the rate of inflation before being discounted to the present.

____15.   The nominal rate to use for DCF computations under inflationary conditions is the sum of the business-risk element and the inflation element.

Multiple-Choice Questions

For each of the following multiple-choice questions, select the best answer(s), and enter the identification letter(s) in the space provided.

_____1.   DCF models include: (a) NPV, (b) IMA, (c) ARR, (d) IRR, (e) AARP.

_____2.   BonMot Co. is considering the purchase of a special-purpose machine for $48,000. The machine has a twelve-year estimated life, a zero salvage value, and expected cash operating savings of $11,000 per year. Compute the payback period: (a) 4.4 years, (b) 7.6 years, (c) 4.8 years, (d) 6.9 years.

_____ 3. See the preceding test item. Compute the accounting rate of return on the initial investment using straight-line depreciation: (a) 20.8%, (b) 22.9%, (c) 14.6%, (d) 13.2%.

_____ 4. MalMot Co. is considering the purchase of equipment for $10,000. The company anticipates annual cash savings of $4,000 for four years with no equipment residual value. Compute NPV at a 10% discount rate. A table shows the annuity discount factor to be 3.170. NPV is: (a) $2,680, (b) $12,680, (c) $6,000, (d) $1,680.

_____ 5. See the preceding test item. Compute the annual cash inflow that would make the net present value equal to zero: (a) $3,170, (b) $13,170, (c) $6,830, (d) $3,155.

_____ 6. A project requires an immediate investment of $60,000 in some new equipment with an estimated useful life of ten years and no residual value. If predicted annual savings of cash operating expenses are $15,000, what is the accounting rate of return based on the initial investment? Use straight-line depreciation and ignore income taxes: (a) 25%, (b) 20%, (c) 15%, (d) 10%.

_____ 7. Appropriate Company acquired a depreciable asset for $72,000. It has an estimated life of eight years with zero terminal salvage value. If the income tax rate is 40%, what is the tax-saving effect of using the accelerated depreciation method instead of the straight-line method for the first year? (a) $4,000 less tax, (b) $4,000 more tax, (c) $3,600 more tax, (d) $3,600 less tax.

_____ 8. Pow Co. sold for $44,000 cash an old piece of equipment. It was purchased eight years ago for $130,000 and was being depreciated on a straight-line basis over a useful life of ten years with an expected terminal scrap value of $10,000. What was the gain or loss on the sale before income taxes? (a) $20,000 gain, (b) $18,000 loss, (c) $10,000 gain, (d) $16,000 loss.

_____ 9. See the preceding test item. Compute the after-tax cash effect of the sale transaction only, assuming a 40% tax rate: (a) $40,000, (b) $17,600, (c) $26,400, (d) $32,000.

Completion

Complete each of the following statements by filling in the blanks.

1. Identify each of the following: DCF_____

   PV_____

   NPV_____

   IRR_____

   ARR_____

2. What the terms above have in common is: _____

   _____

3. The primary difference between IRR and ARR is _____

   _____.

4. When a project has a negative NPV, the present value of the _____

   _____ is _____ than the present value of the

   _____.

5. Accelerated or _____ depreciation is an example of

   _____.

6. Accelerated depreciation ignores _____ values and

   switches to _____ depreciation when

   _____.

7. A gain or loss on the sale of depreciable equipment is equal to _____ less _____.

8. The problem with adjusting depreciation for expected inflation in capital-budgeting analysis is _____.

9. If expected future cash flows are not adjusted for expected _____, then use the _____ rate of interest in DCF models.

10. The nominal rate of interest, also called the _____ rate of interest is the _____ rate plus the _____ rate.

Problems

1. Given for Solar Production Corp.:

Old machine: book value now $60,000, salvage value now	$ 8,000
New replacement machine:	
Price now	$110,000
Predicted useful life	13 years
Predicted residual value at end of useful life	$ 20,000
Predicted annual savings in cash operating expenses (increase in annual cash operating income)	$ 15,000
Minimum desired rate of return	10%
Present value of $1 due 13 years from now, using a 10% interest rate	$ 0.29
Present value of $1 per year due at the end of *each* of 13 years from now, using a 10% interest rate	$ 7.10

Should the old machine be replaced with the new machine? Show supporting computations:

2. Given for Swedish Sun Flower Energy Corporation's 20X4 operations:

Sales	$700,000
Straight-line depreciation expense	30,000
Other operating expenses, including cost of goods sold	600,000
Income tax rate	60%

   a. Compute net income

   b. Compute the annual value of the income tax savings from depreciation:

   c. Compute the after-tax net cash inflow from operations:

3. Given for GeoTherm Equipment Co.:

Initial cost of investing in a special-purpose machine	$540,000
Predicted useful life (no terminal disposal value)	15 years
Predicted annual savings in cash operating expenses	$ 90,000
Present value of an annuity of $1 for 15 years:	
Using a 8% interest rate	$ 8.559
Using a 10% interest rate	7.606
Using GeoTherm's opportunity cost of capital, 12%	6.811
Using a 14% interest rate	6.142
Using a 16% interest rate	5.575

   a. What is the NPV of this investment project?

   b. Is the IRR greater or less than GeoTherm's minimum required rate of return? Explain.

   c. Manually find the project's IRR to the nearest tenth of a percent, ignoring income tax effects. (Hint: begin by computing the payback period.)

Exercises

1. Given for TidalSurge Company

Initial cost of proposed new equipment	$130,000	
Predicted useful life	10	years
Predicted disposal value at end of useful life	$ 10,000	
Predicted savings per year in cash operating expenses	$ 24,000	
Present value of $1 due 10 years from now, using a 10% interest rate, which is TidalSurge's required rate of return	$ 0.385	
Present value of $1 per year due at the end of *each* of 10 years from now, using a 10% interest rate	$ 6.145	

Manually compute each of the following for this project, ignoring income tax effects:

a. NPV

b. Payback period

c. Depreciation expense per year by straight-line method:

d. Predicted increase in future annual net income:

e. ARR based on initial investment:

f. TidalSurge Company is an autonomous division of Consolidated Energy Corp, evaluated as an investment center, and currently has an accounting rate of return of 15%. Would the managers of TidalSurge be inclined to accept or reject this project? Explain.

2.   Zephyr Energy Company has just purchased a special piece of electrical generation equipment for $450,000. It is estimated to have a depreciable life of five years and a terminal scrap value of $30,000. Compute the following:

   a.   Depreciation for the first year:

           Straight-line method

           Accelerated depreciation method

   b.   Depreciation for the second year by accelerated depreciation

   c.   Income tax saving effect of accelerated depreciation compared with the straight-line method for the second year, assuming a 30% income tax rate

CHAPTER 11 SOLUTIONS TO PRACTICE TEST QUESTIONS AND PROBLEMS

True or False Statements

1. True   If the NPV of a project is zero, the project earns the minimum required rate of return and is acceptable.

2. False   The capital-budgeting post-audit process is similar to flexible-budgeting variance analysis. The purpose is to assess the quality of planning and implementation of capital projects and to determine whether continued investment is worthwhile.

3. True   This is the definition of internal rate of return. This IRR would be compared to the required rate of return to determine project acceptability.

4. False   A negative NPV means that the project is earning less than the required rate of return, or the IRR is less than the discount rate.

5. True   A positive NPV means that the project is earning more than the required rate of return; in this case, the IRR is greater than 15%.

6. False   Periodic depreciation is not a cash outflow, so it is not deducted from cash inflows when using DCF techniques. Depreciation is important as a tax shield, however.

7. True   By using an individual's or organization's opportunity cost of capital as the discount rate, DCF techniques measure either the value of a project in terms of equivalent investment required to earn the same cash flows (NPV) or the rate of return forgone if a project is not accepted (IRR).

8. True   Book values of assets really have no relevance for replacement decisions regarding future cash flows, except as they might impact gains or losses for tax purposes.

9. True   The ARR model is the expected net income divided by the average value of the investment; it has nothing to say about the time-value of money.

10. True   Postaudit is easier when the ARR method was used to choose capital projects because the information to compute ARR (and ROI) is readily available from the accounting system. But that does not mean the ARR is the preferred capital budgeting method.

11. True   The definition of the gain or loss on the disposal of depreciable equipment is the disposal value less the net book value of the equipment.

12. False   The gain or loss on the disposal of depreciable equipment has cash tax implications that affect tax payments in the year of disposal that are a function of, but are not equal to, the gain or loss.

13. False   If you use the pure rate of interest, it does not have an inflation component. To be consistent, do not adjust future cash flows for expected inflation, regardless of how bad you expect it to be. You might question whether using the pure rate without addition of a business risk adjustment (to get the "real" rate) is appropriate in this case. Many would argue that it is not appropriate and such low rates contributed to overinvestment in this type of project. Most government bodies now must use a real rate of interest.

14. False   At least in the U.S., depreciation expense for tax purposes is considered to be an allocation of past expense and cannot be adjusted for inflation. Therefore, the amount of the cash savings from depreciation will not be affected by inflation. This represents a loss of purchasing power in the tax savings.

15. False   This is an incomplete definition. The nominal rate or market rate is the sum of the "pure" or riskless rate plus a business-risk element plus an inflation element.

Multiple-Choice Questions

1. a, d   NPV (net present value) and IRR (internal rate of return) are both DCF (discounted cash flow) models. IMA is the Institute of Management Accountants; and ARR is accounting rate of return (a non-DCF approach to capital budgeting). AARP is the American Association of Retired Persons (more lame humor).

2. a   The payback period is $48,000 \div $11,000 = 4.36$ years or approximately 4.4 years.

3. c   The ARR = [$11,000 - ($48,000 \div 12)] \div $48,000 = $7,000 \div $48,000 = 14.6\%$.

4. a   The NPV is ($4,000 \times 3.170) - $10,000 = $2,680$.

5. d   The annual cash inflow would be computed as: $(C \times 3.170) - $10,000 = 0$; $C = $10,000 \div 3.170 = $3,155$.

6. c   The ARR is computed as: $[$15,000 - ($60,000 \div 10)] \div $60,000 = 15\%$.

7. d   The straight-line rate is $100\% \div 8 = 12.5\%$. Straight-line depreciation would be $0.125 \times $72,000 = $9,000$. The double-declining rate is then 25%. First-year accelerated depreciation is $0.25 \times $72,000 = $18,000$. The first-year advantage to using accelerated depreciation is the increase in shielded income times the tax rate: $($18,000 - $9,000) \times 0.4 = $3,600$ less tax.

8. c   The amount of gain or loss is the proceeds less the net book value. The net book value is the initial price less accumulated depreciation: $130,000 - 8 \times ($130,000 - $10,000) \div 10 = $34,000$. The gain on sale is $44,000 - $34,000 = $10,000$.

9. a   The after-tax effect is the proceeds less tax paid on the gain: $44,000 - (0.4 \times $10,000) = $40,000$.

Completion

1.   DCF = discounted cash flow; PV = present value; NPV = net present value; IRR = internal rate of return; ARR = accounting rate-of-return.

2.   All the terms refer to capital-budgeting models.

3.   IRR incorporates the time-value of money, whereas ARR does not.

4.   cash inflows, less, cash outflows (or cash outflows, greater, cash inflows)

5.   double-declining-balance, accelerated depreciation

6.   terminal disposal, straight-line, the accelerated depreciation would be less than straight-line depreciation.

7.   proceeds of the sale, net book value

8.   that it is not allowed for tax purposes in the U.S., so that would overstate the tax shield

9.   inflation, real

10.   market, real, expected inflation

Problems

1. Solar Production Corp.

   Present value of new machine's disposal value:

$20, 000 x 0. 29	$ 5,800

   Present value of annual savings:

$15,000 x 7.10	106,500
Total present value	$112,300

   Less required investment:

$110,000 - $8,000	102,000
Net present value of replacement	$ 10,300

   Decision: replace old machine ($60,000 book value is irrelevant)

2. Swedish Sun Flower Energy Corporation

a. Sales		$700,000
Less:		
Depreciation expense	$ 30,000	
Other operating expenses	600,000	630,000
Income before income taxes		$ 70,000
Less income taxes at 60%		42,000
Net income		$28,000

b. Depreciation	$30,000
Multiply by income tax rate	x 60%
Annual value of income tax savings from depreciation	$ 18,000

c. Sales		$700,000
Less:		
Other operating expenses	$600,000	
Income taxes, from (1) above	42,000	642,000
After-tax net cash inflow from operations		$ 58,000

Alternative computational methods for (c):

(i) Net income, from above	$ 28,000
Add back depreciation	30,000
After-tax net cash inflow from operations	$ 58,000
(ii) Sales	$700,000
Less other operating expenses	600,000
Cash inflows from operations before taxes and the depreciation effect	$100,000
Less applicable income tax outflow at 60%	60,000
After-tax effect of cash inflow from operations before the depreciation effect	$ 40,000
Add annual value of tax savings from depreciation: 60% of $30,000	18,000
After-tax net cash inflow from operations	$ 58,000

3. GeoTherm Equipment Co.

a. NPV = $90,000 x 6.811 - $540,000 = $72,990 (use the company's opportunity cost of capital)

b. The IRR is greater than the minimum rate of return. If the IRR were 12%, the NPV would be zero. The NPV is positive which means that the project earns more than 12%.

c. Payback period is $540,000 divided by $90,000 = 6 years

Because the IRR is greater than 12%, note that the payback period, which is the annuity factor of the IRR, lies between the annuity factors for 14% and 16%.

Present-Value Factors

Rate of return		
14%	6.142	6.142
True rate		6.000
16%	5.575	- .
Differences.	.567	.142

The IRR can be approximated by linear interpolations (which usually is close enough, as shown below):

IRR = 14% + (.142 ÷ .567) x 2% = 14% + (.25 x 2%) = 14.5%

Note: The estimate of IRR from a spreadsheet program is 14.4721%

Exercises

1. TidalSurge Company

   a. NPV

	$24,000 x 6.145	
	+ $10,000 x .385	
	- $130,000	<u>$21,330</u>

   b. Payback period: $130,000 ÷ $24,000   <u>5.4 years</u>

   c. Depreciation expense per year (by straight-line method): $(130,000 – 10,000) ÷ 10 years   <u>$12,000 per year</u>

   d. Predicted increase in future annual net income: $24,000 - $12,000   <u>$12,000</u>

   e. Accounting rate of return based on initial investment: $12,000 ÷ 130,000   <u>9.2%</u>

   f.   If TidalSurge used the ARR, it would be inclined to reject this project because the first-year ARR is less than the required ROI. Thus, accepting the project would reduce the segment's ROI, at least in the early part of the project. This is contrary to the advice from the NPV model which is to accept the project because it has a positive NPV. Also, the IRR must be greater than the required 10% rate of return, and the company as a whole would be better off with the project.

2. Zephyr Energy Company

   a. Straight-line

   ($450,000 - $30,000) ÷ 5 = <u>$84,000</u>

   Accelerated depreciation (ignore terminal value):

   SL rate = 100% ÷ 5 = 20%; ACCELERATED rate = 2 x 20% = 40%;

   Accelerated depreciation = 40% ($450,000) = <u>$180,000</u>

   b. Accelerated second year depreciation = 40% ($450,000 - $180,000) = $108,000

   c. ($108,000 - $84,000) x 30% = $24,000 x 30% = <u>$7,200</u> tax savings using accelerated depreciation

CHAPTER 12

Cost Allocation

OVERVIEW

This chapter focuses on purposes and methods for allocating indirect costs to products and organization segments. It is important to realize that cost allocations can affect behavior and decision making and that it is worthwhile to carefully consider how to perform cost allocations. Your learning objectives are to:

I.   Describe the general framework for cost allocation

II.   Allocate the variable and fixed costs of service departments to other organizational units

III.   Use the direct and step-down methods to allocate service department costs to user departments

IV.   Integrate service-department allocation systems with traditional and ABC systems to allocate total systems costs to product or service cost objects

V.   Allocate costs associated with customer actions to customers

VI.   Allocate the central corporate costs of an organization

VII.   Allocate joint costs to products using the physical-units and relative-sales-value methods

| I. | **Describe the general framework for cost allocation** |

The assignment of costs to cost objectives is called **cost allocation.** The process of cost allocation is fundamental to managerial accounting. It should be done based on careful reasoning.

A. The basic conceptual approach of cost allocation is twofold:

    1. Group similar costs together in a *cost pool*. Costs are similar if they have the same *cost driver(s)* that plausibly links costs with objectives (e.g., from analysis of cost behavior, as discussed in Chapter 3).

    2. Use cost-driver activity as an **allocation base**; that is, divide each cost pool by its allocation base to obtain the **allocation rate**. If budgeted costs and budgeted cost-driver activity are used, the rates are budgeted rates.

    3. Allocate costs to the cost objective based on that objective's *actual* level of cost-driver activity.

B. Major purposes of cost allocation are:

    1. To measure costs and profits of segments and individual products and projects

    2. To help determine output prices or reimbursements that are based on costs

    3. To promote goal congruence and managerial effort, and thus to obtain desired motivation of managers

    4. To predict the economic effects of planning and control decisions

C. The first two purposes of cost allocation will be accomplished (for better or worse) with any arbitrary cost allocation scheme. Carefully designed cost allocations may promote reliable measures of cost and profitability. Only carefully prepared cost allocations can accomplish the last two purposes.

D. Basic types of cost allocations include:

    1. Allocation from central cost pools to responsibility centers for measuring costs of responsibility center operations, as discussed in Chapter 9

    2. Re-allocation from one center to other centers via transfer prices for services or products, as discussed in Chapter 10

    3. Allocation to products or services for sale to customers and clients

E. An important reason to allocate costs is to determine costs for financial reporting or for pricing outputs of tangible products or intangible services. Costs of operating departments, which include costs allocated from service departments, are often allocated to products or services of the operating departments.

F. Indirect costs of a product or a service are allocated using bases that explain how the indirect costs are incurred. Note these should be the same as the cost drivers discussed in Chapter 3. Common allocation bases include:

    1. machine hours

    2. direct labor-hours or cost

    3. number of transactions to complete a product or service

    4. number of components of a product or service.

II. Allocate the variable and fixed costs of service departments to other organizational units

Guidelines for allocating costs are:

A. Allocate costs and evaluate actual results using budgets.

B. If possible, divide the costs of each service department into *two pools:* variable and fixed, with appropriate cost drivers for each cost pool.

    1. Allocate the variable-cost pool to other segments by multiplying the budgeted variable-cost rate by the actual activity level.

    2. The use of predetermined cost rates protects the using departments from operational inefficiencies of service departments and subsequent price changes.

    3. Allocate the fixed-cost pool in lump sums to other segments by multiplying the budgeted total fixed costs by the *budgeted proportions of cost-driver capacity available to users.*

        a. This predetermined *lump-sum* allocation prevents the allocations to user departments from being affected by the actual usage of other departments.

        b. Thus, motivational effects of allocation are less likely to be dysfunctional.

    4. Many critics of current cost allocation practice argue that the allocation base level should be the *practical capacity* of the activity and allocation should be on the basis of activity used, *not* as a lump sum.

        a. That way, any unallocated costs, because operating segments did not utilize the capacity, are an indication of the costs of *excess capacity.*

        b. Using practical capacity also avoids the so-called "death spiral" where decreasing utilization leads to higher budgeted rates, higher costs, higher prices and then lower utilization because of demand decreases and even higher rates, and so on until the service or even the company cannot recover its costs and disappears.

C. Communicate the method and rationale for cost allocation to all affected parties.

    1. Managers will have the opportunity to respond and plan accordingly.

    2. Allocations are more likely to be viewed as fair, and they will be less likely to cause undesirable motivational effects.

D. Organizations typically incur many **central costs** such as expenses of corporate headquarters and various company-wide expenses.

    1. Because of the lack of a plausible allocation scheme, many companies do not allocate such costs.

    2. However, if these costs are to be allocated, an undesirable motivational effect can usually be avoided by using the same approach described above for allocating the fixed costs of a service department.

III.	Use the direct and step-down methods to allocate service department costs to user departments

There are general methods for allocating service costs to other segments: *direct, step-down*, and *reciprocal methods*. **Is "reciprocal" a method? Could only find mention of reciprocal "services"**

A. The **direct method** service costs are allocated directly to segments without consideration of *reciprocal* services among service departments.

B. The **step-down method** first ranks service departments according to their generality of service. The most general service costs are allocated to other service centers and segments and so on until all service costs have been allocated to segments. This method recognizes some reciprocal services, but only from the more general to the less general.

> **Stop and Review**
>
> See and work through textbook
> Exhibits 12-4 and 12-5

> **Study Tip:** *Before going to the next section, review again the guidelines and procedures for allocating service center costs to operating segments.*

IV.	Integrate service-department allocation systems with traditional and ABC systems to allocate total systems costs to product or service cost objects

Activity-based costing is the approach to assigning (or *attributing*) costs to outputs that relies specifically on using cost-driver activities as allocation bases.

A. Traditionally, costs have been allocated in many companies on the basis of some volume activity such as sales or direct labor input that is directly proportional to unit volume.

B. Because of changing technology and competitive pressures, firms are finding that other activities such as complexity and time-related activities also drive costs.

C. Because segments are evaluated as cost or profit centers, better decisions are being made with activity-based costs.

D. Activity-based costing first accumulates costs into cost pools corresponding to basic activities (i.e., driven by the same cost drivers).

E. The second step is to apply costs from the activity-based pools to products and services based on actual usage of cost-driver activity.

F. In concept, this is not a different approach to cost allocation, but it is a different approach to identifying cost pools and allocation bases.

> **Stop and Review**
>
> See textbook Exhibits 12-6 through 12-8

V.	Allocate costs associated with customer actions to customers

To properly allocate costs, accountants must attribute the costs of customer actions to the customers themselves. Customer profitability depends on two factors:

A. Costs incurred to fulfill customer orders and provide services such as order changes, returns, scheduling, and delivery.

    1. A cost-to-serve percentage provides relevant information for cost allocation and is calculated as: cost-to-serve ÷ sales revenue

2. Different customers have different cost-to-serve traits:

Low Cost-to-Serve	High Cost-to-Serve
Large order quantity	Small order quantity
Few order changes	Many order changes
Little pre and post-sales support	Large amounts of pre and post-sales support
Regular scheduling	Expedited scheduling
Standard delivery	Special delivery requirements
Few returns	Frequent returns

B. The next factor in determining customer profitability is the gross margin of the product mix purchased.

> **Stop and Review**
>
> See textbook Exhibits 12-9 through 12-14

> **Study Tip:** *Before going on to the next section, make sure that you understand the factors that determine customer profitability and complete the Summary Problem on p. 546.*

VI.   Allocate the central corporate costs of an organization

A. Cost allocation has four purposes:

1. To predict economic effects of planning and control decisons

2. To motivate managers and employees

3. To measure the costs of inventory and the cost of goods sold

4. To justify costs for pricing or reimbursement

B. The dual method of cost allocation is used for service department costs.

1. Variable costs should be allocated using budgeted cost rates multiplied by the actual cost-driver level.

2. Fixed costs should be allocated using budgeted percent of capacity available for use multiplied by total budgeted fixed costs.

C. Central costs include public relations, top corporate management overhead, legal, data processing, controller's department, and company-wide planning.

1. It is usually best to only allocate the central costs of an organization for which measures of usage by departments are available.

2. Service department costs should be allocated using either the direct or step-down method.

VII.   Allocate joint costs to products using the physical-units and relative-sales-value methods

A. Different allocation bases can lead to greatly different product costs and may lead to greatly different *transfer-pricing* and production decisions by managers who are evaluated by segment margins. (Recall the presentations in Chapters 9 and 10.)

B. Joint production costs are often allocated to joint products:

1. using physical units

2. using relative sales value

3.   more recently, using other cost-driver levels

4.   Note that **by-products** do not receive allocations of joint costs.

Stop and Review

See the textbook examples of joint cost
allocation on pp. 550 and 551

PRACTICE TEST QUESTIONS AND PROBLEMS
True or False Statements

Determine whether each of the following statements is True (T) or False (F), and enter your answer in the space provided.

_____1.   The term *cost driver* is just another name for *cost allocation base.*

_____2.   Prior to allocation, all costs should be gathered in a cost pool for convenience so that the same cost driver can be used.

_____3.   The direct method of allocating service department costs ignores all services rendered by service departments to other service departments.

_____4.   Bases for allocating indirect costs to products are completely arbitrary and should not be made because the products cannot be observed causing the costs.

_____5.   Acceptable ways of dealing with the central costs of an organization include not allocating to organization segments, or allocating by an activity-based cost approach.

_____6.   The step-down method of allocating service department costs ignores the reciprocal services among service departments.

_____7.   Fixed costs should be allocated as a lump sum based on budgeted use, so that costs of excess capacity are evident.

_____8.   Allocations of some central costs on the basis of either budgeted or actual sales is inaccurate because the allocations indicate ability to pay for central costs, not usage of central costs.

_____9.   If a cost in a particular cost pool is found to not be caused by its assigned cost driver, the cost should be placed in the unallocated cost pool.

Multiple-Choice Questions

For each of the following multiple-choice questions, select the best answer(s), and enter the identification letter(s) in the space provided.

_____1.   The major purposes of cost allocation include: (a) obtaining a basis for setting output prices, (b) measuring income and asset valuations, (c) aiding in making planning and control decisions, (d) motivating employees.

_____2.   Basic types of cost allocations include (a) allocation of costs to segments, products, and services, (b) determining inputs for CVP models, (c) establishing cash flows for capital-budgeting analyses, (d) reallocation of costs among service departments.

_____3. A service department in a large company presents the following data:

- budgeted variable costs per direct labor-hour $1.50;

- actual direct labor-hours: 8,000 for Producing Dept. A, 12,000 for B;

- budgeted labor-hours: for A: 9,000, for B: 11,000;

- long-run expected direct-labor hours: for A: 11,000, for B: 9,000.

Compute the allocation of variable costs to A if actual variable costs are $40,000: (a) $16,000, (b) $12,000, (c) $18,000, (d) $13,500.

_____4. Service Departments A and B each have $80,000 of overhead to be allocated. They render 20% of their services to each other. Producing Department C receives 10% of the service of A and 30% of the service of B. Use the step-down method to compute the total overhead to be allocated to C from A and B. Begin with Department B. Service costs allocated to Department C are: (a) $32,000, (b) $40,000, (c) $34,000, (d) $36,000.

_____5. Service Department S has $70,000 of overhead to be allocated. It renders 30% of its service to other service departments, 10% to Producing Department Q, and the remainder to all the other producing departments. The cost to be allocated from S to Q by the direct method is: (a) $7,000, (b) $11,667, (c) $49,000, (d) $10,000.

_____6. Two service departments, S1 and S2, have direct costs of $10,000 and $19,000, respectively. S1 is the more general service department and provides 20% of its service to S2, 40% to P1 and 40% to P2. If S2 provides 10% of its service to S1, 60% to P1, and 30% to P2, the cost allocated from S2 to P1 after the second stage of the step-down method is: (a) $12,600, (b) $11,400, (c) $14,000, (d) $13,300.

_____7. A joint process that cost $6,000 results in two products: 100 units of A and 50 units of B. Using a physical-units basis, the allocated cost per unit is: (a) A: $60, B: $120, (b) A: $20, B: $20, (c) A: $40, B: $40, (d) A: $80, B: $80.

Completion

Complete each of the following statements by filling in the blanks.

1. A convincing or plausible link between costs and cost objectives is called a _____.

2. Before allocating costs, one should usually group like costs into _____ that are determined by _____.

3. The contribution margin by segments is _____ less _____.

4. In the allocation of costs of such services as power, the variable-cost element may be distributed by a _____ and the fixed-cost element may be distributed as a _____.

5. In order to prevent the fixed-cost charges to a given operating department from depending on the quantity of services actually consumed by other operating departments, one can use allocation amounts based on _____ hours and costs.

6. Using a cost allocation base that reflects the _____ of indirect costs can promote _____.

7. By-products of joint processes never receive _____.

8. Activity-based cost allocations are based on _____.

9.	ABC cost allocations should lead to _____ because
	_____.

10.	Decisions about joint products should never _____.

Problems

1. Shrub Company's own power plant provides electricity for its two producing departments, X and Y. The 20X4 budget for the power plant shows:

Budgeted fixed costs $70,000

Budgeted variable costs per kilowatt hour (KWH) $ 0.18

Additional data for 20X4:	Dept. X	Dept. Y
Long-run demand (KWH)	420,000	280,000
Budgeted for 20X4 (KWH)	310,000	200,000
Actual for 20X4 (KWH)	320,000	160,000

Actual power plant costs for 20X4 are:

Fixed $78,000

Variable $90,000

Compute the 20X4 allocation of power plant costs to Departments X and Y:

	a. Fixed	b. Variable
Dept. X	$	$
Dept. Y	$	$

2. Expert Innovations, Inc., provides the following information:

	Service Dept. 1	Service Dept. 2	Production Dept. X	All Other Production Depts.
Overhead costs before allocation	$4,000	$4,600	$5,000	$51,000
Proportions of service furnished by Dept. 1	-	20%	30%	50%
Proportions of service furnished by Dept. 2	10%	-	40%	50%

a. Use the *direct method* to allocate costs and determine the total overhead of Dept. X after allocation.

	Dept. 1	Dept. 2	Dept. X	Others
Overhead costs before allocation	$4,000	$4,600	$5,000	$51,000

b. Use the *step-down method* to allocate costs and determine the total overhead of Dept. X after allocation. *Begin with Dept. 1.*

	Dept. 1	Dept. 2	Dept. X	Others
Overhead costs before allocation	$4,000	$4,600	$5,000	$51,000

Exercises

1. Lewis Company uses a $5,000 joint process to produce X, Y, and Z. Use the following data to compute the cost per unit of each product using (a) physical units and then (b) relative sales value.

Product	Units	Sales price per unit	Separable costs after split-off
X	500	$12.00	$1,000
Y	700	$ 5.00	$3,000
Z	50	$ 1.00	0

   a. Physical units:

   b. Relative sales value:

2. TunnelView Services has three basic service products, Alpha, Beta, and Gamma. Overhead has been applied to products on the basis of 150% of direct design cost. The controller of TunnelView has determined from activity analysis that overhead costs should be split in at least three separate cost pools and allocated according to separate cost drivers.

The following information is now available:

	Alpha	Beta	Gamma	New overhead rates
Direct design cost	$900	$2,000	$1,000	@20% of design cost
Computer time	8 hours	14 hours	3 hours	@ $65 per hour
Systems integration	10 hours	26 hours	5 hours	@ $110 per hour

   a. Compute the overhead cost of each product using the old overhead rate of 150% of direct design cost.

   b. Compute the cost of each product using the new overhead rates.

   c. Discuss the implications of the differences in product costs.

True or False Statements

1. False   The term cost driver implies a cause-and-effect relationship between a particular cost and an underlying activity. A cost allocation base can be any basis for assigning costs. It is believed that using cost drivers as allocation bases will result in better decision making, because the allocated costs will more closely represent "true" cost behavior.

2. False   The issue is more than convenience. Each cost pool should contain costs that can be affected by different usage of the assigned cost drivers.

3. True   The direct method allocates all service department costs directly to operating segments. If there are significant interdependencies among service departments, this could lead to somewhat different cost allocation than using the step-down method.

4. False   Because indirect costs cannot be observed as they are incurred, there is some element of subjectivity in allocating them. However, the techniques of activity analysis, discussed in Chapter 3, can go a long way toward making the process of allocating indirect costs more objective—effectively transforming indirect into direct costs. Besides, even subjectively determined allocations could create desired motivations and behaviors.

5. True   If cost drivers cannot be identified, then perhaps it is best not to allocate central costs. However, if appropriate cost drivers can be identified, planning and control of central costs are enhanced by allocating them to operating segments. Some believe that central costs should be allocated if only to make operating segments aware of the magnitude of central costs and so that they will complain if central costs seem to be greater than necessary.

6. True   The step-down method recognizes one-way services among service departments, but not true reciprocal services.

7. False   Allocations of fixed costs as lump sums on budgeted use prevents distortions of cost allocations due to other departments' usage. However, this does not indicate the magnitude of excess capacity. Allocations based on units of capacity used might leave some capacity costs unallocated, which would indicate excess capacity.

8. True   Few central costs are *caused* by segment sales levels; thus most allocations based on either budgeted or actual sales levels are based on a "deep pockets" approach to allocation. These allocations, though common in practice because they are convenient, are unlikely to fulfill the purposes of cost allocation.

9. False   This is one response, but a better one would be to try to find the appropriate cost driver. Failing that, the cost may be assigned to the unallocated pool.

Multiple-Choice Questions

1. a,b,c,d   All of these are purposes of cost allocations; whether cost allocations succeed depends on the care and effort taken to design the allocations.

2. a, d   Cost allocations are not suitable for either CVP modeling or capital budgeting; for these purposes, costs should be separated by cost behavior only. Allocations are intended to assign costs to segments, products, and services and to re-allocate costs among service centers for income measurement, pricing, and motivational purposes.

3. b   The allocation of variable costs to operating departments should be at budgeted rates and actual usage: $1.50 x 8,000 = $12,000.

4. d   Use the following approach:

	A	B	C	Others
Overhead	$ 80,000	$ 80,000		
Allocate B (.2, .3, .5)	16,000	(80,000)	$ 24,000	$ 40,000
Allocate A [0.1/(1.0-0.2) = 1/8 to C; (1.0 – 0.1 –0.2)/(1.0 – 0.2) = 7/8 to others]	$(96,000)		12,000	84,000
Totals			$36,000 (d)	$124,000

5. d   Ignore uses by other service departments. 100% - 30% = 70%; 10% ÷ 70% = 1/7, $70,000 x 1/7 = $10,000 (d)

6. c   Allocation of S1 to S2: 0.2 x $10,000 = $2,000. Allocation of S2 to P1: [0.6/(0.6 + 0.3)] x ($2,000 + $19,000) = 0.6667 x $21,000 = $14,000 (c).

7. c   Using the only physical basis available in this problem, number of units, the joint cost per unit is $6,000 ÷ 150 units = $40 per unit.

Completion

1.   cost driver or cost allocation base

2.   cost pools, common cost drivers

3.   net sales, variable costs

4.   budgeted (or standard) rate per unit of services consumed, lump-sum predetermined monthly charge

5.   predetermined (or budgeted)

6.   cause or cost driver, improved cost control and decision making

7.   allocations of joint costs

8.   usage of cost drivers

9.   better decision making, product costs more closely reflect how costs are incurred

10.   be based on allocated joint costs

Problems

1. Shrub Company

   a. Use long-run demand to allocate budgeted fixed costs

   (total KWH: 420,000 + 280,000 = 700,000):

   Dept. X: (420,000/700,000) x $70,000 = $42,000

   Dept. Y: (280,000/700,000) x $70,000 = $28,000

   b. Use predetermined rates and actual KWH to allocate variable costs:

   Dept. X: $0.18 x 320,000 = $57,600

   Dept. Y: $0.18 x 160,000 = $28,800

   (Unallocated actual costs for 20X4 may be written off to expense at end of year.)

2. Expert Innovations, Inc.

   a. direct method

	Dept. 1	Dept. 2	Dept. X	Others
Overhead costs before allocation	$ 4,000	$ 4,600	$5,000	$51,000
Dept. 1 costs allocated, 3/8 and 5/8	($4,000)		1,500	2,500
Dept. 2 costs allocated, 4/9 and 5/9		(4,600)	2,044	2,556
Totals			$8,544	$56,056

   b. step-down method

	Dept. 1	Dept. 2	Dept. X	Others
Overhead costs before allocation	$ 4,000	$ 4,600	$5,000	$51,000
Dept. 1 costs allocated, .2, .3, .5	(4,000)	800	1,200	2,000
Dept. 2 costs allocated, 4/9, 5/9		(5,400)	2,400	3,000
Totals			$8,600	$56,000

Exercises

1. Lewis Company

a. Physical units

Product	Units	Weighting	Allocation of Joint Cost	Separable Costs	Cost per Unit
X	500	5/12 x $5,000 =	$2,083	$1,000	(2,083 +1,000)/ 500 = $6.17
Y	700	7/12 x $5,000 =	2,917	3,000	(2,917 + 3,000)/ 700 = $8.45
Z*	-				
Total	1200		$5,000		

b. Relative sales value

Product	Revenue	Relative sales value less Separable Costs	Weighting	Allocation of Joint Cost	Cost per Unit
X	500 x $12 = $6,000	$6,000 - $1,000 = $5,000	$5,000 ÷ $5,500 = 90.9%	$5,000 x 0.909 = $4,545	($1,000+$4,545)÷500= $11.09
Y	700 x $5 = $3,500	$3,500 - $3,000 = $500	$500 ÷ $5,500 = 9.1%	$5,000 x 0.091 = $455	($3,000 + $455) ÷ 700 = $4.94
Z*	50 x $1 = $50				
totals		$5,500	100%	$5,000	

*Z should be treated as a by-product.

2. TunnelView Services

    a. Using 150% of direct design cost:

	Alpha	Beta	Gamma
Direct design cost	$900	$2,000	$1,000
Overhead @ 150%	$1,350	$3,000	$1,500

    b. Using new overhead rates:

	New overhead rates	Alpha	Beta	Gamma
Design cost overhead	@20% of design cost	0.2 x $900 =$180	0.2 x $2,000 =$400	0.2 x $1,000 =$200
Computer time overhead	@ $65 per hour	8x$65 = $520	14x$65 = $910	3x$65 = $195
Systems integration	@ $110 per hour	10x$110=$1,100	26x$110=$2,860	5x$110 = $550
Total overhead cost		$1,800	$4,170	$ 945

c. All of the overhead costs differ, several dramatically. The overhead cost of Alpha is 33% higher using the new overhead rates. The cost of Beta is 39% higher, but the cost of Gamma is 37% lower using the new rates. The reason for these differences in costs is that each service uses relatively different amounts of the three cost drivers. The new overhead rates charge services for their usage of the activities that drive costs. Direct design cost was shown to drive much less overhead cost than previously believed. The old, single rate penalized relatively high design-cost products but did not consider that these services may use relatively less computer time or systems integration. Conversely, the old rate unfairly shielded services with low direct-design time but high levels of computer and systems-integration time. If the activity analysis is valid, the new service costs are more accurate. These new service costs should lead to improved decision making (e.g., pricing, service mix, and so on).

CHAPTER 13

Accounting for Overhead Costs

OVERVIEW

This chapter examines the application of overhead costs to products and services. Much of this chapter discusses the difference between two approaches to income measurement: variable costing and absorption costing. The difference between them is the treatment of fixed factory-overhead costs as either noninventoriable (period) costs by variable costing or inventoriable (product) costs by absorption costing. Your learning objectives are to:

I.   Compute budgeted factory-overhead rates and apply factory overhead to production

II.   Determine and use appropriate cost-allocation bases for overhead application to products and services

III.   Identify the meaning and purpose of normalized overhead rates

IV.   Construct an income statement using the variable-costing approach

V.   Construct an income statement using the absorption-costing approach

VI.   Compute the production-volume variance and show how it should appear in the income statement

VII.   Explain why a company might prefer to use a variable-costing approach

I.	**Compute budgeted factory-overhead rates and apply factory overhead to production**

A.   Factory overhead is usually applied by a budgeted rate.

B.   Many factory costs are indirect manufacturing costs and thus cannot be traced easily to specific jobs. (ABC seeks to improve cost tracing.)

C.   Therefore, the amounts of factory-overhead cost applicable to specific jobs must be allocated by a reasonable procedure that measures consumption of basic resources and activities.

D.   A budgeted rate is preferred to an actual rate because:

         1.   budgeted rates are more timely, if less accurate, than actual rates

         2.   budgeted rates promote efficiency

E.   Separate fixed-cost and variable-cost allocations are preferable, but a more traditional practice is to use a single overhead rate to cover total overhead.

F.   Organizations usually budget a rate on an annual basis by dividing budgeted factory overhead by the budgeted activity base (that is, the budgeted cost-driver level or cost-allocation base). Such predetermined overhead rates are typically used on an annualized basis rather than a monthly basis in order to avoid month-to-month fluctuations in overhead cost rates.

G.   Ideally, the cost-allocation base used in a particular production process should be the principal cost driver, that is, the activity that causes the cost.

H.   *Applied overhead* is the budgeted rate times the *actual* usage of cost-driver activity.

I.   The *excess* of the applied overhead over the actual overhead incurred is called *overapplied overhead* or overabsorbed overhead.

J.   If the actual amount of overhead incurred *exceeds* the applied amount, the difference is called *underapplied* or underabsorbed overhead.

K.   The amount of underapplied or overapplied overhead is disposed of in two alternative ways: with an end of the year write-off to the period or *proration* over inventories.

         1.   **Immediate write-off:** If the underapplied or overapplied amount is relatively small, as it typically is, the entire amount is treated as an adjustment of the year's net income.

                 a.   This means that it is simply written off directly to cost of goods sold (an addition if factory overhead is underapplied, a subtraction if overapplied).

                 b.   Such an immediate write-off is largely justified because most of the manufactured products usually have been sold by the end of the year.

                 c.   Another justification for such treatment is that when there is underapplied overhead, it is due mostly to *inefficiencies* or to the *underutilization of available facilities* (which would not be appropriate costs of the inventory assets).

         2.   **Proration:** If there is a *relatively large* amount of underapplied or overapplied overhead, it may be **prorated.**

                 a.   This means that the amount is allocated to the three balances that were affected by the use of budgeted overhead rates: work-in-process inventory, finished-goods inventory, and cost of goods sold.

      b.   This method tends to adjust applied costs to an actual basis and is therefore conceptually appealing if the difference is due to large forecasting errors.

II.   Determine and use appropriate cost-allocation bases for overhead application to products and services

    A.   No one cost driver is appropriate in all situations.

    B.   Cost drivers should reflect cause-and-effect relations between costs and cost drivers.

    C.   The number of cost pools used to allocate overhead should be the same as the number of cost drivers used.

III.   Identify the meaning and purpose of normalized overhead rates

The cost system we are describing is sometimes called an *actual cost system.*

    A.   However, it is more accurately called a **normal costing system** because the factory overhead included in product costs is not the actual amount incurred but is the amount applied by means of *budgeted* overhead rates.

    B.   Typically, the normal system is used to cost products during the year, and the year-end procedures described above are used to reconcile total results to an approximate actual-cost basis.

> **Study Tip:** *Before going on to the next section, review this long section and be sure that you understand how costs are applied to products, batches, and jobs using job-order costing. Do you understand the calculation, meaning and disposition of underapplied or overapplied overhead?*

IV.   Construct an income statement using the variable-costing approach

    A.   There are two major approaches in the application of costs to products for measuring net income:

        1.   The contribution approach to income measurement uses **variable costing,** less accurately called **direct costing.**

            a.   Recall that in variable costing, *fixed manufacturing overhead costs* are treated immediately as *expense* and therefore are *excluded from product inventories,* which include *only* direct material, direct labor, and *variable* factory overhead costs.

            b.   Variable costing is growing in use for internal performance reports to management, but it is not acceptable for income tax purposes or external reporting.

        2.   The second approach is absorption costing. The essential difference between these two costing methods is *timing* of the recognition of the expense of fixed manufacturing overhead costs.

> **Stop and Review**
>
> See textbook Exhibit 13-2

            a.   In absorption costing, fixed manufacturing overhead is *first included in inventory* and therefore is treated as an *unexpired cost* (an *asset*) until the period in which the inventory is sold and included in cost of goods sold (an *expense*).

b. However, in variable costing, fixed manufacturing overhead is regarded as an *expired cost* and is *charged against sales immediately,* only *variable* manufacturing costs being included in product inventories.

3. These two approaches can produce different reported figures for net income.

a. Notice that when the *quantity of inventory increases* during a period, absorption costing will generally report *more net income* than variable costing. This is because a portion of the period's fixed manufacturing overhead cost was assigned to products that *remain* in inventory, whereas in variable costing all the period's fixed manufacturing overhead was recognized as expense.

b. However, when the *quantity of inventory decreases* during a period, absorption costing will generally report *less net income* than variable costing. Each unit was assigned a portion of fixed manufacturing overhead, and some units had been produced in a prior period. Because more units were sold than were produced, the total fixed manufacturing overhead included in cost of goods sold was greater than the *current* period's fixed manufacturing overhead *cost.* In variable costing, only the current period's fixed manufacturing overhead cost was expensed, none from a previous period.

c. You should also note that the absorption-costing approach includes a plus or minus adjustment to gross profit for the *production-volume variance* in fixed factory overhead (this will be covered later).

4. Two principal purposes of a cost-accounting system are for planning and control and for product costing. As mentioned in earlier chapters, some firms use multiple cost systems to accomplish these separate purposes.

a. If the proper cost drivers are identified, virtually any cost system can assist in planning, controlling, and applying *variable* costs to products and services.

i. This is because, as activity levels increase, the total variable costs rise proportionately.

ii. Difficulties in working with variable costs arise when appropriate cost drivers are not known, or it is too costly to use them for accounting purposes.

b. On the other hand, planning, controlling, and applying fixed costs for product-costing purposes can be more confusing.

i. For planning and control purposes, total fixed costs may be predicted and evaluated as constant levels of expenditure within a specific relevant range.

ii. If variable costing is used, the role of fixed costs in product costing is also simple—it is expensed as a cost of the period.

iii. However, for financial reporting using absorption-costing, fixed costs are applied on a *per-unit* basis, and the method of allocating fixed costs to units of product or service will affect product costs and reported, absorption-cost-based income.

iv. Fixed cost applied to products under absorption costing is a function of the fixed overhead rate:

Fixed cost applied = actual activity level × fixed-overhead rate

V. Construct an income statement using the absorption-costing method

A.   The full-costing, functional, or traditional approach uses **absorption costing.**

   1.   Recall that in absorption costing, *fixed manufacturing overhead costs* are treated initially as *product costs* and therefore are *included in product inventories* and cost of goods manufactured and sold, along with direct material, direct labor, and *variable* manufacturing overhead costs.

   2.   Absorption costing must be used for U.S. income tax purposes and is generally accepted for making financial reports to stockholders and other external parties.

B.   To obtain an absorption product cost for pricing and inventory uses, one must select an expected level of activity as the basis for applying fixed overhead.

   1.   A budgeted rate for applying fixed factory overhead is then predetermined for a given year:

   Fixed-overhead rate = budgeted fixed overhead ÷ expected activity level.

   2.   Most absorption-cost systems, since they are primarily for financial reporting rather than internal decision making, use *expected* unit production volume as the allocation base.

      a.   Because the resulting rates and unit costs have limited significance for planning, pricing, and control purposes, many companies are beginning to use activity analysis and activity-based costing (Chapters 3 and 4) to determine more appropriate cost drivers for variable costs and for applying fixed costs.

      b.   The analysis that follows, however, applies conceptually to absorption costing, regardless of the nature of the fixed overhead allocation base.

      c.   Some accountants argue that the best fixed overhead allocation base is **practical capacity**, which is the level of production activity that would utilize facilities optimally.   When expected or actual production is less than optimal, the production-volume variance is an indication of the cost of excess capacity— excess fixed cost that is incurred because production is lower than the facility was designed for.

VI. Compute the production-volume variance and show how it should appear in the income statement

A **production-volume variance** arises whenever the actual production volume deviates from the expected or practical-capacity level. (For ease of discussion, we will use only expected levels from here on.)

A.   When actual production volume is *less* than the expected volume, the fixed overhead production-volume variance is *unfavorable* because fixed overhead expected is greater than applied (or fixed overhead is *underapplied*).

B.   When actual production volume is *greater* than the expected volume, the volume variance is *favorable* because fixed overhead applied is greater than expected (or fixed overhead is *overapplied*).

Production-volume variance =   Applied fixed overhead - budgeted fixed overhead

=   (actual volume x fixed-overhead rate) - (expected volume x

fixed-overhead rate)

=   (actual volume - expected volume) x fixed-overhead rate

C. This variance is similar in nature to the sales-activity variance discussed in Chapter 8. It is the result of actual activity (production volume in this case) differing from the expected level. When the two production levels are equal, there is no production-volume variance.

VII.	Explain why a company might prefer to use a variable-costing approach

Many companies use the variable-costing approach for their internal income statements.

A. One reason is that an increase in the quantity of product manufactured would, of course, not affect reported operating income because there would be no effect on the amount of fixed overhead expensed in the period.

    1. On the other hand, if the absorption-costing approach is used, an increase in the quantity of goods manufactured would reduce an unfavorable production-volume variance (an expense).

    2. Thus, there would be an increase in reported operating income, which might be falsely interpreted as an improvement in operating performance.

B. Another reason, as mentioned in earlier chapters, is that variable costing is consistent with CVP planning models, and evaluating performance by comparing plans with actual results is easier.

PRACTICE TEST QUESTIONS AND PROBLEMS
True or False Statements

Determine whether each of the following statements is True (T) or False (F), and enter your answer in the space provided.

_____1. In the U.S., the variable-costing approach is an acceptable alternative to absorption costing for internal reporting, income tax reporting, and external reporting.

_____2. Actual factory overhead incurred should be charged to work-in-process.

_____3. Manufacturing overhead costs are treated as expenses of the period by both the absorption-costing and the variable-costing methods.

_____4. If underapplied overhead is caused by forecasting errors, the year-end treatment that is most justified is the proration method.

_____5. Unfavorable production-volume variances in fixed factory overhead costs that occur in the absorption-costing approach should be reported as expenses.

_____6. If direct-labor factory workers are paid unequal hourly wage rates, direct-labor dollars would most likely be a better base for applying overhead to labor-intensive jobs than direct-labor hours.

_____7. The fixed overhead spending variance occurs only in absorption costing.

_____8. Variable costing and absorption costing differ in the way variances are disposed of.

_____9. When inventories increase, variable-cost-based income is greater than absorption-cost-based income.

_____10. During a particular period, factory overhead was overapplied by $10,000, and total credits to factory overhead were $150,000. Therefore, total debits to factory overhead for the period were $140,000.

Multiple-Choice Questions

For each of the following multiple-choice questions, select the best answer(s), and enter the identification letter(s) in the space provided.

Use these selected data (in millions) for the first three test items:

Fixed selling expenses	$ 10
Variable selling expenses	$ 30
Fixed factory overhead	$ 50
Variable factory overhead	$ 15

_____1.   In a variable-costing income statement, the total of the above amounts to be included as part of the contribution margin is: (a) $30, (b) $40, (c) $45, (d) $60.

_____2.   In a variable-costing income statement, the total of the above amounts to be excluded from the contribution margin is: (a) $40, (b) $45, (c) $60, (d) $65.

_____3.   In an absorption-costing income statement, the total of the above amounts to be included in gross profit is: (a) $40, (b) $45, (c) $60, (d) $65.

_____4.   Factory overhead applied should be: (a) debited to finished goods, (b) debited to cost of goods sold, (c) credited to cost of goods manufactured, (d) debited to work-in-process.

_____5.   A labor-intensive service company budgeted for 20X3 a total of 40,000 direct-labor hours and $220,000 of overhead costs. However, the actual 20X3 amounts were 44,000 hours and $240,000 cost, respectively. Compute the proper rate for applying overhead to programs: (a) $5.00, (b) $5.45, (c) $5.50, (d) $6.00.

_____6.   See the preceding test item. The applied overhead should be: (a) $220,000, (b) $240,000, (c) $242,000, (d) $264,000.

_____7.   See items 5 and 6 above. Overhead in 20X3 was: (a) $2,000 overapplied, (b) $2,000 underapplied, (c) $20,000 overapplied, (d) $20,000 underapplied.

_____8.   A company reported for 20X4 sales of $790,000, cost of goods sold $500,000, $190,000 of applied overhead, and overapplied overhead amounting to $10,000. The actual factory overhead incurred was: (a) $190,000, (b) $200,000, (c) $180,000, (d) $515,000.

_____9.   See the preceding test item. If the year-end overhead difference was not prorated, the gross profit would be (a) $300,000, (b) $265,000, (c) $275,000, (d) $288,000.

_____10.   See test item 8. If the year-end difference was prorated across cost of goods sold $500,000, and finished goods of $300,000, the gross profit would be (a) $306,250, (b) $296,250, (c) $286,250, (d) $276,250.

Completion

Complete each of the following statements by filling in the blanks.

1.   The predicted activity level for determining the fixed overhead rate is the _____.

2.   Budgeted factory-overhead rates can be computed by dividing _____ cost by _____.

3.   Absorption costing and variable costing differ because _____.

4.　　　At the end of the year, if the underapplied or overapplied factory-overhead cost is to be treated in a theoretically correct and precise manner, it should be prorated over three accounts:

(a)_____

(b)_____

(c)_____

5.　　　When the actual production level is less than the predicted level, the fixed overhead _____variance is _____.

6.　　　Application of manufacturing overhead to a job requires a _____ entry to the _____ account.

7.　　　Overapplied overhead is disposed of with a debit entry to the _____ account.

8.　　　Overhead is applied to jobs using a _____ overhead rate multiplied by _____.

9.　　　There are two fixed manufacturing overhead variances; the _____ variance occurs only in _____ costing, but the _____ variance occurs in both _____ and _____ costing.

10.　　　When_____ decrease, _____-cost-based income is greater than _____-cost-based income.

Problems

1. Given for the first year of operations of Random Products, a manufacturer of a uniform product:

	Fixed	Variable
Direct labor cost	$ -	$140,000
Selling and administrative expenses	10,000	70,000
Direct materials used	-	100,000
Factory overhead	72,000	36,000

The company manufactured 12,000 units and sold 9,000 of these units for $380,000. There was no ending inventory of work-in-process. Compute these amounts:

a. Ending inventory of finished goods:

Absorption-costing method

Variable-costing method

b. Gross profit on sales (absorption costing)

c. Contribution margin (variable costing)

d. Operating income:

Absorption-costing method

Variable-costing method

2. Given for Hancock Products, Inc. (in millions):

Budgeted factory overhead cost	$280
Budgeted machine-hours	70 hrs.
Actual factory-overhead cost incurred	$293
Actual machine-hours used	72 hrs.

a. Compute:

   Budgeted overhead rate:

   Applied factory-overhead cost:

   Amount of overhead underapplied or overapplied:

b. Prepare the journal entry to write off the overhead difference at year end (without proration):

Exercises

1. Given for Martingale Corporation for 19X7:

Beginning inventory	none
Production	10,000 units
Sales at $40 each	8,000 units
Ending inventory	2,000 units

Standard manufacturing costs per unit:

Variable manufacturing costs	$12
Fixed factory overhead	4
Total	$16

Selling and administrative expenses:

Variable	$95,000
Fixed	45,000
Total	$140,000

    a.   Prepare an income statement using absorption costing. Ignore income taxes, and assume no production-volume variance:

    b.   Prepare an income statement, using variable costing and ignoring income taxes:

c.   Reconcile the difference in net income shown by these two methods:

2. Given for Harrison Company (in millions):

Sales	$540
Cost of goods sold at normal cost	325
Overapplied factory overhead	12

Compute the gross profit for the year, assuming that the overapplied factory overhead is written off in one lump sum without proration.

CHAPTER 13 SOLUTIONS TO PRACTICE TEST QUESTIONS AND PROBLEMS

True or False Statements

1. False   In the U.S., the variable-costing approach is not "generally accepted accounting practice" and is therefore not allowed for either tax or financial reporting. Any method, including variable-costing, is acceptable for internal reporting.

2. False   Actual factory overhead is charged to a factory overhead account, which is a temporary asset account that records a period's overhead costs. *Applied factory overhead* is charged to work-in-process.

3. False   Fixed manufacturing overhead is treated by variable costing as an expense of the period, but as an inventoriable product cost by absorption costing. Both costing methods regard variable manufacturing overhead as inventoriable product cost.

4. False   The source of the error is less important than the magnitude of the error. If the error is large enough that inventory balances would be seriously misstated by writing off the error, the underapplied overhead should be prorated. If the error is small, the error should be charged to the period and written off (usually as part of cost of goods sold).

5. True   All production-volume variances are treated as adjustments to the period's income— whether they are favorable or unfavorable.

6. False   The issue is which is the better cost driver—direct-labor hours or direct-labor cost. This could be established by statistical analyses.

7. False   The fixed overhead spending variance occurs whenever actual fixed overhead exceeds budgeted fixed overhead, regardless of the costing system.

8. Unclear Variable costing can use either actual or standard variable costs, so the question is not specific enough. If the variable costing uses actual costs, then there are no variances to dispose of. However, if variable costing uses standard costs, then the variances are, as is usually the case, charged to periodic income.

9. False   When inventories increase, a portion of the period's fixed manufacturing overhead remains in inventory, which increases absorption-cost income relative to variable-cost income. When inventories decrease, just the opposite effect and result occur.

10. True   An overapplied factory overhead balance means that credits (overhead applied) exceed the debits (overhead incurred). Therefore, if total factory overhead applied was $150,000 and $10,000 overapplied, the factory overhead incurred must have been $140,000.

Multiple-Choice Questions

1. c   Variable costs of the period are counted as part of contribution margin: $30 + $15 = $45.

2. c   Fixed costs are deducted after contribution margin is computed: $10 + $50 = $60.

3. d   Gross profit includes all product costs, including: $50 + $15 = $65.

4. d   Factory overhead applied is the amount of overhead cost added to jobs. This addition requires a debit to work-in-process and a credit to factory overhead.

5. c   The proper rate should be the budgeted rate: $220,000 ÷ 40,000 hours = $5.50 per hour.

6. c   The amount applied is the budgeted rate multiplied by the actual cost-driver activity: $5.50 x 44,000 = $242,000.

7. a   Actual overhead was $240,000, and applied overhead was $242,000. Thus overhead was $2,000 overapplied.

8. c	Overhead applied was $190,000, and it was overapplied by $10,000. Therefore, actual overhead was $180,000.
9. a	Cost of goods sold would be reduced by the amount of overapplied overhead from $500,000 to $490,000. Thus gross profit would be $10,000 greater, or $300,000.
10. b	The difference would be prorated on the basis of account balances: 3/8 to finished goods, and 5/8 to cost of goods sold. The portion to subtract from cost of goods sold is 5/8 x $10,000 = $6,250. Therefore gross profit would be $6,250 higher or $290,000 + $6,250 = $296,250.

Completion

1. expected, normal, or practical capacity level
2. budgeted factory overhead, budgeted cost-driver activity
3. of the way that fixed factory overhead is treated
4. work-in-process, finished goods, cost of goods sold
5. volume, unfavorable
6. debit, work-in-process; or credit, factory overhead
7. factory overhead
8. budgeted, actual cost-driver usage
9. volume, absorption, spending, absorption, variable
10. inventories, variable, absorption

Problems

1. Random Products

    a. The ending inventory is 12,000 - 9,000 = 3,000 units.

    Absorption-costing:

    The cost per unit = ($140 + $100 + $36 + $72) ÷ 12 = $348 ÷ 12 = $29

    Ending finished-goods inventory = 3,000 x $29 = $87,000.

    Variable-costing:

    The cost per unit = ($140 + $100 + $36) ÷ 12 = $276 ÷ 12 = $23

    Ending finished-goods inventory = 3,000 x $23 = $69,000

    b. Cost of goods sold is $348,000 - $87,000 = $261,000. Gross profit is $380,000 - $261,000 = $119,000.

    c. Variable cost of goods sold is $276,000 - 69,000 = $207,000. Total variable expenses are 207,000 + 70,000 = $277,000. Contribution margin is 380,000 - 277,000 = $103,000.

d. Operating income:

Absorption-costing:

Operating income = $119,000 - ($10,000 + $70,000) = $119,000 - $80,000 = $39,000

Variable-costing:

Operating income = $103,000 - ($10,000 + $72,000) = $103,000 - $82,000 = $21,000

Proof: Profit difference $39,000 - $21,000 = $18,000

Fixed overhead rate = $72,000 ÷ $12,000 = $6 per unit

$18,000 = $6 x 3,000 units increase in inventory

2. Hancock Products, Inc. (in millions)

a. Budgeted overhead rate: Divide budgeted factory overhead cost by budgeted machine hours: $280 ÷ 70 hrs = $4 per hour.

Applied factory-overhead cost: Multiply the actual machine-hours used by the budgeted overhead rate; 72 hrs x $4 = $288

Underapplied overhead: Subtract the applied factory-overhead cost incurred from the actual factory-overhead cost: $293 - $288 = $5 underapplied overhead.

b. Cost of goods sold   5

    Factory department overhead   5

Exercises

1. Martingale Corporation

   a. Absorption-costing income statement:

Sales: 8,000 units @ $40		$320,000
Less standard cost of goods sold:		
Cost of goods manufactured at standard:		
10,000 units @ $16	$160,000	
Less ending inventory: 2,000 units @ $16	32,000	128,000
Gross profit at standard		$192,000
Less selling and administrative expenses:		
Variable expenses	$ 95,000	
Fixed expenses	45,000	140,000
Operating income		$ 52,000

   b. Variable-costing income statement:

Sales: 8,000 units @ $40		$320,000
Variable manufacturing cost of goods produced:		
10,000 units @ $12	$120,000	
Less ending inventory: 2,000 units @$12	24,000	
Variable manufacturing cost of goods sold:		
8,000 units @ $12	$ 96,000	
Variable selling and administrative expenses	95,000	
Total variable expenses		191,000
Contribution margin		$129,000
Less fixed costs:		
Factory overhead: 10,000 units @ $4	$ 40,000	
Selling and administrative expenses	45,000	85,000
Operating income		$44,000

   c. Reconciliation of difference in operating income:

   Operating income difference: $52,000 - $44,000 = $8,000

   Ending inventory difference: 2,000 units x ($16 - $12) = 2,000 x $4 fixed overhead cost per unit = $8,000

2. Harrison Company (in millions):

Sales	$540
Cost of goods sold at normal cost	325
Less overapplied overhead	12
Cost of goods sold at actual cost	313
Gross profit	$227

CHAPTER 14

Job-Costing and Process-Costing Systems

OVERVIEW

This chapter examines and differentiates between the job-costing system and the other basic system for costing products: process costing. The key concept to learn about process costing is to understand equivalent units produced, the measure of the amount of work done in a process in a given period. Your learning objectives are to:

I.   Distinguish between job-order and process costing

II.   Prepare summary journal entries for the typical transactions of a job-costing system

III.   Use an ABC system in a job-order environment

IV.   Show how service organizations use job costing

V.   Explain the basic ideas underlying process costing and how they differ from job costing

VI.   Compute output in terms of equivalent units

VII.   Compute costs and prepare journal entries for the principal transactions in a process-costing system

VIII.   Demonstrate how the presence of beginning inventories affects the computation of unit costs under the weighted-average method

IX.   Use backflush costing with a JIT production system

I.   Distinguish between job-order and process costing

A.   Two product-costing systems are widely used:

1.   **Job-order costing** is suitable for controlling the costs of custom-made products or services that are readily identified by individual units or batches, each of which receives varying degrees of attention and skill.

    a.   The *cost object* is the individual product, a batch of like products, or a job or order for a particular customer or client.

    b.   Some examples are products such as furniture, machinery, highway bridges, and drilling platforms for off-shore oil exploration; or services such as systems installations, management consulting, auditing, legal consultation.

2.   In contrast, **process costing** is appropriate for the mass production of uniform units, which usually flow continuously through a series of standard production steps called operations or processes; for example: textiles, chemicals, petroleum products, cement, bricks, newsprint, ice cream, and breakfast foods.

B.   Job-order costing essentially involves **cost application,** which is the identification of accumulated costs with specific jobs or orders of products or services.

1.   Job-order costing was first designed for manufacturing, but it can be used equally well by service companies. The first examples in the chapter are manufacturing, but later examples are costing for services.

> **Stop and Review**
>
> See textbook Exhibit 14-1

II.   Prepare summary journal entries for the typical transactions of a job-costing system

A.   The primary record of the job-cost system is the **job-cost record**, which contains accumulated costs for *each* product, batch, or job according to the definition of the cost object using these supporting documents:

1.   Material requisitions, used to apply *direct-material costs.*

2.   Time tickets, used to apply *direct-labor costs.*

3.   Budgeted rates, used to apply *factory-overhead costs.*

B.   The typical transactions for manufacturing activities describe the flow of resources and costs to the cost object, during its manufacture or development, and after completion.

1.   Note carefully the formal *journal entries* and the accompanying detailed transaction analyses in the textbook.

> **Stop and Review**
>
> See textbook Exhibit 14-2

2.   Observe the *cost flows* through the general ledger (T-) accounts.

III. Use an ABC system in a job-order environment

There are two motives for management to adopt an activity-based costing (ABC) system:

A. The aggressive cost reduction targets set by top management

B. The need to understand product-line profitability

> **Study Tip:** *For a better understanding of activity-based costing systems, see the textbook objective three example using Dell Computer Corporation and Exhibit 14-3.*

IV. Show how service organizations use job costing

The job costing approach described for manufacturing companies is also used in service and nonprofit organizations.

A. Costs are allocated to projects or programs, which are identifiable groups of activities that produce *services*.

> **Stop and Review**
>
> See the textbook example on p. 648

B. Service organizations are just as concerned with identifying appropriate cost drivers for their delivered services as manufacturers are.

   1. In service organizations, which are typically labor-intensive, one of the primary cost drivers is *time*.

   2. Understanding how employees spend their time is important for several reasons:

      a. If time spent drives costs, then knowing time allocations is prerequisite to knowing cost allocations (for all its purposes, as discussed above).

      b. Identifying how and where employees spend time is an important step in eliminating nonvalue-added activities in delivering service.

         • If certain activities can be identified as redundant or nonvalue added, the human resources spent on those activities can be redeployed to value-added activities.

         • Some managers of large companies believe that their most significant improvements in efficiency will come from eliminating non-value-added service activities and enhancing value-added ones.

V. Explain the basic ideas underlying process costing and how they differ from job costing

Again, the two basic systems of product costing are:

A. **Job-order costing** is appropriate when different products are manufactured in identifiable batches called *jobs*.

   1. Job-order costing is used when it is economically feasible to trace direct costs to identifiable products.

   2. Indirect costs are allocated to products as described in Chapters 12 and 13.

   3. The cost object is the *product*.

B. **Process costing** is appropriate when uniform product units are manufactured in a continuous flow through a series of standard operations called *processes*.

1.   Process costing is used when it is not feasible to trace direct costs to individual products or batches of products—the product is uniform and the process is more or less continuous.

2.   The initial cost object is the *work done in some time period*.

3.   In essence, all product costs in process costing are treated as costs of the period, and then costs of the products are averages for the period because it is not feasible to trace costs directly to individual products.

C.   The flow of costs through each process differs somewhat, though the general progression follows the production process:

1.   Resources are applied to the process from direct material, direct labor, and manufacturing overhead.

2.   The costs of resources when combined in the process become work-in-process.

3.   When products are completed, the costs become finished goods.

4.   When products are sold, the costs become cost of goods sold.

> **Stop and Review**
>
> See textbook Exhibits 14-5 and 14-6

D.   Both cost systems follow the application of costs through work-in-process, finished goods (or goods transferred out), and cost of goods sold. The primary difference between the two systems is the method of measuring unit costs.

1.   Job-order costing traces the costs to identifiable units, batches, or jobs of products.

2.   Process costing traces the costs to the process or parts of the process during a specified time period and divides the costs by units produced to get unit costs.

> **Study Tip:** *Before going on to the next section, be sure that you understand the basic rationales of and the difference between job-order costing and process costing.*

VI.   Compute output in terms of equivalent units

The key to understanding how process costing assigns costs to units of product is understanding the concept of *equivalent units produced.*

A.   **Equivalent units** produced measures the amount of resources applied during a time period that could have *fully processed* units of product.

1.   Process costing computes equivalent units produced for each category of assigned cost.

2.   The usual cost categories are direct material and conversion costs (direct labor and manufacturing overhead), but there are many variations in practice. For example, different materials may be traced separately to the process.

3.   By computing equivalent units produced, process costing answers the question: "If I had applied all the materials (or conversion) used during the period toward the completion of products, how many could I have fully completed?"

4.   For example, a product takes two hours of direct labor to fully complete. The process used 2,000 direct-labor hours. How many units could have been fully processed by labor effort? Enough labor effort was applied to fully complete the equivalent of:

2,000 hours ÷ 2 hours per unit = 1,000 *equivalent units.*

5.	This is the essence of computing equivalent units produced: divide the resources applied during a period by the expected (or standard) resource necessary to fully complete a single unit of product.

B.	In contrast, the number of *physical units* worked on during a period is usually greater than the equivalent units because not all units worked on are actually fully processed during a time period.

1.	In the previous simple example, 2,000 physical units may have been started during the period.

2.	What if not a single unit had been transferred out of the process (as finished goods or to the next process stage)? What would you infer about the status of completion of those 2,000 units begun during the period but still counted as work-in-process?

3.	Two thousand physical units have received 1,000 equivalent units of labor, so on average, they should be 50% complete.

4.	In practice, we try to obtain better information about the degree of completion of work-in-process.

C.	Process costing keeps track of the number of physical units worked on, accumulates costs of resources used during a time period, and assigns these costs to *equivalent units produced*, not physical units.

1.	The calculation of cost per equivalent unit is simple: divide the costs of the period by the equivalent units produced.

2.	Continuing the simple example, suppose total direct-labor cost of the period was $10,000. The direct-labor cost per equivalent unit was $10,000 ÷ 1,000 equivalent units = $10 direct-labor cost per equivalent unit.

3.	The meaning of this *cost per equivalent unit* is that every unit that was fully completed cost $10 in direct labor to do so. Any unit that was 50% completed now has $5 of direct labor cost attached to it, and so on.

D.	A systematic approach to process costing involves five steps:

Step 1.	Account for the physical units of production into the process and out of the process:

(1)	Units in process in the beginning of the period*

+	Units started during the period

=	Total units worked on during the period

(2)	Units completed during the period

+	Units still in process at the end of the period

=	Total units worked on during the period

* *Note:* At first we assume that there are no units in process at the beginning of the period, so only the second calculation is required to account for units.

Step 2.	Compute equivalent units of production applied *in each category of cost*: usually direct materials and conversion cost, *separately*.

Stop and Review
See textbook Exhibit 14-7

VII. Compute costs and prepare journal entries for the principal transactions in a process-costing system

This objective involves steps 3-5 in the calculation of production costs.

Step 3. Summarize the total costs to be accounted for in each cost category.

Step 4. Compute the costs per equivalent unit in each cost category.

Step 5. Use these unit costs to allocate and reconcile the total costs of goods completed and ending work-in-process.

> **Stop and Review**
>
> See textbook Exhibit 14-8

> **Study Tip:** *Before going on, carefully work through the Summary Problem on p. 657 in the text. Be sure that you understand each calculation and how each calculation flows into the next one. Learn to set up these analyses systematically, and the entire process will be easier and more intuitive. Please do not go on until you are ready.*

VIII. Demonstrate how the presence of beginning inventories affects the computation of unit costs under the weighted-average method

If the process begins a period with partially completed units from the preceding period (this is typically the case), process costing becomes only a little more complicated.

A. The problem is that because the cost object is the *process during a specific time period*, costs may be different in different periods.

B. Process costing has two common approaches to accounting for the costs of separate periods: the *weighted-average* costing method and the *first-in, first-out* (FIFO) method. Here we focus on the weighted-average method.

C. The **weighted-average method** treats the beginning inventory of work-in-process as though it were begun and finished during the current period.

1. Beginning-inventory costs for each type of cost are mingled with the respective current period costs.

2. These costs include **transferred-in costs** (or *previous-department costs*), as well as the present department's currently added costs of material, labor, and overhead.

> **Stop and Review**
>
> See textbook Exhibit 14-9

3. Therefore, the divisor for computing per equivalent unit costs is the *total equivalent units*, that is, the equivalent units from the previous work on the beginning inventory as well as the current work.

4. Thus, monthly unit costs actually represent *weighted averages* of beginning-inventory costs and currently added costs.

IX.	Use backflush costing with a JIT production system

Just-in-time manufacturing companies can simplify their process-costing method because inventories are minimal.

A. If there are zero inventories, **backflush costing** applies all costs of production directly to cost of goods sold.

B. In practice, many JIT firms in the U.S. maintain some inventories, so some inventory accounting is required for financial control.

> **Study Tip:** *Before going on to the practice exam, carefully work through the Summary Problem on p. 664 in the text.*

PRACTICE TEST QUESTIONS AND PROBLEMS

True or False Statements

Determine whether each of the following statements is True (T) or False (F), and enter your answer in the space provided.

_____ 1. Examples of products for which a process-cost system would probably be suitable include chemicals and textiles.

_____ 2. Equivalent units of production are computed as the physical units worked on multiplied by the expected cost per unit in each cost category.

_____ 3. In process-cost calculations, the completion percentages of work-in-process inventories typically pertain to conversion costs.

_____ 4. The process-cost method that treats the beginning inventory of work-in-process as though it were begun and finished during the current period is first-in, first-out.

_____ 5. The primary difference between job-order costing and process costing is the specification of the appropriate cost object.

_____ 6. Backflush costing works best when physical inventories are negligible.

_____ 7. A cost driver in a job-cost system is the same as an indirect cost application base.

_____ 8. Within a normal costing system, the costs charged to job-cost records would include normal applied factory overhead and normal direct material.

_____ 9. Job-order costing, with its emphasis on direct-labor-based allocations, cannot be used with activity-based costing.

_____ 10. Individual products are the cost objects in job-order costing.

Multiple-Choice Questions

For each of the following multiple-choice questions, select the best answer(s), and enter the identification letter(s) in the space provided.

_____1. In job-order costing systems, the issuance of direct materials to production requires a debit to: (a) materials used, (b) direct-materials inventory, (c) finished goods inventory, (d) work-in-process inventory.

_____2. See the preceding item. The credit should be to: (a) accounts payable, (b) work-in-process inventory, (c) direct-materials inventory, (d) materials used.

_____3. Cost of goods manufactured should be: (a) debited to finished goods, (b) debited to cost of goods sold, (c) credited to direct-materials inventory, (d) debited to work-in-process.

_____4. (*Hint*: Set up a worksheet.) A certain process that adds all material at the beginning of the process had a beginning inventory of 5,000 units that were 40% completed as to conversion costs and an ending inventory of 1,000 units that were 50% completed. Units started were 20,000, and units completed were 24,000. The total equivalent units of conversion produced using the weighted-average method was: (a) 24,500, (b) 22,000, (c) 22,500, (d) 20,000.

_____5. See item 4 above. The equivalent units produced for materials, using the weighted-average method, were: (a) 24,500, (b) 25,000, (c) 22,500, (d) 20,000.

_____6. When direct materials are added to the *second* process in a series of three manufacturing processes, the journal entry would include: (a) a credit to the second process, (b) a credit to the first process, (c) a debit to the first process, (d) a debit to material inventory.

Completion

Complete each of the following statements by filling in the blanks.

1. _____costing is appropriate when the _____ are individual products or batches, but _____is appropriate when the _____ are _____.

2. Costs of materials used in production are carried through three accounts:

   (a)_____

   (b)_____

   (c)_____

3. The fundamental record in a job-order cost system is the _____.

4. One effect of using activity-based costing is to shift the classification of some indirect costs to a _____.

5. For product/service costing purposes, the difference between an auto repair shop and a custom-home builder is the _____. The similarity between them is _____.

6. When there are no beginning _____ inventories, equivalent units produced are the same as _____.

7.   The five steps in the analysis of process costing are:

(a)_____

(b)_____

(c)_____

(d)_____

(e)_____

8.   The total costs to account for are the sum of _____ and
_____.

9.   Many companies with _____ manufacturing methods use
_____ costing because they have virtually no inventories.

10.   Companies with multiple, linked processes generally have three categories of costs:
_____, _____, and
_____.

Problems

1. Given for the Bleaching Process for July (all materials added at the beginning of the process):

	Units
Inventory in process, November 1, 70% completed for conversion costs	300
Transferred into process in November	600
Completed and transferred out of process in November	700
Inventory in process, November 30, 60% completed for conversion costs	200

Beginning work-in-process (40% complete)

Started

Total units to account for

Units completed

Ending work-in-process

Total units accounted for

a. Find the equivalent units produced for computing unit costs by the *weighted-average* method:

Physical units	Materials	Conversion

2. Given for the Milling Process for March (all materials added at the beginning of the process):

Inventory in process, January 1, 40% completed for conversion costs	300 units
Started in January	600 units
Completed and transferred out of process in January.	700 units
Inventory in process, January 31, 50% completed for conversion costs.	200 units
January 1 inventory costs:	
Direct materials costs	$3,900
Conversion costs	$2,800
Costs added in January:	
Direct materials	$5,100
Conversion costs	$3,600

Using the *weighted-average* method, calculate the cost of work transferred out in March and the cost of the March 31 inventory of work-in-process:

Step 1: Summarize physical units:

Step 2: Compute output in equivalent units:

Direct Materials	Conversion

Step 3: Summarize total costs to account for:

Direct Materials Costs	Conversion Costs	Total Costs

Step 4: Compute unit costs:

	Direct Materials Cost	Conversion Cost	Total Unit Cost

Step 5: Compute total costs of work completed and in-process:

Exercise

1. For each of these transaction types of Aaron Company, make a journal entry (without explanation) to fit the following data (all beginning inventories are zero):

Material purchases on credit	$14,000
Direct labor used and paid:	$ 8,000
Factory utilities paid	$ 2,000
Supervisory salaries on account	$ 4,000
Indirect labor paid	$ 3,000
Supplies purchased and used	$ 1,000
Materials issued	$10,000
Factory overhead applied @ 120% of material used	?
Ending work-in-process	$ 2,000
Ending finished goods	$ 3,000
Sales	$45,000

	Accounts:	Debit:	Credit:
a. Direct materials purchased:			
b. Direct labor incurred:			
c. Factory overhead incurred:			
d. Direct materials used:			
e. Factory overhead applied:			
f. Work-in-process completed:			
g. Cost of goods sold:			
h. Product sales on account:			
i. Close overhead account			

CHAPTER 13 SOLUTIONS TO PRACTICE TEST QUESTIONS AND PROBLEMS

True or False Statements

1. True — These are examples of products that are undifferentiated (e.g., one yard of fabric is just like any other of its type, hopefully) and result from a continuous process. In this case, the most feasible cost object is the process during the time period--using process costing.

2. False — Equivalent units of production are the number of units that could have been fully completed from the resources applied. Equivalent units could be computed by the amount of the resource applied divided by the standard or expected resource required per completed unit.

3. False — Completion percentages also reflect materials. Usually there are separate materials and conversion cost calculations.

4. False — Weighted-average process costing is the method that blurs the distinction between the prior period's work and the current period's work. FIFO costing assumes that beginning work-in-process was begun in a prior period and partially completed at the prior period's unit cost.

5. True — Job-order costing applies costs to individual products or batches of product. Process costing applies costs to the process operating for a specific period of time and then to products by dividing the period's costs by equivalent units.

6. True — Backflush costing requires negligible inventories because it charges all manufacturing costs of the period to finished goods or preferably to cost of goods sold directly. Backflush costing makes JIT manufacturing firms look much like service firms, which cannot inventory their services.

7. True — Or at least it should be. Many companies still use direct-labor hours or cost as the only cost driver and allocation base for indirect costs, when it is likely that other cost drivers would be more appropriate allocation bases.

8. False — A normal costing system charges factory overhead at budgeted rates and actual direct labor. A system that charged normal direct material sounds like a standard cost system.

9. False — It is true that job-order costing has historically and traditionally applied overhead on the basis of direct labor, but there is no rule that says this must be so. Job-order costing can and should use the most appropriate cost drivers to apply overhead to jobs.

10. True — But sometimes batches of product or specific orders are cost objects. It depends on the feasibility of tracing costs and on the nature of the business.

Multiple-Choice Questions

1. d — Issuance of direct materials requires a credit to materials and a debit to work-in-process inventory.

2. c — credit to materials inventory

3. a — Cost of goods manufactured represents the costs of products completed, and therefore transferred from work-in-process to finished goods. The complete entry would debit finished goods and credit work-in-process.

4. computations:

Beginning work-in-process (40% complete)	5,000 units
Started	20,000 units
Total units to account for	25,000 units

Units completed	24,000 units
Ending work-in-process	1,000 units
Total units accounted for	25,000 units

		Equivalent units	
	Physical units	Materials	Conversion
Completed	24,000	24,000	24,000
Ending work-in-process	1,000	1,000	500
Weighted-average total equivalent units	25,000	25,000	24,500

4. a

5. b

6. b   The journal entry would debit the second process to record the costs transferred in and credit the first process to record the costs transferred out.

Completion

1.   Job-order, cost objects, process costing, cost objects, processes during a period of time

2.   work-in-process, finished goods, cost of goods sold

3.   job-cost record

4.   direct cost classification because the cost can be traced by cost-driver usage

5.   terminology and the nature of the product, both produce something of value to a particular customer requiring accounting by customer or order

6.   work-in-process, the current equivalent units

7.   (a) summarize the flow of physical units

(b) calculate output in terms of equivalent units

(c) summarize total costs to account for

(d) calculate unit costs

(e) apply costs to units completed and ending work-in-process

8.   costs of beginning work-in-process, current costs

9.   JIT, backflush

10.   transferred-in cost, direct-materials cost, conversion cost

Problems

1. Bleaching Process

	Physical units	Material Cost	Conversion Cost
a. Transferred out	700	700	700
Ending inventory: 200 x 100%	200	200	
200 x 60%	200	-	120
Equivalent units produced		900	820

2. Milling Process

    Step 1: Units of physical flow

Work-in-process, beginning	300 (40%)	Units completed	700
Units started	600	Work-in-process, end	200 (50%)
Units to account for	900	Units accounted for	900

Step 2: Equivalent units

	Direct Materials	Conversion Costs
Completed and transferred out	700	700
Ending work-in-process: 200 x 100%	200	
200 x 50%		100
Work done to date (equivalent units produced for weighted-average method)	900	800

Step 3: Summary of total costs to account for

	Direct Materials	Conversion Costs	Total Costs
Work-in-process, beginning	$ 3,900	$ 2,800	$ 6,700
Costs added currently	5,100	3,600	8,700
Total costs to account for	$ 9,000	$6,400	$15,400

Step 4: Unit costs

	Direct Materials	Conversion Costs	Total Unit Cost
Total costs to account for (Step 3)	$ 9,000	$ 6,400	
Divide by equivalent units (Step 2)	÷ 900	÷800	
Unit costs	$ 10.00	$ 8.00	$18.00

Step 5: Total costs of work completed and in-process

Units completed: (700)($18)		$12,600
Work-in-process, end:		
Direct-materials costs: (200)($10)	$2,000	
Conversion costs: (200)(50%)($8)	800	2,800
Total costs accounted for		$15,400

Exercise

1.   Aaron Company, journal entries:

	Accounts:	Debit:	Credit:
a. Direct materials purchased:	Materials	$14,000	
	Accounts payable		$14,000
b. Direct labor incurred:	Work-in-process	8,000	
	Cash		8,000
c. Factory overhead incurred:	Factory overhead	10,000	
	Cash		6,000
	Salaries payable		4,000
d. Direct materials used:	Work-in-process	10,000	
	Materials		10,000
e. Factory overhead applied:	Work-in-process	12,000	
	Factory overhead		12,000
f. Work-in-process completed:	Finished goods	28,000	
	Work-in-process		28,000
g. Cost of goods sold:	Cost of goods sold	25,000	
	Finished goods		25,000
h. Product sales on account:	Accounts receivable	45,000	
	Sales		45,000
i. Close overhead account	Factory overhead	2,000	
	Cost of goods sold		2,000

CHAPTER **15**

Basic Accounting: Concepts, Techniques, and Conventions

OVERVIEW

This chapter focuses on the accounting equation. The fundamental task of an accounting system is to make every economic transaction balance the equation. This chapter demonstrates how balancing the accounting equation not only is a powerful control device, but it also results in the generation of three of the principal financial statements used for external reporting. Note that this chapter discusses the accounting equation without the use of journal entries. An introduction to journal entries is in the study guide appendix and in textbook Appendix 15B. Your learning objectives are to:

I.   Read and interpret basic financial statements

II.   Analyze typical business transactions using the balance sheet equation

III.   Distinguish between the accrual basis of accounting and the cash basis of accounting

IV.   Relate the measurement of expenses to the expiration of assets

V.   Explain the nature of dividends and retained earnings

VI.   Select relevant items from a set of data and assemble them into a balance sheet and an income statement

VII.   Distinguish between the reporting of corporate owners' equity and the reporting of owners' equity for partnerships and sole proprietorships

VIII.   Identify how the measurement conventions of recognition, matching and cost recovery, and stable monetary unit affect financial reporting

I. Read and interpret basic financial statements

Through the financial accounting process, the accountant accumulates data on the operations of an organization for use by managers, investors, and other interested groups.

A. The focus is on the *entity* and its *transactions*.

    1. An **entity** is a specific area of accountability. The principal form of business entity is the **corporation**, which is owned by its stockholders.

    2. **Transactions** are events that affect the financial position of an entity and require recording by the entity.

B. Accountants summarize transactions in the form of two main **financial statements**:

    1. The **balance sheet,** also called the **statement of financial position,** summarizes at a given *date* the economic resources owned by a company **(assets)** and the claims against them **(equities).**

    2. The **income statement** summarizes for a given *period* the results of the profit-seeking operations of a company in order to measure **net income:** the excess of sales **(revenues)** over the costs of obtaining them **(expenses).**

    3. These two financial statements have a direct relation to each other because the net income reported in the income statement for a given period increases the owners' equity, which is shown in the balance sheet at the end of the period.

II. Analyze typical business transactions using the balance sheet equation

The accounting process records the transactions and events of the **entity,** which may be a business unit, often referred to as a **segment**, **firm, company,** or **corporation**, depending on its organization.

A. Accounting systems are based on the fundamental **balance sheet equation:**

Assets = Equities, or

Assets = Liabilities + Owners' Equity

    1. **Assets** are the economic resources owned by the entity and expected to benefit its future activities, for example, money, merchandise, and machinery. **Accounts receivable** are sales made on account where cash is received on a later date, accounts receivable fall into the asset side of the balance sheet equation.

    2. **Equities** are the total claims against, or interests in, the assets of the entity.

    3. **Liabilities** are the debts owed by the entity to its creditors and other non-owners. **Accounts payable** is a liability because goods or services have been received by the entity and payment has yet to be made.

    4. **Owners' equity** measures the investment interest of owners and is the excess of a company's assets over its liabilities. For a corporation, this is called **stockholders' equity.**

    5. Stockholders' equity consists of **paid-in capital** and **retained earnings (income).**

    6. Retained income is increased periodically by **net income,** the excess of **revenues** over **expenses.**

B.   Every economic transaction affects some components of the balance sheet equation, and the *accounting system ensures that the equation is balanced at all times*; that is, assets always equal the total of liabilities and owners' equity.

> **Stop and Review**
>
> See textbook Exhibit 15-1

> **Study Tip:** *Before going on to the next section, be sure that you understand the working of the accounting equation and its primary elements.*

III.   Distinguish between the accrual basis of accounting and the cash basis of accounting

Net income is generally measured on the accrual basis of accounting, that is, by matching related revenues and expenses by periods.

A.   Revenues generally arise from increases in assets caused by sales of goods and services to customers.

B.   Revenues are **earned** or **realized** (recognized in the accounting records and formal financial statements) when:

1.   The goods or services sold are "fully rendered" (for example, delivered to customers).

2.   An actual exchange of resources has occurred (in terms of either cash or credit).

3.   There is a reasonable assurance that credit sales will be collected.

C.   Expenses are **incurred** (recognized in the accounting records and formal financial statements) as goods or services are used to obtain revenues. Expenses generally arise from used-up assets.

D.   The **accrual basis** of accounting, which recognizes revenues as they are earned and expenses as they are incurred, should be distinguished from the **cash basis** of accounting.

1.   The cash basis does not match revenues and expenses by periods.

2.   The recognition of revenues and expenses on a cash basis would depend solely on the timing of various cash receipts and disbursements, thus omitting changes in some assets and liabilities such as increases in accounts receivable and payable due to sales or expenses.

> **Study Tip:** *Can you express the difference between a cash-based and an accrual-based accounting system?*

IV.   Relate the measurement of expenses to the expiration of assets

A.   It is helpful to view assets as **bundles of economic services** held for future use.

1.   When unexpired or stored costs, such as merchandise inventory and equipment, are used in the production of revenue, the expired cost portions are transferred from assets to expenses, which are summarized in the income statement.

2.   In practice, however, some costs are not charged to assets when they are acquired but are charged immediately to expenses because they measure services that usually are too difficult to match to anything but the accounting period; for example, research and development expense, advertising expense, and interest expense.

B.   At the end of an accounting period, in order to complete the implementation of the accrual method, the accountant must make **adjustments** for some **implicit transactions** that are mostly the result of the passing of time.

1. Formal entries for these adjustments must be made in the accounting records at the end of an accounting period before the financial statements are constructed.

2. The adjustments form an essential element of the accrual process because they increase the precision of measurements and help provide more complete and realistic reports of operations and financial position.

3. The principal adjustments are classified into four distinctive types:

   a. Expiration of unexpired costs

   b. Recognition (earning) of unearned revenues

   c. Accrual of unrecorded expenses

   d. Accrual of unrecorded revenues

4. Examples of the first type include write-offs to expense of the expiration of such assets as *plant and equipment, office supplies*, and *prepaid insurance.*

5. **Recognition of unearned or deferred revenues** means the earning of revenues previously collected in advance.

   a. When cash collections are made in advance by sellers for certain types of services to be rendered later to their customers, these *explicit transactions* create *liabilities* of the sellers called *unearned revenues;* for example, rent collected in advance and insurance premiums collected in advance.

   b. As time passes, the services are rendered to customers, and *periodic adjustments* must therefore be made to reflect the *implicit transactions:* the decreases in these liabilities and the increases in such revenues as rent earned and insurance premiums earned.

6. **Accrual of unrecorded expenses** means incurring expenses and accumulating the related liabilities as time passes or as some services are continuously acquired and used.

   a. Common examples are wages, salaries, commissions, taxes, interest on money borrowed, utility services such as electricity, and other operating expenses that are ordinarily not paid in cash until *shortly after* the consumption of the services.

   b. *Periodic adjustments* are made for the *implicit transactions* to increase expenses and the corresponding liabilities for the amounts accrued and not yet entered in the accounting records.

7. **Accrual of unrecorded revenues** means earning revenues and accumulating the related assets as time passes or as some services are continuously rendered to customers.

   a. Common examples are interest on money loaned, fees for services rendered, *and* other revenues that are ordinarily not collected in cash until shortly after they have been earned.

   b. *Periodic adjustments* are made for the *implicit transactions* to increase revenues and the corresponding assets for the amounts accrued and not yet earned in the accounting records.

V.	**Explain the nature of dividends and retained earnings**

A. Generally, **dividends** are distributions of cash to stockholders that decrease the company's retained income.

1. Don't make the mistake of confusing dividends with expenses. Dividends are not a cost of producing revenues.

2. Expenses are deducted from revenues to arrive at net income, which in turn is *added* to retained income.

3. Dividends are deducted *directly* from retained income because they represent asset withdrawals that reduce the ownership claims against the business entity.

4. *Dividends do not decrease net income but do reduce retained income.*

B. For partnerships and sole proprietorships, the equity of each individual owner is measured, but the distinction between contributed capital and retained income is seldom reported.

VI. Select relevant items from a set of data and assemble them into a balance sheet and an income statement

The finished products of the accounting process are the formal financial statements.

A. The **income statement** may show a single-step deduction of expenses from revenues in determining net income, or the statement may use a multiple-step approach in arriving at the net income figure:

1. **Gross profit** (or **gross margin**) is the excess of sales over the cost of goods sold.

2. **Net income** is the gross profit minus operating expenses (also minus income taxes, which are not covered in this introductory presentation).

B. **The balance sheet** summarizes an entity's assets, liabilities, and owners' equity.

1. For a corporation, the owners' equity is divided into two main elements.

2. One of these is **contributed capital** or **paid-in capital.** This includes **capital stock,** which usually measures the investment paid into the corporation by its shareholders.

3. The other element is **retained earnings, retained income,** or **reinvested earnings.** This is the *accumulated increase* in the stockholders' equity caused by the total net income earned since the company was formed less *all dividends* paid to stockholders during that time.

4. Retained income is part of the stockholders' equity and therefore is not cash or any kind of asset. Moreover, retained income is not a measure of any other *particular* asset; it is part of the stockholders' general claim against, or undivided interest in, the *total* assets of the corporation.

> **Study Tip:** *Do you understand how financial statements are derived from entries to the basic accounting equation? If not, review this section and work through Exhibit 15-2 again.*
>
> **Study Tip:** *Before going on to the next section, be sure that you understand the role of implicit accounting entries or adjusting entries.*

VII. Distinguish between the reporting of corporateowners' equity and the reporting of owners' equity for partnerships and sole proprietorships

Owners can organize businesses in many forms, including corporations, partnerships, and sole proprietorships. The different organizational forms have many implications for governance and financial and tax reporting.

A. Basic accounting practices are similar for each type of business organization. For example the residual of total assets less total liabilities is the measure of accounting **net worth** of the company – but not its economic net worth or market value.

B. One area of accounting difference is the treatment of the company's accounting net worth.

    1. The net worth of a corporation is called stockholders' equity (or shareholders' equity) and is composed of capital stock (or paid-in capital) and retained earnings (undistributed earnings). Legally a corporation can pay dividends to owners only out of retained earnings.

    2. The net worth of a **partnership** also separates partners' capital contributions and undistributed earnings.

    3. The net worth of a **sole proprietorship** has only a single net worth account, owner's equity, which contains the owner's capital contributions and undistributed earnings.

VIII. Identify how the measurement conventions of recognition, matching and cost recovery, and stable monetary unit affects financial reporting

A. When independent auditors express their opinion of the presentation of a company's financial statements, they specify whether the statements conform to **generally accepted accounting principles (GAAP)**. GAAP includes certain accounting assumptions and conventions.

    1. GAAP evolved over many years from widespread usage.

        a. This usage has been significantly influenced by the companies that report to external users and rule-making bodies such as the ABP, FASB, and SEC.

        b. In essence, although the rule-making power lies with the federal government through the SEC, most of the current rulings are made by the FASB, an independent nongovernmental entity.

        c. GAAP can be said to be a collection of successful accounting practices.

B. Additional generally accepted accounting conventions and assumptions:

    1. An important accounting *convention* is **recognition** or **realization** of revenues when goods or services are delivered to customers.

    2. A second important convention is the periodic **matching of revenues and expenses**, as represented by the accrual basis of accounting.

    3. A third important convention is the assumption that we use the **monetary unit** as a **stable measure** of the financial or economic effects of transactions. This assumption is, of course, subject to serious challenge in many parts of the world in the face of continued inflation.

    4. The **continuity** or **going-concern assumption** views the business entity as continuing indefinitely with no intention to sell all of its assets and discontinue operations.

    5. The **principle of objectivity** or **verifiability** requires accounting measurements to be unbiased, supported by convincing evidence, subject to independent check, and therefore reliable.

    6. The **materiality convention** permits relatively small dollar amounts to be accounted for and reported in an expedient manner (even though some other basic GAAP might be ignored).

    7. The **conservatism convention** means, in case of doubt concerning the appropriate measurement, that accountants must use the more pessimistic alternatives.

    8. **Cost-benefit** means that the benefits from increased precision in accounting for and reporting business transactions must be weighed against the costs of achieving the benefits.

9. These and other GAAP are important guidelines that still permit the use of **considerable judgment** in measuring financial data.

10. **Accounts** are used to accumulate the effects of transactions on the **individual items** that are summarized by the terms in the balance sheet equation.

   a. Increases in **asset** accounts are recorded on the left (debit) side, decreases on the right (credit).

   b. Increases in **liability and stockholders' equity** accounts are recorded on the right side (credit), decreases on the left (debit).

   c. The **balance** of an account is the excess of the sum of the dollar entries on one side of the account over the sum of the dollar entries on the other side.

11. To understand the use of the debit-credit rules in analyzing the effects of transactions on the accounts and financial statements, turn to the appendix to this study guide.

> **Study Tip:** *If understanding journal entries is important to your study of accounting, do not go on unless you are comfortable with the basics of recording accounting transactions.*

PRACTICE TEST QUESTIONS AND PROBLEMS
True or False Statements

Determine whether each of the following statements is True (T) or False (F), and enter your answer in the space provided.

_____1. A company could not operate at a net loss during a given period and yet increase its cash balance during that period.

_____2. The stockholders' equity shown in the balance sheet of a corporation is a measure of items of property owned by the corporation.

_____3. Unexpired costs are called assets.

_____4. Expired costs are called expenses.

_____5. Items typically reported in a statement of retained income include net income and dividends to stockholders.

_____6. Generally accepted accounting principles are the result of careful logical analysis by rule-making bodies such as the FASB and the SEC.

_____7. The realization or recognition convention means that costs are not expired until revenues are earned.

_____8. The accounting convention of relying on a stable monetary unit is violated in practice in the U.S., which means that accounting financial statements are invalid.

_____9. Credit entries are used to record increases in revenue accounts.

_____10. An entry on the left side of any account may be called a debit.

Multiple-Choice Questions

For each of the following multiple-choice questions, select the best answer(s), and enter the identification letter(s) in the space provided. (Hint: Use the accounting equation.)

_____1.   Korsikov Corp. purchased merchandise on account for $85,000. As a result, there was: (a) no change in the total amount of its assets, (b) no change in its total liabilities, (c) an increase in the total amount of its assets, (d) an increase in its liabilities.

_____2.   Ravel Co. purchased merchandise with $200,000 of its cash. As a result, there was: (a) no change in the total amount of its assets, (b) an increase in its stockholders' equity, (c) an increase in the total amount of its assets, (d) a decrease in its stockholders' equity.

_____3.   Vaughn-Williams Co. has total assets of $420,000 and stockholders' equity of $280,000. It purchased $60,000 of merchandise on account and collected $20,000 on account from its customers. As a result, the company's total liabilities would be: (a) $200,000, (b) $80,000, (c) $480,000, (d) $460,000.

_____4.   See the preceding test item. The company's total assets would be: (a) $500,000, (b) $460,000, (c) $400,000, (d) $480,000.

_____5.   A materials-inventory account had a beginning balance of $75,000, purchase of materials was $35,000, and usage of materials was $100,000. The ending inventory balance was: (a) $140,000 credit, (b) $10,000 debit, (c) $10,000 credit, (d) $140,000 debit.

_____6.   During one period a corporation earned income of $40,000, received paid-in capital of $50,000, paid dividends of $30,000, and retired debt of $10,000. The retained income account: (a) increased $50,000, (b) stayed the same, (c) increased $10,000, (d) increased $30,000.

Completion

Complete each of the following statements by filling in the blanks.

1.   If a company purchases merchandise inventory on account (for credit), its total assets would be _____, its total liabilities would be _____ and its stockholders' equity would be _____.

2.   When unexpired or stored costs, such as merchandise inventory or equipment, are used in the production of revenue, the expired cost portions are transferred from _____ accounts to _____ accounts, which are summarized in _____.

3.   Gross profit is the excess of _____ over _____.

4.   The three tests that must be met before revenues may be recognized in the accounting records are:

(a)_____

(b)_____

(c)_____

5.   The balance sheet equation requires that _____ equal _____ plus _____ at all times.

6.   Identify the following terms:

   GAAP _____

   APB_____

   FASB_____

   SEC_____

   What they have in common is _____.

7.   Two accounting conventions that are critical to the measurement of operating income are
     _____ and _____.

8.   The conservatism convention means that when in doubt _____.

9.   Decreases in liability accounts are recorded by _____ entries.

10. An entry on the _____ side of an account is called a credit; conversely an
     entry to the _____ side is called a _____.

Problems

1. You are given the following transaction and account balance data (in thousands) for Gnu Co. at the
   end of 2003. Prepare an income statement and a balance sheet, ignoring income taxes.

Accounts payable	$12,000	Furniture and fixtures	$15,300
Accounts receivable	21,000	Inventory	14,400
Accrued interest payable	60	Notes payable	6,000
Accrued salaries payable	900	Prepaid rent	1,050
Advertising expense	600	Rent expense	2,100
Capital stock	54,000	Retained income	1,500
Cash	22,950	Salaries expense	7,500
Cost of goods sold	15,000	Sales	27,000
Depreciation expense	300	Unearned rent revenue	240

2. Given the following selected data for Eland Publishers, Inc., compute:

     (a) net income for 20x4,

     (b) retained income at December 31, 20x4.

Retained income at January 1, 20x4	$240,000
Cash dividends declared and paid to stockholders in 20x4	110,000
All other cash payments in 20x4	750,000
Total cash receipts in 20x4	825,000
Depreciation expense in 20x4	20,000
All other 20x4 expenses	815,000
Total revenues for 20x4	970,000

Exercise

1. a. Complete this transaction-analysis framework:

| | Assets | | | | | = | Liabilities and Stockholders' Equity | | |
	Cash	Accounts Receivable	Merchandise Inventory	Prepaid Rent	Equipment		Accounts Payable	Paid-in Capital	Retained Income
1. Issued capital stock for cash, $100,000									
2. Issued capital stock for store equipment, $50,000									
3. Purchased store equipment for cash, $10,000									
4. Purchased merchandise on account, $70,000									
5. Sold merchandise on account, $35,000									
6. Recorded cost of merchandise sold, $20,000									
7. Sold part of store equipment at cost on account, $2,000									
8. Collected cash on account for previous credit sales recorded, $13,000									
9. Recorded depreciation of store equipment, $1,000									
10. Paid cash for six months' rent in advance, $9,000									

	Cash	Accounts Receivable	Merchandise Inventory	Prepaid Rent	Equipment	Accounts Payable	Paid-in Capital	Retained Income
11. Recorded current month's rent expense, $1,500								
12. Paid cash for current month's salaries, advertising, utilities, and miscellaneous office supplies purchased and used, $8,500								
13. Paid cash on account to suppliers for merchandise purchases previously made and recorded, $40,000								
14. Declared and paid cash dividends to stockholders, $3,000								
Totals								

b. Compute:

Total assets_____

Total stockholders' equity_____

Total liabilities_____

Total equities_____

Net income _____

2. End-of-Period Adjustments. Use only the words *increase, decrease,* or *no effect* to fill each of the blanks below to indicate the usual effect of these end-of-period adjustments on a company's reported assets, liabilities, revenues, and expenses:

	Assets	Liabilities	Revenues	Expenses
a. Expiration of unexpired costs	____	____	____	____
b. Realization (earning) of previously deferred revenues	____	____	____	____
c. Accrual of previously unrecorded expenses	____	____	____	____
d. Accrual of previously unrecorded revenues	____	____	____	____
e. Depreciation	____	____	____	____

CHAPTER 15 SOLUTIONS TO PRACTICE TEST QUESTIONS AND PROBLEMS

True or False Statements

1. False   It is possible to have a net loss yet increase the cash balance if a relatively large portion of expenses is the expiration of unexpired costs such as depreciation. Another possibility is an increase in cash from borrowing or additional paid-in capital, which do not affect income but would affect cash.

2. False   Stockholders' equity is a measure of the claim stockholders have against the general assets of the firm; no dollar of stockholders' equity is traced to any specific item of property.

3. True   A firm may acquire inventory or prepaid expenses, which are assets because they have not yet expired.

4. True   When an asset is consumed or used for productive purposes (e.g., generating income), that asset becomes an expense.

5. True   The statement of retained income describes the changes that have occurred in this section of owners' equity. Income increases the account, and dividends decrease the account.

6. False   Though accounting logic certainly plays a role in setting GAAP, the process is quite political and depends on the strength of lobbying by affected parties as much as logic.

7. False   The realization or recognition principle means that revenues may not be counted as earned unless the transaction meets three tests: goods or services delivered, exchange of resources, collectibility assured. The matching principle means that costs are not expired until revenues are earned.

8. False   Though the monetary unit is not stable, users still derive significant usefulness from the financial disclosures based on that unstable monetary unit, and that is the most relevant measure of validity. It is possible that usefulness could be improved by using an adjusted monetary unit to account for inflation, but we do not have much evidence of this.

9. True   Revenue represents an increase in owners' equity; thus a credit entry.

10. True   It is customary to call an entry to the left side of any account (asset, liability, expense, or revenue) a debit. Entries to the right of any account are called credits. The names, debit and credit, have no more meaning than left and right, and are used to conceptually balance the accounting equation.

Multiple-Choice Questions

1. c, d   The transaction increased merchandise inventory, an asset, and also increased accounts payable, a liability.

2. a   This transaction was an exchange of assets, with no effect on total assets.

3. a   Before the transaction total liabilities (in $000s) = $420 - $280 = $140. To analyze this with the accounting equation, proceed as follows:

	Assets	= Liabilities +	Stockholders' equity
beg. bal.	420	= 140	+ 280
purchase	60	= 60	+ 0
collection	20 - 20	= 0	+ 0
end bal.	480	= 200	+ 280

4. d   See above.

5. b   Use a T-account to analyze this account:

Materials
Inventory

75	
35	
	100
<u>10</u>	

6. c   Use a T-account to analyze this account:

Retained
Income

	40
30	
	<u>10</u>

Completion

1.   increased, increased, unchanged

2.   asset, expense, income

3.   sales revenue, total cost of goods sold

4.   products or services must be delivered, there must be an exchange of resources, revenues must be collectible

5.   total assets, total liabilities, total owners' equity

6.   Generally Accepted Accounting Principles, Accounting Principles Board, Financial Accounting Standards Board, Securities and Exchange Commission. The last three are groups that have or had authority to set accounting principles (GAAP) for U.S. publicly-traded corporations.

7.   realization or recognition, matching

8.   use the most pessimistic estimates of the values of assets, expenses, liabilities, revenues, and equities.

9.   debit

10.   right, left, debit

Problems

1.

Gnu Co.

INCOME STATEMENT

For the Year Ended December 31, 2003

Revenue:

    Sales $27,000

Expenses:

Cost of goods sold	$15,000	
Depreciation expense	300	
Rent expense	2,100	
Salaries expense	7,500	
Advertising expense	600	25,500
Net income		$1,500

Alternative form of income statement (multiple-step form):

Sales		$27,000
Cost of goods sold		15,000
Gross profit		$12,000
Operating expenses:		
Depreciation expense	$ 300	
Rent expense	2,100	
Advertising expense	600	
Salaries expense	7,500	10,500
Net income		$ 1,500

Gnu Co.

BALANCE SHEET

December 31, 2003

Assets		Liabilities and Stockholders' Equity		
		Liabilities:		
Cash	$22,950	Accounts payable		$12,000
Accounts receivable	21,000	Notes payable		6,000
Inventory	14,400	Accrued interest payable		60
Prepaid rent	1,050	Accrued salaries payable		900
Furniture and fixtures	15,300	Unearned rent revenue		240
		Total liabilities		$19,200
		Stockholders' equity:		
		Capital stock	$54,000	
		Retained income	1,500	55,500
Total	$74,700	Total		$74,700

2. Eland Publishers, Inc.

   a. Net Income

Revenues		$970,000
Less expenses:		
Depreciation	$ 20,000	
Other expenses	815,000	835,000
Net Income		$135,000

   b. Retained income

Retained income, January 1, 20x4	$240,000
Net income for 20x4	135,000
Total	375,000
Cash dividends for 20x4	110,000
Retained income, December 31, 20x4	$265,000

Note: The $750,000 cash payments and the $825,000 cash receipts are not relevant to the solution.

Exercises

1. a. Transaction Analysis

		Assets					=	Liabilities + Stockholders' Equity		
		Cash	Accounts Receivable	Merchandise Inventory	Prepaid Rent	Store Equipment		Accounts Payable	Paid-in Capital	Retained Income
1.	Issued capital stock for cash, $100,000	100,000							100,000	
2.	Issued capital stock for store equipment, $50,000					50,000			50,000	
3.	Purchased store equipment for cash, $10,000	(10,000)				10,000				
4.	Purchased merchandise on account, $70,000			70,000				70,000		
5.	Sold merchandise on account, $35,000		35,000							35,000
6.	Recorded cost of merchandise sold, $20,000			(20,000)						(20,000)
7.	Sold part of store equipment at cost on account, $2,000		2,000			(2,000)				
8.	Collected cash on account for previous credit sales recorded, $13,000	13,000	(13,000)							

	Cash	Accounts Receivable	Merchandise Inventory	Prepaid Rent	Store Equipment	Accounts Payable	Paid-in Capital	Retained Income
9. Recorded depreciation of store equipment, $1,000					(1,000)			(1,000)
10. Paid cash for six months' rent in advance, $9,000	(9,000)			9,000				
11. Recorded current month's rent expense, $1,500				(1,500)				(1,500)
12. Paid cash for current month's salaries, advertising, utilities, and miscellaneous office supplies purchased and used, $8,500	(8,500)							(8,500)
13. Paid cash on account to suppliers for merchandise purchases previously made and recorded, $40,000	(40,000)					(40,000)		
14. Declared and paid cash dividends to stockholders, $3,000	(3,000)							(3,000)
Totals	42,500	24,000	50,000	7,500	57,000	30,000	150,000	1,000

b. Compute: Total assets $ 181,000   Total stockholders' equity $151,000

               Total liabilities $ 30,000   Total equities $181,000

               Net income $ 4,000 (look at owners' equity column)

2.   End-of-Period Adjustments:

	Assets	Liabilities	Revenues	Expenses
a.	decrease	no effect	no effect	increase
b.	no effect	decrease	increase	no effect
c.	no effect	increase	no effect	increase
d.	increase	no effect	increase	no effect
e.	decrease	no effect	no effect	increase

Understanding Corporate Annual Reports: Basic Financial Statements

OVERVIEW

This chapter presents the construction of and the relationships among the principal financial statements prepared for external users. The major new focus of this chapter is the statement of cash flows. Your learning objectives are to:

I. Recognize and define the main types of assets in the balance sheet of a corporation

II. Recognize and define the main types of liabilities in the balance sheet of a corporation

III. Recognize and define the main elements of the stockholders' equity section of the balance sheet of a corporation

IV. Recognize and define the principal elements in the income statement of a corporation

V. Recognize and define the elements in the statement of retained earnings

VI. Identify activities that affect cash and classify them as operating, investing, or financing activities

VII. Assess financing and investing activities using the statement of cash flows

VIII. Use both the direct method and the indirect method to explain cash flows from operating activities

IX. Explain the role of depreciation in the statement of cash flows

X. Describe and assess the effects of the four major methods of accounting for inventories (Appendix 16A)

I.   Recognize and define the main types of assets in the balance sheet of a corporation

Corporate *balance sheets* are usually prepared in *classified form,* which means that accounts are separated according to major groups. Main groups are:

A.   *Assets:* the economic resources owned by the corporation:

      1.   **Current assets** are the assets directly involved in the **operating cycle** (also called a **working-capital cycle**) and usually include: cash, temporary investments in marketable securities, accounts receivable less allowance for doubtful accounts, merchandise inventories, and prepaid expenses.

      2.   **Property, plant, and equipment** (sometimes called **fixed assets, tangible assets** or **plant assets)** include the original cost of land and the original cost of other long-term tangible assets less accumulated depreciation (cost allocated to expense since acquisition of the assets). The remainder is called **net book value. Leasehold improvements** and **natural resources** are often reported as plant assets.

Stop and Review
See textbook Exhibit 16-1

      3.   **Intangible assets** include **goodwill**, patents, franchises, trademarks, and copyrights. These are reported at original cost, less accumulated amortization where applicable.

II.   Recognize and define the main types of liabilities in the balance sheet of a corporation

Liabilities: the monetary obligations of the corporation.

A.   **Current liabilities** are company debts falling due within the coming year or within the normal operating cycle if longer than a year. They include: accounts payable to suppliers, notes payable to banks and others, accrued expenses payable, and income taxes payable.

B.   **Long-term liabilities** fall due beyond the coming year and include mortgage bonds and *debentures*.

Stop and Review
See textbook Exhibit 16-4

III.   Recognize and define the main elements of the stockholders' equity section of the balance sheet of a corporation

Stockholders' equity (also called *ownership equity, capital,* or *net worth*): the owners' residual interest in the business, that is, the excess of total assets over total liabilities.

A.   **Preferred stock** is the par or stated value paid in by investors who purchased stock with a priority over common stock for periodic dividends or liquidating distributions. Preferred stock usually has a *predetermined dividend rate* with a *cumulative feature* and *no voting rights* in stockholders' meetings.

B.   **Common stock** is the par or stated value paid in by investors in common stock. Although this stock has *no predetermined dividend rate,* it typically *has voting rights,* an *unlimited potential participation in earnings,* and a *limited liability* for debts owed by the corporation to its creditors.

C. **Paid-in capital in excess of par or stated value** was formerly called **surplus** or **paid-in surplus.** This is the excess received by the corporation over the par or stated or legal value of the shares issued.

D. **Retained income** (also called **retained earnings** or **reinvested earnings)** is the part of stockholders' equity measured by the excess of accumulated profits over accumulated dividends distributed to stockholders since the company was formed.

E. In addition to such **positive** elements as the above four items, the stockholders' equity section may include a **negative** item called **treasury stock,** the company's cost of reacquiring some of its own capital stock that had previously been issued.

IV.   Recognize and define the principal elements in the income statement of a corporation

---

The *income statement* reports a company's revenues (sales) and expenses and the net income or net loss that represents the difference between revenues and expenses and the change in the firm's wealth over time. The absorption form of the income statement is used for financial reporting.

> **Stop and Review**
>
> See textbook Exhibit 16-5

A. Note how this multiple-step income statement arrives at a figure called *income from operations* by deducting selling and administrative expenses from gross profit.

   1. Interest expense is deducted from this figure.

   2. The statement reflects the distinction between *operating management* and *financial management.*

B. The income statement must also show the **earnings per share of common stock**. In the simplest capital structure, the earnings-per-share figure is net income divided by the number of common shares outstanding.

C. Net income links the beginning and ending balance sheets because it is the difference between beginning and ending stockholders' equity (except as modified by dividends as discussed below).

V.   Recognize and define the elements in the statement of retained earnings

---

The **statement of retained earnings** (also called **statement of retained income**) reports the effects of net income and dividends on the balance of retained income.

> **Stop and Review**
>
> See textbook Exhibit 16-6

A. Net income increases retained earnings.

B. Dividends to stockholders decrease retained earnings but are *not expenses* (not deductions in computing net income).

VI. Identify activities that affect cash and classify them as operating, investing, or financing activities

The **statement of cash flows** typically summarizes the sources and uses of cash and cash equivalents during a fiscal period, and it must be presented as a basic financial statement in corporate annual reports.

> **Stop and Review**
>
> See textbook Exhibit 16-7

A. The statement of cash flows is supposed to aid users of financial statements who want to:

   1. Predict future cash flows

   2. Evaluate management of cash

   3. Determine the ability of a company to pay interest, debt, and dividends.

B. *Cash equivalents* are liquid short-term investments such as money market funds and treasury bills.

C. Changes in cash are grouped into *operating, investing,* and *financing* activities to aid in understanding the sources and uses of cash.

   1. *Operating activities* include collections from customers, interest earned (both inflows) and payments to suppliers, employees, banks and the IRS (all outflows).

   2. *Investing activities* include sales of assets and investments (inflows) and purchases of assets and investments (outflows), other than cash equivalents.

   3. *Financing activities* include borrowing and issuing stock (inflows) and repayments and repurchases of debt or equity (outflows).

VII. Assess financing and investing activities using the statement of cash flows

A. Cash flows from investing activities can be either inflows or outflows.

   1. Increases (inflows) in the cash account of an organization's balance sheet from investing activities are the result of increases in liabilities or paid-in-capital.

   2. Decreases (outflows) in the cash account of the balance sheet from investing activities are the result of decreases in liabilities or paid-in-capital or the payment of dividends.

B. Cash flows from financing activities can also be either inflows or outflows.

   1. Increases (inflows) in the cash account of an organization's balance sheet from financing activities are the result of decreases in long-lived assets, loans, and investments.

   2. Decreases (outflows) in the cash account of the balance sheet from financing activities are the result of increases in long-lived assets, loans, and investments.

C. Investing and financing activities that do not affect the cash account of an organization's balance sheet but are similar to cash flow activities are reported in a separate schedule that accompanies the statement of cash flows.

VIII. Use both the direct method and the indirect method to explain cash flows from operating activities

The statement of cash flows may be prepared using either the *direct* or *indirect* method, but the format is the same.

A.   The **direct method** *analyzes changes in balance sheet accounts* to determine their effects on cash flow.

> **Stop and Review**
>
> See textbook Exhibit 16-11

B.   First, analyze the accounts that affect income to determine cash flow from operations. For example, cash inflows may be from reductions in accounts receivable, and cash outflows may be from reductions in interest payable.

C.   Next, determine cash flows from investing and financing activities by analyzing all balance sheet accounts other than cash.

   1.   Increases in cash are from increases in liabilities or stockholders' equity (e.g., new debt or issue of securities) or from decreases in noncash assets (e.g., sales of fixed assets).

   2.   Decreases in cash are from decreases in liabilities or stockholders' equity (e.g., retirement of debt or payment of dividends) or from increases in noncash assets (e.g., investment in fixed assets).

D.   The **indirect method** *adjusts reported net income for all noncash accruals* contained in net income. If this method is used, net income must be reconciled to net cash flow.

> **Stop and Review**
>
> See textbook Exhibits 16-12 and 16-13

E.   The general rules for reconciling net income to cash flow are:

   1.   Add depreciation

   2.   Add decreases in noncash current assets

   3.   Add increases in current liabilities

   4.   Deduct increases in noncash current assets

   5.   Deduct decreases in current liabilities

   6.   Add loss (or deduct gain) from sale of fixed assets

   7.   Add loss (or deduct gain) on retirement of debt

> **Stop and Review**
>
> See textbook Exhibit 16-17

IX. Explain the role of depreciation in the statement of cash flows

Remember that because depreciation was not a cash outflow of the period (it is an allocation of an historical cost), it is added back to income to determine cash flow.

X.	Describe and assess the effects of the four major methods of accounting for inventories (Appendix 16A)

There are four inventory methods that are accepted by U.S. GAAP: *specific identification, weighted-average cost, FIFO, and LIFO.* The inventory method chosen by a company can significantly affect the amounts reported as gross profit and net income.

A.   The **specific identification** method uses the actual cost paid for inventory to account for sales. Each inventory item is labeled so the vendor can tell which item has been sold. This method makes sense for high priced items but is not practical for high-volume sales.

B.   The **weighted-average cost** method of accounting for inventory assigns the same per-unit cost to all indistinguishable products in the inventory. It is called the weighted-average cost method because the higher the number of units purchased at any one price the more bearing that purchase has on the per-unit cost used to account for the inventory.

weighted average = [(# at price 1 x price 1) + (# at price 2 x price 2) + (# at price 3 x price 3)]

÷ (# at price 1 + # at price 2 + # at price 3)

C.   Using the **first-in, first-out (FIFO)** inventory method, companies sell all of their oldest inventory first, using original purchase price as the cost of goods sold, and then sell the next "layer" using its purchase price as cost of goods sold, and so on. Using FIFO can lead to higher gross profits if prices are rising because the old inventory was purchased at a lower cost than the newer "layers."

D.   In contrast, the **last-in, first-out (LIFO)** inventory method uses the purchase price of the most recently acquired inventory as the cost of good sold. Many companies prefer to use LIFO because, in periods of rising prices, gross profits are smaller than if other methods were used. This is because the higher price of recent inventory purchases is used as cost of goods sold, and smaller reported gross profits mean less income tax.

Stop and Review
See textbook Exhibit 16-18

PRACTICE TEST QUESTIONS AND PROBLEMS WITH SOLUTIONS

True or False Statements

Determine whether each of the following statements is True (T) or False (F), and enter your answer in the space provided.

_____1.   Depreciation accounting is both a cost-allocation process and a valuation process.

_____2.   Accumulated depreciation serves the purpose of a fund for replacement or expansion of plant and equipment.

_____3.   The intangible asset classification used in financial statements includes trademarks and goodwill.

_____4.   The goodwill asset should be measured by the excess of the fair value of net identifiable assets of businesses acquired over the total purchase price of the businesses acquired.

_____5.   When a company develops goodwill through advertising, managerial ability, and maintenance of high-quality products and services, the goodwill should be placed on the books and carried as an asset in the balance sheet.

_____6.   The cost of treasury stock held by a corporation is an asset of the corporation.

_____7.   Retained income is the portion of total stockholders' equity that measures the accumulation of profits over the life of the corporation.

_____8.   The amount of a company's cash flow from operations is not affected by whether it buys merchandise for cash or on credit.

_____9.   Financing activity outflows would include retirement of long-term debt and declaration and payment of dividends.

_____10.   The purchase of noncurrent assets is an operating activity.

Multiple-Choice Questions

For each of the following multiple-choice questions, select the best answer(s), and enter the identification letter(s) in the space provided.

_____1.   Current assets include: (a) cash and land, (b) accounts receivable, (c) trademarks and equipment, (d) merchandise inventories and prepaid expenses.

_____2.   Current liabilities include: (a) accounts payable, (b) long-term debt, (c) goodwill, (d) notes payable.

_____3.   In computing the amount of cash provided by operations, one should add depreciation to net income because depreciation: (a) generates funds, (b) provides cash, (c) is not an expense, (d) does not require a current cash outlay.

_____4.   The cash flow statement of Tantra, Inc., showed a $50,000 increase in inventory and a $40,000 decrease in liabilities. Thus there was a cash: (a) increase of $10,000, (b) decrease of $10,000, (c) decrease of $90,000, (d) increase of $90,000.

_____5.   The activities of Arapahoe Corp. included (in thousands): purchase of fixed assets, $360, net income, $540; $30 gain on cash sale of equipment carried at $50; increase notes payable, $100; cash dividends, $60; depreciation, $60. Cash from operating activities totaled: (a) $600, (b) $700, (c) $670, (d) $570.

_____6.   See the preceding test item. Cash from investing activities totaled: (a) $360 outflow, (b) $280 outflow, (c) $140 inflow, (d) $80 inflow.

_____7.   See item number 5. Cash from financing activities totaled: (a) $240 inflow, (b) $300 inflow, (c) $60 outflow, (d) $40 outflow.

_____8.   See item number 5. Total net cash flow was: (a) $530 inflow, (b) $740 inflow, (c) $420 outflow, (d) $60 outflow.

Completion

Complete each of the following statements by filling in the blanks.

1.   The four principal financial statements that appear in annual reports are:

(a) _____

(b) _____

(c) _____

(d) _____

2.   The cost of plant and equipment less accumulated depreciation leaves an amount commonly called _____ .

3.   Goodwill, patents, and copyrights are _____ assets, which means they have _____ but are not _____ in nature.

4.   The operating cycle is the time span during which _____ to acquire _____ used to produce goods and services for sale to customers who _____ .

5.   Retained income, also called _____ or _____ is the increase in stockholders' equity from the excess of accumulated _____ over accumulated _____ since the company was formed.

6.   A company's own capital stock once issued and later reacquired by the company is called _____ and is treated as _____ on the balance sheet.

7.   A   payment   to   owners   from   retained   income   is   called   a _____ .

8.   The issuance of long-term debt is _____ activity; it _____ cash.

9.   If outflows of cash from operations and investing exceed inflows for a given company during a certain period, there is _____ .

10.   The amount of cash provided by operations is _____ plus _____ .

Problems

1. Given for Kalmia Trading Company's operations for 20x4 (in thousands):

Total cash receipts	$700
Total cash disbursements	590
Total revenues earned	516
Total expenses incurred (including cost of goods sold)	455
Total dividends declared and distributed to stockholders	40
Additional capital stock issued at par	50
Treasury capital stock acquired at cost	20

a. Compute the net income for 20x4:

b. Compute the net change in retained income for 20x4:

c. Compute the net change in stockholders' equity for 20x4:

2. For each of the transactions listed below for the Bosque Corporation, use plus, minus, or zero symbols to indicate the effect on net income, total owners' equity, and cash. The first is given as an example.

	Net Income	Total Owners' Equity	Cash
Issued capital stock for cash	0	+	+
Paid bonds payable with cash			
Declared and distributed cash dividends			
Recorded bad debt expense			
Collected accounts receivable in cash			
Paid accounts payable with cash			
Purchased land and buildings with cash			
Purchased treasury stock with $900 cash			
Sold treasury stock (above) for $700 cash			
Created a reserve for contingencies			
Recorded depreciation of machinery			
Increased bond sinking fund (a noncurrent asset)			
Recorded accrued salaries			
Purchased merchandise on account			
Collected rents in advance in cash			
Sold merchandise on account (for credit) at a profit			

Exercise

1. From the following data, prepare a statement of 20x4 cash flows for Genesee Company. Use the indirect method. Assume changes in account balances are due to cash transactions.

	December 31	
	20x4	20x3
Inventories	$870,000	$840,000
Accounts payable	150,000	240,000
Land	115,000	130,000
Equipment, net	435,000	440,000
Bonds payable	200,000	300,000
Capital stock	550,000	400,000
Retained income	590,000	500,000

For 20x4 Year:

Net income	$160,000
Depreciation expense	25,000
Dividends on capital stock	70,000
Gain or loss on sale of land	none

CHAPTER 16 SOLUTIONS TO PRACTICE TEST QUESTIONS AND PROBLEMS

True or False Statements

1. False   Depreciation is an allocation of an historical cost; it is not meant to measure the decline in economic value of an asset.

2. False   The accumulated depreciation account in no way creates an asset fund that could be used for replacement or expansion of assets. A separate *sinking* fund would be established for that purpose.

3. True   Intangible assets are resources with long lives, but are not physical in nature.

4. False   Just the opposite: goodwill is measured as the excess of the purchase price of assets over their fair market value.

5. False   Although tempting; goodwill recognized on a balance sheet results from an economic transaction, not managers' judgment.

6. False   Treasury stock reduces the amount of traded stock and is counted as a reduction of stockholders' equity.

7. False   Retained income is accumulated earnings less accumulated dividends.

8. False   Cash flow from operations can be computed (in part) by net income plus increases in current liabilities.

9. True   Financing activities include all transactions that affect the suppliers or supply of capital.

10. False   The purchase of long-term assets qualifies as an investing activity because the assets are expected to benefit more than the current period.

Multiple-Choice Questions

1. b, d   Accounts receivable and merchandise inventories and prepaid expenses will benefit the current period, whereas the other answers are noncurrent assets.

2. a, d   Accounts payable and notes payable are due in the current period, but the other answers are either a noncurrent liability (long-term debt) or asset (goodwill).

3. d   Net income understates cash flow by the amount of depreciation (and other noncash expenses), so depreciation is added back to net income to move toward net cash flow.

4. c   There are two possible explanations: Acquiring $50,000 of inventory required a cash payment of $50,000, and reducing liabilities required another $40,000. Alternatively, the inventory was acquired on credit, but overall liabilities decreased by $40,000, requiring a total of $90,000.

5. c   Adjust net by adding depreciation, adding increase in notes payable, deducting the gain on sale of equipment: $540 + $60 + $100 - $30 = $670.

6. b   Investing activities include: purchase $360 outflow, sale of equipment $30 + $50 inflow = $280 outflow.

7. a   Financing activities include: issuance of debt $300 inflow and cash dividends $60 outflow = $240 inflow.

8. a   Net cash flow equals cash from operations plus investment and financing activities: $570 - 280 + 240 = $530 inflow.

Completion

1.   (a) balance sheet, (b) income statement, (c) statement of retained income, (d) statement of cash flows

2.   net book value

3.   intangible, long lives or value, physical

4.   cash is spent, resources and services, pay for them with cash

5.   retained earnings, reinvested earnings, profits (or earnings, or net income), dividends distributed

6.   treasury stock, a reduction of stockholders' equity

7.   dividend

8.   financing, increases

9.   a need for borrowing

10.   net income, depreciation and net changes to current accounts

Problems

1. Kalmia Trading Company

    a. 20x4 net income:

Total revenues earned	$516
Less total expenses incurred	455
Net income	$ 61

    (Cash receipts and disbursements are not relevant here.)

    b. Change in retained income for 20x4:

Net income as above	$61
Less dividends to stockholders	40
Increase in retained income	$21

    c. Change in stockholders' equity

Increase in retained income as above	$21
Additional capital stock issued	50
Total	$71
Less treasury stock acquired	20
Increase in stockholders' equity	$51

2. Bosque Corporation

	Net Income	Total Owners' Equity	Cash
Issued capital stock for cash	0	+	+
Paid bonds payable with cash	0	0	-
Declared and distributed cash dividends	0	-	-
Recorded bad debt expense	-	-	0
Collected accounts receivable in cash	0	0	+
Paid accounts payable with cash	0	0	-
Purchased land and buildings with cash	0	0	-
Purchased treasury stock with $900 cash	0	-	-
Sold treasury stock (above) for $700 cash	0	+	+
Created a reserve for contingencies	0	0	0
Recorded depreciation of machinery	-	-	0
Increased bond sinking fund (a noncurrent asset)	0	0	-
Recorded accrued salaries	-	-	0
Purchased merchandise on account	0	0	0
Collected rents in advance in cash	0	0	+
Sold merchandise on account (for credit) at a profit	+	+	0

Exercise

1.

Genesee Company

Statement of Cash Flows

For the Year Ended December 31, 20x4

Cash provided (used) by operations:

Net income	$ 160,000	
Income charges (credits) not affecting cash:		
Depreciation expense	25,000	
Charges in certain working-capital components		
Increase in inventories	(30,000)	
Decrease in accounts payable	(90,000)	
Cash provided by operations		$65,000
Cash provided (used) by investing activities:		
Sale of land	$15,000	
Purchases of equipment	(20,000)*	
Cash used by investing activities		$(5,000)
Cash provided (used) by financing activities:		
Reductions in long-term debt	$ (100,000)	
Payments of dividends	(70,000)	
Issuance of capital stock	$ 150,000	
Cash used by financing activities		$ (20,000)
Net increase (decrease) in cash		$ 40,000

*$435,000 + $25,000 - $440,000 = $20,000 increase in equipment (a decrease in cash).

Understanding and Analyzing Consolidated Financial Statements

OVERVIEW

The first part of the chapter explains how investments in other companies are disclosed in financial statements. When certain criteria are met, firms disclose these investments using the cost, equity, or consolidation methods. Coverage of the last method explores the relationship between parent and subsidiary companies and their consolidated corporate financial statements. The second part of the chapter examines well-known financial ratios for analyzing reported corporate data and the concept of capital market efficiency. Your learning objectives are to:

I.   Contrast accounting for investments using the equity method and the market-value method

II.   Explain the basic ideas and methods used to prepare consolidated financial statements

III. Describe how goodwill arises and how to account for it

IV.   Explain and use a variety of popular financial ratios

V.   Identify the major implications that efficient stock markets have for accounting

VI.   Explain and illustrate four methods of measuring income (Appendix 17)

I. Contrast accounting for investments using the equity method and the market-value method

When one company has a long-term investment in the equity securities (capital stock) of another company, there are two methods of accounting for the investment:

A.   *If the ownership is less than 20%,* the **market-value method** may ordinarily be used.

    1.   The initial investment is recorded at acquisition cost, and dividends received from the investee are treated as income.

    2.   Thus the carrying amount of the investment is unaffected by the dividends or profits of the investee.

B.   Marketable securities are classified either as *trading securities* or as *available-for-sale securities.*

    1.   **Trading securities** are investments that are made with the intention to sell in the near future. Changes in the market prices of trading securities are reported in the company's income statement.

    2.   **Available-for-sale securities** are purchased with no intent to sell in the near future. Unrealized gains or losses resulting from changes in the market prices of available-for-sale securities are reported in the stockholder's equity section of the balance sheet.

C.   *If the ownership is 20% to 50%,* (sometimes called *investments in affiliates*) the **equity method** must ordinarily be used, because it would usually be assumed that the owner has the ability to influence significantly the operations of the investee.

    1.   The initial investment is recorded at acquisition cost, but this basis is adjusted for the investor's share of the earnings and losses of the investee after the investment date.

    2.   Dividends received from the investee are treated as reductions of the cost basis of the investment.

    3.   Under this method, the net income of the investor could not be directly affected by manipulating the dividend policies of the investee, because dividends received by the investor are not treated as income.

II. Explain the basic ideas and methods used to prepare consolidated financial statements

A.   *When a corporation owns more than 50%* of the outstanding voting shares of another corporation, there is a **parent-subsidiary relationship** that usually results in the operation of these two separate legal entities in the manner of a **single economic unit.**

    1.   Therefore the financial data of such companies would be combined into **consolidated statements.**

    2.   Consolidation is required even if parent and subsidiary companies have markedly different types of businesses (for example, banking and transportation).

B.   In *consolidated financial statements,* the assets and equities in the individual balance sheets of the parent and subsidiary companies are *added together* except for the *eliminations of the intercompany transfers* to avoid double-counting (e.g., sales between the parent and the subsidiary do not generate revenue for the consolidated entity).

1. Thus the parent company's asset, investment in subsidiary, is canceled against the subsidiary's stockholders' equity (or the appropriate proportion of it).

2. If part of the subsidiary's capital stock is *not owned* by the parent company (a **minority interest**), the consolidated balance sheet would ordinarily include this outside interest just above the stockholders' equity section.

3. This minority interest represents the ownership interest of the minority stockholders in one or more of the subsidiary companies in which they own stock.

C. In the consolidated income statement, the expenses and revenues of the two companies are also combined, but there would be a deduction for any minority share of subsidiary net income.

> **Stop and Review**
>
> See textbook Exhibits 17-2 and
> 17-3

D. Note two important points concerning consolidated statements:

1. The separate legal entities continue to operate, each with its own set of accounts.

2. For periodic reporting purposes, the accounts of parent and subsidiary are merely added together, after eliminating double-counting.

E. When one company purchases another, often called a **merger,** the purchasing company should record the assets obtained at **acquisition cost** (the agreed amount of money to be paid, or the fair value of other assets exchanged).

III. Describe how goodwill arises and how to account for it

A. If the total purchase price exceeds the sum of the fair value of the identifiable individual assets acquired less the liabilities, the excess, often called **purchased goodwill,** is an asset that should be reported on the consolidated balance sheet as "excess of cost over fair value of net identifiable assets of businesses acquired."

B. Such goodwill should be carried as a separate intangible asset on the consolidated balance sheet until management determines that the advantages of the acquisition are no longer present, at which point the value of the asset would be written down.

> **Study Tip:** *Before going on to the next section, be sure that you understand the principles of the different methods of combining financial statements of related companies. Work through the Summary Problem in the text using the balance sheet equation approach.*

IV. Explain and use a variety of popular financial ratios

Financial statement analysis is the study of relationships contained in financial statements for the purposes of evaluating past performance of the entity, predicting future performance of the entity, or evaluating the risk of the entity.

A. Techniques of financial statement analysis include:

1. Comparing financial information over time (*time-series* **comparisons**) with that of similar companies, with "rules of thumb" (*benchmark* **comparisons**), and against industry averages (*cross-sectional* **comparisons**). **See query re time-series definition*

2. Measuring differences from budgets and cash-flow projections.

3. Computing ratios and *common-size statements* to aid in *profit evaluation* and *solvency determination.*

B. **Common-size statements** are really ratios of individual financial statement amounts to a base of sales (for the income statement) or total assets (for the balance sheet).

1. Note how the elements in the common-size income statement are related to the dollar amount of *sales*, which is used as the *base figure* for the *common* sizes. Each dollar figure in the statement can be expressed as a percentage of sales.

2. In the balance sheet, the *total asset* dollar amount is used as the *base* for determining the common sizes of the major balance sheet items. Each balance sheet is expressed as a percentage of total assets (or total equities, of course).

3. These ratios may be compared, over time, with competitors, and against industry averages to evaluate the entity.

C. Below are definitions of some typical ratios, but note that there are many variations in practice.

1. **Short-term ratios** help in assessing a company's ability to pay its current debts on time and manage its current assets:

    Current ratio: Current assets ÷ Current liabilities

    Average collection period in days: (Average accounts receivable x 365) ÷ Sales on account

2. **Debt-to-equity ratios** help in judging the risks of insolvency and disappearance of profits:

    Current debt to equity: Current liabilities ÷ Stockholders' equity

    Total debt to equity: Total liabilities ÷ Stockholders' equity

3. **Profitability ratios** aid in measuring operating success and overall accomplishment:

    Gross profit rate or percentage: Gross profit ÷ Sales

    Return on sales: Net income ÷ Sales

    Return on stockholders' equity: Net income ÷ Average stockholders' equity

    Earnings per share: Net income less preferred dividends ÷ Average common shares outstanding

    Price-earnings ratio: Common market price per share ÷ Earnings per common share

4. **Dividend ratios** relate profit distributions to common stock prices and earnings:

    Dividend yield: Dividends per common share ÷ Market price per common share

    Dividend-payout ratio: Dividends per common share ÷ Earnings per common share

5. The pretax operating rate of **return on total assets** (also called **ROI**—see Chapter 10) helps measure operating performance:

    Operating income ÷ Average total assets available

    This ratio can also be computed by multiplying the two following ratios:

    Return on sales: Operating income ÷ Sales

    Total asset turnover: Sales ÷ Average total assets available

    See the discussion on ROI in Chapter 10.

> **Study Tip:** *Before going on, review the construction of these common financial ratios and, just as important, review in the text their meaning for decision making. Be sure that you understand how to calculate the ratios in textbook Exhibit 17-7 from the data in the financial statements in Exhibits 17-4, 5, and 6. Note also how to compare these ratios to industry averages.*

V. Identify the major implications that efficient stock markets have for accounting

Research over the past 30 years has indicated that **capital markets** are reasonably **efficient** with respect to accounting information.

A. This means that stock market prices "fully reflect" relevant data that are publicly available. Be aware that financial statements are just one of many sources of information about the prospects of a firm.

B. Thus financial ratios and other reported data are, in effect, "translated" by or combined with other information by informed readers and analysts, regardless of the different accounting and reporting methods that may be used.

C. This assumes, of course, that there are *adequate disclosures* of such methods, either in the body of the financial statements or in the accompanying footnotes (e.g., as required by GAAP and the SEC).

D. Research in recent years, however, indicates that not all accounting information may be utilized by capital markets. For example, it may be that careful analysis of financial statement ratios can yield insights that others do not have. Of course, financial analysts have been making good livings doing just that for many years.

VI. Explain and illustrate four methods of measuring income (Appendix 17)

Most financial statements account for assets using **historical cost** (the amount originally paid to acquire an asset) and **nominal dollars** (price measurements not adjusted for inflation). However, because prices may change and the purchasing power of the dollar fluctuates with inflation, many accountants feel that it makes more sense to prepare financial statements using **current cost** (the cost to replace an asset at current market value, not historical cost) and **constant dollars** (nominal dollars adjusted to reflect price changes due to inflation). There are four combinations of the above concepts used to measure income and capital:

A. *Historical cost /Nominal dollars* (HC/ND), or simply the historical-cost method, is the traditional method used to measure invested capital and income. Assets are accounted for using historical cost and dollar measurements use nominal dollars. This method ignores price fluctuations and inflation.

B. *Current cost/Nominal dollars* (CC/ND), or the current-cost method uses current market prices to account for changes in inventory. This means that cost of goods sold is not measured in historical cost and income reflects the new market price that must be paid to replace inventory. Nominal dollars are still used, so inflation is not taken into account.

C. *Historical cost/Constant dollars* (HC/CD) uses historical cost to account for assets, but a general price index is used to adjust nominal dollars to current dollar values. This means that changes in price level due to the devaluation of the dollar are taken into consideration but price changes unrelated to inflation are not.

D. *Current cost/Constant dollars* (CC/CD) uses dollar amounts adjusted for both fluctuations in price of the asset and changes in the value of the dollar. When CC/CD is used it becomes possible to determine how much of a holding gain on inventory is the result of inflation and how much is due to the difference between historical and current costs.

Stop and Review
See textbook Exhibit 17-9

PRACTICE TEST QUESTIONS AND PROBLEMS WITH SOLUTIONS

True or False Statements

Determine whether each of the following statements is True (T) or False (F), and enter your answer in the space provided.

_____1.   The equity method must generally be used when the equity ownership by one company of another company is less than 20%.

_____2.   When two companies have a parent-subsidiary relationship, they are a single economic entity.

_____3.   The minority interest measures the interest of parent company stockholders in the subsidiary company.

_____4.   When parent and subsidiary companies have totally different types of business, the parent company should carry its investment in the subsidiary by the equity method.

_____5.   When a company develops "goodwill" internally, it should be placed on the books and reported as an asset in the balance sheet

_____6.   Purchased goodwill should be amortized over a period not to exceed 20 years.

_____7.   Nix Co. had a current ratio of two to one. It paid part of its accounts payable. As a result, the current ratio increased.

_____8.   The dividend yield multiplied by the price-earnings ratio would be equal to the dividend-payout ratio.

_____9.   When common-size income statements are constructed, the base figure is usually net income.

_____10.   Your company's average collection period increased. This suggests greater risk of being unable to pay current liabilities.

Multiple-Choice Questions

For each of the following multiple-choice questions, select the best answer(s), and enter the identification letter(s) in the space provided.

_____1.   First Company owns 30% of the voting stock of Second Company, which reported a net income in Year One of $10 million and paid $4 million of cash dividends. Compute the increase in the retained income of First Company in Year One from Second Company's operations, using the **market method**: (a) $3.0 million, (b) $1.8 million, (c) $1.2 million, (d) $4 million.

_____2.   See the preceding test item. Compute the increase in the retained income of First Company in Year One from Second Company's operations, using the **equity** method: (a) $3.0 million, (b) $1.8 million, (c) $1.2 million, (d) $4 million.

_____3. See item 1 above. Assume that the acquisition cost of First Company's investment was $100 million. Compute the year-end balance of First Company's investment account, using the equity method: (a) $103.0 million, (b) $101.8 million, (c) $101.2 million, (d) $102 million.

_____4. Big Company acquired a 90% voting interest in SmallCo for $150 million. The stockholders' equity of SmallCo was $160 million at acquisition, and the book values of its individual assets were equal to their fair market values. Compute the consolidated goodwill: (a) $16 million, (b) $10 million, (c) $6 million, (d) negative $10 million.

_____5. See the preceding test item. The minority interest is: (a) $16 million, (b) $15 million, (c) $15 million, (d) negative $15 million. **b and c are the same – need another choice**

_____6. The individual net incomes of a company and its 75% owned subsidiary were each $16 million. Compute the consolidated net income: (a) $32 million, (b) $20 million, (c) $24 million, (d) $28 million.

_____7. Nomad Co. has $12,000 current assets, $150,000 sales, $75,000 total assets, and $24,000 net income. What is the common-size percentage for $3,000 accounts payable? (a) 12.5%, (b) 2%, (c) 25%, (d) 4%.

_____8. Farrone Company has a return on sales of 12% and asset turnover of four times. Its return on total assets is: (a) 12%, (b) 3%, (c) 24%, (d) 48%.

_____9. Bodin Corp. has a return on total assets of 12% and return on sales of 6%. Its asset turnover is: (a) 7.2 times, (b) .5 times, (c) 2 times, (d) 9 times.

_____10. Current-cost accounting differs from historical cost accounting because (a) current-cost reflects general price level changes, (b) historical costs are irrelevant for current valuation, (c) current-costs reflect current replacement costs rather than historical purchase price, (d) historical costs are depreciated whereas current costs are not.

Completion

Complete each of the following statements by filling in the blanks.

1. The three methods of combining financial statements are:

   (a)_____

   (b)_____

   (c)_____

2. Under the equity method of accounting for a parent company's interest in a subsidiary, the investment in the subsidiary should be carried as _____ in the parent company's balance sheet at _____plus the consolidated group's share of accumulated _____ since acquisition.

3. An account called "minority interest" on a consolidated balance sheet measures _____.

4. When one company buys another, the excess of the total purchase price over the fair values of the identifiable individual assets acquired less the liabilities is often called _____. This is an asset that should be reported in the acquiring company's balance sheet as _____.

5. The pretax operating rate of return on total assets can be computed by multiplying the _____ by the _____. This ratio can be improved by increasing either _____ or _____.

6.   The total asset turnover is _____ divided by average total assets available. When this ratio is less than that of a competitor it signals _____.

7.   The dividend-payout ratio for common stock is _____ divided into _____. When this ratio is lower than the industry average, it signals _____.

8.   The average collection period is _____ divided by _____. When this ratio decreases over time, it signals _____.

9.   The return on stockholders equity is _____ divided by _____. When this ratio is lower than competitors', it signals _____.

Problems

1. Company P owns 40% of the voting stock of Company S. Given in millions of dollars:

Cost of P's 40% ownership	$180
Net income of S in year one	20
Cash dividends of S in year one	10

Compute:

a. Year-end balance of P's investment account:

    Using the equity method

    Using the market method

b. Increase in retained income of P in year one from S operations:

    Using the equity method

    Using the market method

2. Tamarisk Company acquired 20% of the voting stock of Aspen Company for $60 million. During the following year, Aspen reported a net income of $25 million and distributed total cash dividends of $15 million.

     a.   Assume that Tamarisk Company uses the **market method**. Compute:

           The carrying amount of the investment at the end of the year

           The increase in Tamarisk's reported stockholders' equity because of Aspen's operations during the year

     b.   Assume that the **equity method** is used by Tamarisk Company. Compute:

           The carrying amount of the investment at the end of the year

           The increase in Tamarisk's reported stockholders' equity because of Aspen's operations during the year

Exercises

1. Table Mesa Company acquired Piedra Company. Before the acquisition the companies had neither debt nor preferred stock outstanding. Their annual reports before the acquisition revealed the following data:

	Table Mesa	Piedra
Net assets	$80,000	$20,000
Stockholders' equity	80,000	20,000
Net income	8,000	7,000

Table Mesa Company issued capital stock with a market value of $50,000 in exchange for all the stock of Piedra Company. Assume that the book value and the current value of the individual assets of Piedra were equal before the acquisition. Also assume the purchase method is used.

a.   Compute the following for the consolidated company immediately after acquisition:

Purchased goodwill

Net assets (including goodwill)

Stockholders' equity

b.   Compute the prospective annual net income of the consolidated company, assuming that purchased goodwill is not to be amortized.

2. Company P has just acquired a 90% voting interest in Company S for the amount shown below in the investment account (all amounts in millions of dollars):

P Co.:	Investment in S	$180
	Cash and other assets	440
	Liabilities	200
	Stockholders' equity	420
S Co.:	Cash and other assets	500
	Liabilities	300
	Stockholders' equity	200

a. Prepare a consolidated balance sheet. (No work sheet is required, but show support for all figures.) Assume that the book values of S individual assets are equal to their fair market values.

b. Compute the consolidated goodwill, assuming that a 75% voting interest had been acquired, but use all the **same dollar numbers** shown above. Also assume that the book values of the S individual assets are equal to their fair market values. Prepare the consolidated balance sheet (work sheet not required).

3. Selected data for Roaring Fork Corporation (in millions):

Sales	$800	Cost of goods sold	$500
Current assets	240	Current liabilities	120
Stockholders' equity	200	Merchandise inventory	125
Accounts receivable	80	Accounts payable	60
Retained income	150	Net income	36

Assume that all sales were on account. Compute each of the ratios indicated below. It is not necessary to compute any average amounts for balance sheet figures.

Current ratio:

Inventory turnover:

Collection period for accounts receivable:

Gross profit rate:

Return on sales:

Return on stockholders' equity:

4. Given for Gunnison Corporation (in millions):

Operating income	$ 54
Sales	900
Average total assets available	500

Find:

a. Operating income percentage of sales

b. Total asset turnover

c. Pretax operating rate of return on total assets

5. San Luis Corporation recorded the following transactions and the following price information during the past year. The general price level index at the start of the year was 170, 188 at the end of the year, and 105 when the property and equipment was purchased five years ago. Current sales prices reflect the current general price level. The inventory for sale was purchased at the beginning of the year, and the current replacement cost of inventory is $6,000. There are no beginning or ending inventories. The current replacement cost of the equipment is twice the historical cost. Current general and administrative costs reflect the general price level. Restate historical cost-based operating income to current cost and general price level adjusted operating incomes.

	Historical cost	Price level adjusted	Current cost
Sales revenue................................. (earned uniformly throughout the year)	$ 20,000		
Cost of goods sold........................... (purchased at the start of the year)	5000		
Depreciation.................................... (on 5-year old property & equipment)	4000		
General & administrative costs............. (used uniformly throughout the year)	6000		
Operating income............................	$ 5,000		

CHAPTER 17 SOLUTIONS TO PRACTICE TEST QUESTIONS AND PROBLEMS

True or False Statements

1. False   The market method must be used when ownership is less than 20%. The equity method is used when ownership is between 20% and 50%.

2. True   Parent and subsidiary decisions are likely to be so intertwined that they are effectively a single economic unit. Thus, consolidation of financial statements is required.

3. False   A minority interest measures ownership by a third party, not the parent.

4. False   Even when parent and subsidiary are in unrelated businesses, the financial statements must be consolidated.

5. False   Goodwill results from actual, "arms-length" economic transactions not internal developments.

6. False   Goodwill is not amortized, but companies annually must verify that its value is unimpaired.

7. True   Though both current assets and current liabilities decreased by the transaction, because current assets are larger, they decreased proportionately less, and the current ratio increased.

8. True   Dividend yield x price-earnings ratio = (dividend per share ÷ price per share) x (price per share ÷ earnings per share) = dividend per share ÷ earnings per share = dividend-payout ratio.

9. False   The base is usually sales.

10. True   A larger collection period means that your company is being less aggressive or successful in collecting payments on credit sales. This can precede lower cash flows and less ability to pay current obligations.

Multiple-Choice Questions

1. c   First's share of Second's dividends is 0.3 x $4 million = $1.2 million. Because the market method is used, Second's income does not affect First.

2. a   Using the equity method, First's retained income increases by its share of Second's income: 0.3 x $10 million = $3 million. Dividends are treated as a reduction in the cost basis of the investment.

3. b   The new cost basis is adjusted by income and dividends: $100 + $3 - $1.2 = $101.8.

4. c   Goodwill is the purchase price less Big's share of SmallCo's owners' equity: $150 – 0.9 x $160 = $6 million

5. a   The minority interest is 0.10 x $160 million = $16 million.

6. d   The consolidated net income is the parent's net income plus its share of the subsidiary's income: $16 + 0.75 x $16 = $28 million.

7. d   The component percentage of this balance sheet account is $3 ÷ $75 = 4%.

8. d   The return on assets is equal to the product of these two ratios: 4 x 12% = 48%.

9. c   Turning the above calculation around means the asset turnover is equal to return on assets divided by return on sales: 12% ÷ 6% = 2 times.

10. c   Current costs reflect specific price changes, not general. Historical costs might be relevant for current valuation, but usually are not. Current costs **do** reflect replacement costs. Whether historical costs are depreciation is irrelevant to the issue.

Completion

1.   the market method, equity method, consolidation

2.   an asset, original cost, retained income

3.   a third party's investment in a subsidiary.

4.   purchased goodwill, excess of cost over fair value of net identifiable assets of businesses acquired

5.   return on sales, total asset turnover, return on sales, total asset turnover

6.   sales, that the firm's assets are not being utilized as well as a competitor's

7.   common earnings per share, common dividends per share, that the firm is retaining more income for internal investment than the industry norm (assuming income and cash levels are comparable)

8.   (average accounts receivable x 365), sales on account, increasingly aggressive or successful collections of credit sales

9.   net income, average stockholders' equity, less efficient use of resources

Problems

1. Company P and Company S (in millions of dollars)

   a.   Year-end balance of P's investment

   Equity method: $180 + 40\%(\$20 - \$10) = \$180 + \$4 = \$184$

   Market method: $180

   b.   Increase in P's retained income

   Equity method: $40\%(\$20) = \$8$

   Market method: $40\%(10) = \$4$

2. Tamarisk Company

   a.   Market method:

   Investment carrying amount: $60 million

   Increase in stockholders' equity: 20% x $15 million of dividends = $3 million

   b.   Equity method:

   Carrying amount of investment: $60 million + (20% x $25 million) - (20% x $15 million)

   = $60 million + $5 million - $3 million = $62 million

   Increase in stockholders' equity: 20% x $25 million = $5 million

Exercises

1. Table Mesa Company and Piedra Company

   a.

Market value of capital stock exchanged	$ 50,000
Less current *value* of individual assets of Piedra	20,000
Goodwill	$ 30,000

Net assets of Table Mesa before acquisition	$ 80,000
Individual assets of Piedra before acquisition	20,000
Goodwill, as above	30,000
Net assets after acquisition (including goodwill)	$130,000

Stockholders' equity of Table Mesa before acquisition	$ 80,000
Market value of additional Table Mesa capital stock issued	50,000
Stockholders' equity after acquisition	$130,000

   b.

Net income of Table Mesa before acquisition	$ 8,000
Net income of Piedra before acquisition	7,000
Prospective annual net income after acquisition	$ 15,000

2. Company P and Company S

    a.

	Assets		Liabilities and Stockholders' Equity	
Cash and other assets (440 + 500) =	$940		Liabilities (200 + 300)=	$500
			Minority interest (10%)(200) =	20
			Stockholders' equity	420
Total assets	$940		Total equities	$940

    b.

	Assets		Liabilities and Stockholders' Equity	
Cash and other assets (400 + 500)	$940		Liabilities (200 + 300)	$500
			Minority interest (25%)(200)	50
Consolidated goodwill*	30		Stockholders' equity	420
Total assets	$970		Total equities	$970

    *Consolidated goodwill: 180 - 75 %(200) = 180 - 150 = $30

3. Roaring Fork Corporation

    Current ratio: $240 ÷ $120 = 2 to 1, or 2

    Inventory turnover: $500 ÷ $125 = 4 times

    Collection period: ($80 x 365) ÷ $800 = 36.5 days

    Gross profit rate: ($800 - $500) ÷ $800 = 37.5%

    Return on sales: $36 ÷ $800 = 4.5%

    Return on stockholders' equity: $36 ÷ $200 = 18%

4. Gunnison Corporation

    a. Operating income percentage of sales: $54 ÷ $900 = 6%

    b. Total asset turnover: $900 ÷ $500 = 1.8 times

    c. Pretax operating rate of return on total assets: $54 ÷ $500 = 10.8%

        alternative calculation from part b:

        6% x 1.8 = 10.8%

5. San Luis Corp.

	Historical cost	Price level adjusted	Current cost
Sales revenue.............................. (earned uniformly throughout the year)*	$ 20,000	x (188/((188+170)/2) = $21,006	x (188/((188+170)/2) = $ 21,006
Cost of goods sold......................... (purchased at the start of the year)	5000	x (188/170) = 5,529	(given) 6,000
Depreciation................................ (on 5-year old property & equipment)	4000	x (188/105) = 7,162	x 2 = 8,000
General & administrative costs............. (used uniformly throughout the year)*	6000	x (188/((188+170)/2) = 6,302	x (188/((188+170)/2) = 6,302
Operating income...........................	$ 5,000	$ 2,013	$ 1,816

* Revenues earned or expenses used throughout the year are assumed to increase in cost from the average price level index for the year, ((188+170)/2).

Introduction to Journal Entries and T-Accounts

OVERVIEW

The purpose of this appendix is to introduce the primary means of recording data in double-entry accounting systems—journal entries. As an aid to explaining the effects of journal entries, the appendix uses so-called T-accounts, which are useful conceptual devices and which represent actual balance sheet and income statement accounts.

REVIEW OF KEY CONCEPTS

A. Most accounting systems are designed to record data simultaneously to all *accounts* affected by a single transaction. Though more than two accounts may be affected, these systems are called **double-entry systems** because at least two entries are required to record every transaction.

   1. The double-entry system is built on the accounting equation for every privately owned company, which is:
       Assets = Liabilities + Owners' Equity

   2. Every economic transaction affects this equation, and at all times the equation must be balanced.

   3. The continual balancing of the accounting equation is what makes accounting systems such effective control devices: if the system is designed with appropriate accounts and tended by competent (and honest) personnel, it is almost impossible to lose track of costs and revenues. In addition, the system almost automatically produces useful (and required) financial statements.

   4. The accounting equation is balanced by recognizing that an increase or a decrease in one account *must* be accompanied by an offsetting increase or decrease in another account (hence the double-entry designation).

       a. For example, purchase of materials results in an increase in the material inventory account. The offsetting or balancing entry would show where the resources were obtained to purchase the material: either by decreasing *cash* (another asset) or by increasing the *accounts payable* account (a liability, or promise to pay cash in the future).

       b. As another example, application of labor to the construction of a custom-built house results in an increase of an asset, *work-* (or *construction-*) *in-process* accomplished by either a decrease in *cash* (another asset) or an increase in *wages payable* (a liability).

       c. As a third example, credit sales of products result in the increase of the asset account, *accounts receivable*, and a corresponding increase in *owners' equity* (an equity account; though the typical system funnels revenues through *temporary* accounts, such as *sales* or *income* in order to have a ready means of computing periodic income).

   5. In every case, an increase in an asset account must be accomplished by (1) a corresponding decrease in another asset or (2) a corresponding increase in a liability or equity account, or (3) a combination of the two effects.

       a. Likewise, a decrease in an asset is accompanied by an increase in another asset, a decrease in a liability or equity, or a combination of the two.

       b. Similarly, an increase in a liability or equity is accompanied by a decrease in another liability or equity, a decrease in an asset, or a combination of the two.

       c. How is a decrease in a liability balanced?

B. Most accounting systems accomplish the double entries by means of making *journal entries* as transactions occur and by *posting* these entries to the affected accounts (also called *ledger accounts* after the large books or ledgers in which these accounts used to be kept in manual systems of not too long ago).

1. A **journal entry** is the means of recording (at one time literally in a daily journal, but now of course mostly via computer input) the amounts of a transaction and the identity of all accounts affected by the transaction.

   a. The journal entry would identify which accounts were increased or decreased and by how much.

   b. For example, to record the purchase of materials, the journal entry would record that material inventory was increased, and that either or both cash and accounts payable were decreased or increased, respectively.

2. For many, many years accountants and bookkeepers have employed logical devices to help them keep track of which accounts were increased and which were decreased by transactions. Most computerized accounting systems retain this logic, if not the physical devices.

   a. *Ledger accounts* exist for every balance sheet account and temporary account (used primarily to record income statement items). There also may be *subsidiary* ledgers, such as job-cost records that are subsidiary to work-in-process accounts. (See Chapter 14. Many of the examples of this appendix reflect the context of Chapter 14 and job-order costing).

   b. Ledger accounts for assets record *increases* in *assets* on the *left* side (or **debit** side, from a Latin word meaning "what is owed") of the account.

   c. Likewise, *decreases* in *assets* are recorded on the *right* side (or **credit** side, which is just an accounting term for "the other side") of the account.

   d. Because liability and equity accounts are on the other side of the accounting equation, the designation of increases and decreases is reversed for these accounts:

      • *Increases* in *liabilities* or *equities* result in *credit* entries to those accounts.

      • *Decreases* in *liabilities* or *equities* result in *debit* entries to those accounts.

   e. The probably familiar phrase "debits equal the credits" explains that in order to keep the accounting equation balanced, all debit entries (e.g., increases in assets) must be accompanied by an equal amount of credit entries (e.g., reductions in other assets or increases in liabilities or equities).

3. Journal entries for every separate transaction, by convention, list the debit entry first and the credit entry second (indented to the right), accompanied by a brief explanation of the transaction.

a. For example, a transaction to record the purchase of $14,000 of materials on credit would be recorded in the journal as:

Accounts	Debit	Credit
July 22, 19X6 Purchase of materials:		
Materials inventory	$14,000	
Accounts payable		$14,000

b. Issuing $10,000 of this material to a job would be recorded as follows:

Accounts	Debit	Credit
July 23, 19X6 Issuance of material		
Work-in-process inventory	$10,000	
Materials inventory		$10,000

c. Use of $8,000 direct labor (half cash and half payable at the end of the month) on a job would be recorded as:

Accounts	Debit	Credit
July 23, 19X6 Application of labor:		
Work-in-process inventory	$8,000	
Cash		$4,000
Wages payable		$4,000

d. Recording incurrence of a $2,000 utilities bill, part of factory overhead, would be recorded:

Accounts	Debit	Credit
July 23, 19X6 Factory utilities:		
Factory overhead control	$2,000	
Utilities payable		$2,000

e. Applying factory overhead at 150% of direct labor cost would be recorded:

Accounts	Debit	Credit
July 23, 19X6 Application of factory overhead:		
Work-in-process inventory	$12,000	
Factory overhead control		$12,000

f. Credit sales of products resulting in revenues of $45,000:

Accounts	Debit	Credit
July 24, 19X6 Sales of products:		
Accounts receivable	$45,000	
Sales		$45,000

4.   Each journal entry is *posted* or written to the debit or credit sides of the affected ledger accounts, so that at virtually any time a glance at a ledger account shows its current balance, much as you are able to do with your balanced checkbook, or more likely these days as you are able to do at the mini-teller.

   a.   Ledger accounts can be represented by T-accounts (in fact many manual ledgers look just like T-accounts), which are so-called because of their T shape.

   b.   The account title goes on top of the T, and debit entries (and beginning positive balances for assets) go on the left or debit side. Likewise, credit entries (and beginning positive balances for liabilities and equities) go on the right side of the T. For example, a T-account for work-in-process inventory would look like this before any entries:

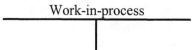

   c.   The journal entries above that would be posted to the work-in-process ledger account can be shown on the T-account as:

Work-in-process

July beginning balance	0
7/22/X6 Application of material	$10,000
7/23/X6 Application of labor	8,000
7/23/X6 Application of overhead	12,000
7/23/X6 Balance	$30,000

   d.   As shown above, at any time an account balance can be determined by totaling all the entries (debit and credit).

   e.   In the above example, when goods are completed, the journal entry for the cost of goods completed would *debit* (increase) *finished-goods* inventory and *credit* (decrease) *work-in-process*. Assume that products costing $20,000 were completed on July 24; the T-accounts would look like:

Work-in-process

July beginning balance	0	
7/22/X6 Application of material	$10,000	
7/23/X6 Application of labor	8,000	
7/23/X6 Application of overhead	12,000	
7/24/X6 Completion of products		$20,000
7/24/X6 Balance	$10,000	

Finished goods

July beginning balance	0
7/24/X6 Completion of products	$20,000

f.   When those goods are sold, say in a single transaction, you would debit cost of goods sold (a temporary income account), and credit finished goods:

Finished goods		
July beginning balance	0	
7/24/X6 Completion of products	$20,000	
7/25/X6 Sale of products		$20,000
7/25/X6 Balance	0	

Cost of goods sold	
7/25/X6 Sale of products	$20,000	

C.   This appendix has been a brief introduction to the mechanics of recording accounting transactions. Though real accounting systems can be very complex and the transactions they record can be even more complex, be assured that every transaction can be recorded by balancing the accounting equation, by insuring that the debits equal the credits. The real accounting problem can be deciding where the debits and credits *should* go!